FUNDAMENTALS OF

RURAL DEVELOPMENT

FUNDAMENTALS OF
RURAL DEVELOPMENT

Prof. Tahir Hussain
M.A., PGDC., Ph.D.
Department of Geography
and
Environmental Studies
Adigrat University, Adigrat
Ethiopia, North East Africa

Prof. Mary Tahir
M.A., M.Phil., Ph.D.
Department of Geography
Jamia Millia Islamia
(Central University)
New Delhi

Riya Tahir
M.A. Economics
Research Assistant, LBSNAA

TECHSAR™
NEW DELHI

Published and Printed by

Techsar Pvt. Ltd.
4435-36/7, Ansari Road, Daryaganj
New Delhi–110 002 (India)
E-mail: tech_info@techsarworld.com
Website: www.techsarworld.com

ISBN: 978-93-85909-63-4

Reprint 2025

Preface

Despite economic progress in the post-independence period, five year plans and heavy investments, the living condition of the rural poor has not improved, instead it has deteriorated with inflation and widespread unemployment. Dissatisfaction with the quality of life and creeping changes in economic strata are contributing to an undercurrent of frustration that's starting to affect basic rural people's attitudes and social harmony.

In the era of planned economic development, the concept of Rural Development has been defined to bring about economic and social changes in the rural areas, especially for the benefit of poorer sections. As is natural in a democratic system, the initial attempts at rural development, in this sense, were to set up an administrative infrastructure which would devise and implement developmental programmes as also stimulate voluntary community effort for self-betterment.

Rural Development, over the years, has emerged as "a strategy designed to improve the economic and social life of a specific group of people –the rural poor. It involves extending the benefits of development to the poorest among those who seek a livelihood in the rural areas. The group includes small and marginal farmers, tenants, landless labourers, rural artisans, etc." The objectives of rural development encompass improved productivities, increased employment, higher incomes for target groups as well as a minimum acceptable levels of food, clothing, shelter, education and health. Growth with social justice is the objective of Indian economic planning. But the compulsions of the economic situation, as they unfolded themselves over the years, characterized by a high rate of population growth and less than commensurate increase in food production, adverse weather, etc. made pursuit of the growth aspect more imperative than the social justice aspect of development programmes.

The removal of poverty remains a central concern of planning in India. The stress continues to be on complementary strategies increasing employment, meeting basic needs, reduction in the inequalities in income and wealth, and raising the productivity of the poor—all integrated with human development.

Consistent with this objective, the 12th five year plan (2012-17) development strategy and the pattern of growth emerging from it are expected to lead to a reduction in absolute poverty at a faster rate than in the past. The plan envisages an expanded coverage under the various anti-poverty programmes. The plan pays special attention to the problem faced by the more vulnerable sections of our society, such as BPL families, senior citizens, SC/STs, women and children. As a result of these measures, the government aims to reduce poverty estimates by 2 per cent annually on a sustainable basis during the Plan period.

According to the Tendulkar methodology, the percentage of population below the poverty line was 29.8 per cent at the end of 2009-10. This number includes 33.8 per cent in the rural areas and 20.9 per cent in the urban areas. The total number of poor in 2009-10 was 301.7 million, lower than 321.3 million in 1979-74 by about 19.6 million during the long span of 35 year which cannot be described as a creditable achievement. Sixty years after independence, more than a quarter of population continues to be poor. It is therefore essential that the five year plans address the task of reducing the numbers of the poor frontally. It is clear that rapid growth will be essential to reduce the number of the poor and for sustainable poverty reduction, but for growth to benefit the poor disproportionately, it will have to be accompanied by more rapid employment expansion than hitherto, greater investment in health, education, water/sanitation, and child nutrition than so far, and directly targeted poverty-reduction programmes.

Rural development implies both the economic betterment of people as well as greater social transformation. In order to provide the rural people with better prospects for economic development, increased participation of people in the rural development programmes, decentralization of planning, better enforcement of land reforms and greater access to credit are needed.

Since rural poverty and rural development are multidimensional problems, the emphasis should be on the importance of constituting a decentralized planning authority and setting up machinery at the district level to formulate an integrated development plans which would combine both the development and beneficiary aspects, with the shared objective of amelioration of poverty. Secondly, regions where land-man ratio is the lowest, effective land reforms and provision of agricultural services need special emphasis. Thirdly, there is a large dependence on casual labour. These workers get low wages and are unable to find employment throughout the year. Most of them belong to SC and STs. A programme like the Mahatma Gandhi National Rural Employment Guarantee Programme (MGNREGP) can provide better wages and enhance the number of working days for this category. Fourthly, the poor have to be enabled to increase their incomes by diversifying away from agriculture to non-farm work as a source of subsidiary income. Fifthly, education and skill development among the poor should be enhanced so that they can seek employment in emerging sectors like information technology, and other occupations requiring better skills. Last but not the least, the structure of production has to be employment generating, especially in non-agricultural occupations.

More importantly, stress should be on rural development in an integrated manner. The need of the hour is that rural development programme must be devised to synchronize with self-reliance and self-respect. The plan of action should be re-oriented to operate their own programme and ensure rural development on an ongoing basis.

The book is divided into twelve chapters. The analysis, discussion, information and statistics provide a new insight to the students of rural development, rural economists as well as readers in general.

We shall welcome any suggestions from any quarter which may improve the usefulness of this book.

We would be failing in our duty if we do not thank our parents for love and blessings.

Prof. Tahir Hussain
Prof. Mary Tahir
Riya Tahir

Contents

CHAPTER 1

Introduction

CHAPTER OUTLINE

- What is Development?
- Difference between Development and Growth
- Development Studies as a Discipline
- Meaning and Dimensions of Rural Poverty
- Concept of Rural Development
- Integrated Rural Development
- Approaches to Rural Development

1.1 WHAT IS DEVELOPMENT?

Development means different things to different people. However, by looking at different views of development we can draw some conclusions about what is broadly agreed as being development, while still bearing in mind the impossibility of having a purely objective definition of development.

Traditionally, development was synonymous with economic growth. As such development was defined narrowly as the ability of a country to sustain growth. This view of development was associated with the *modernisation* of the economy's structure, whereby agriculture's share of the economy would decline and that of manufacturing and services would increase. Such a definition of development underpinned strategies to promote industrialisation and urbanisation, usually at the expense of agriculture and rural development. The principal measures of development were economic although social indicators related to health, education and so on supplemented these. However, the main objective of development was economic growth; and problems of poverty, unemployment and income distribution were of secondary importance.

The experience of the 1950s and 1960s, during which many developing countries enjoyed significant economic growth, but conditions for the majority of their populations did not improve, led to widespread questioning of this narrow economic view of development. An early development economist, Dudley Seers, articulated this concern in a famous journal article by raising the question of whether it was possible to say there had been development if poverty, unemployment and inequality worsened even though GNP per capita grew. As a response to such concerns, in the 1970s economic development came to be redefined in terms of a reduction/elimination of poverty, inequality and unemployment in the context of a growing economy.

Over time the definition of development has been expanded beyond the narrow confines of economic well-being to include concerns such as satisfying human needs, and aspiring to ideals of sustainability, realisation of human potential, equity, political participation, cultural diversity and freedom. The way development is defined and the emphasis placed on certain components of its definition plays a determining role in defining what approaches and policies are pursued in the name of development.

It is reasonable to establish that development is now considered a multidimensional process involving the reorganisation and reorientation of entire economic and social systems. The aims of such a process of development should include:

- to increase living standards, and impact positively on quality of life;
- to expand the range of social and economic choices available to individuals; and
- to reduce inequality and exclusion.

1.2 DIFFERENCE BETWEEN DEVELOPMENT AND GROWTH

The terms development and growth are wrongly used as synonyms for each other while development is much more than economic growth. Development is a multidimensional process which involves reorientation and reorganization of the entire economic and social system. Development means all-round development of the society while economic growth means only the financial condition of the people/society.

Development represents the entire gamut of changes by which the entire socio-economic system turned to the diverse basic needs and wants of individuals or society as a whole move from unsatisfactory level towards materially and spiritually better living conditions.

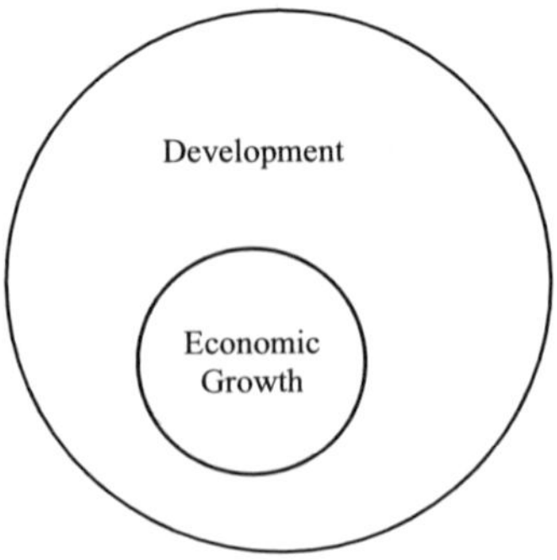

So economic growth is an essential component of development. Mathematically, economic growth is a sub-set of development which can be represented diagrammatically as given on page 2.

1.3 DEVELOPMENT STUDIES AS A DISCIPLINE

The study of development is a broad discipline, which looks at the economic, social, cultural, scientific and political processes aimed at improving the well-being of people in society. The study of the problems and processes of development in Africa, Asia and Latin America has emerged in the last fifty years. Development Studies is one of the recent and most challenging branches of studies in the social sciences.

All students of development must be sensitive to the uniqueness and diversity of different societies and areas where each one works. It is also important to recognise that in development studies there are few, if any, true principles or laws as there are in the physical sciences. At best there are tendencies and approaches that offer insights and possibilities on how things can be done better. Also, because of the diversity of the countries and regions there is no single or universal approach that can be applicable to all situations. Instead, it is necessary to combine concepts, theories, experiences, approaches and evidences and apply them appropriately to local realities.

The study of development also needs to be considered within a broader context than traditional disciplines. Development policy needs to be analysed within the context of both the local social system and the global environment. Despite such diversity, the common purpose of this discipline is **to understand the concepts and process of development and to develop skills in order to contribute to improving the well-being of people.**

An appreciation of the subjective nature of development both in theory and practice is important to bear in mind. As a social science, development is concerned with people and social systems whereby people organise themselves to satisfy both material needs (such as food, water, clothing shelter) and non-material needs (such as education, health, entertainment, spiritual fulfilment). Unlike the physical sciences, social sciences cannot claim scientific laws and principles. But wide ranging personal experiences and a keen sense of observation can yield better approaches of doing things. But even then, what has worked well in one place may not be applicable to different places, situations or times. Likewise, where science and technology is applied to development problems they cannot be considered in isolation from the social and cultural contexts that can influence the success or failure of the application of such scientific techniques. Therefore, development theory, policy and practice cannot be isolated from the institutional, social and political context.

Value judgments also play an important role in influencing what is desirable or not when considering development. The very concept of development represents value judgments about desirable goals. Concepts or goals such as economic and social equality, elimination of poverty, universal education, national independence, grassroots participation, democracy, rising standards of living and gender equity are based on value judgments of what is considered desirable and when. As such the study of development cannot be value free in the same way as the physical sciences. As values are an integral part of development policy, analysis and practice, this needs to be borne in mind when studying the topic.

Once subjective values about what development is have widespread agreement amongst the citizens of a nation and those responsible for policy making, then specific goals such as greater income equality can be set and corresponding public policies can be pursued such as increasing taxation on wealthier segments of the population. However, in the real world, gaining consensus around goals and policies is difficult. Where widespread value differences exist, establishing desirable goals and appropriate policy becomes extremely difficult. This is specially true in the Indian context wherein the difficulties arising out of political, socio-economic constraints, the whole process, right from policy making to its implementation becomes a cumbersome task. Added to this is the well-known fact of rampant corruption prevalent at every stage.

1.4 MEANING AND DIMENSION OF RURAL POVERTY

There have always been differences of view on 'what' poverty means in conceptual terms. In simple meaning, **poverty** is the quality or state of having no money and no material possession. People are poor whose incomes do not allow two meals a day, two sets of clothes in a year, do not have a settled residence, cannot send their children for education and those people whose access to resources and skills necessary to earn a livelihood is denied. Poverty is a condition of lacking both money and basic necessities such as food, water, education, healthcare and shelter. In India, poorest families are those who are unable to buy or produce enough food for their own consumption.

The World Bank defines "Poverty as the inability of people to attain a minimum standard of living".

According to Amartya Sen (1992), "Poverty is the failure of basic capabilities to reach certain minimally acceptable levels".

A current and widely used definition of poverty given by the Organization for Economic Co-operation and Development (OECD) is: "Poverty encompasses different dimensions of deprivation that relate to human capabilities including consumption and food security, health, education, rights, voice, security, dignity and decent work."

Poverty goes beyond lack of income. The poor are not only deprived of income, but also of resources, political, social, cultural and other opportunities.

Income is not the only measurement of poverty and economic growth alone will not end poverty. Removal of poverty depends on improving personal capacities and increasing access to resources, institutions and support. There are different dimensions (economic, political, and social) of poverty as given below:

1. Economic-Income/consumption
2. Health
3. Education
4. Security
5. Empowerment

These dimensions determine the livelihood of the poor. Poor health, illiteracy, inadequate schooling, social exclusion, powerlessness and gender discrimination contribute to poverty. So, investments in health, education and gender equality are vital to eradicate poverty. These social investments attack poverty directly and empower individuals especially women. Because of the multidimensional character of poverty, different conjunctive actions are essential in several areas to annihilate poverty.

1.5 CONCEPT OF RURAL DEVELOPMENT

The concept of Rural Development has attracted the attention of government and international agencies, NGOs and social organizations because national development depends on the development of rural areas. Rural Development is one of the most critical issues of the day. Post-Independence Indian cities and towns were in an early growing stage and thus could easily assimilate the migrants from rural areas in search of employment and better living conditions. But at present (70 years after freedom), and in spite of the past 11 Five Year Plans and 12th running (2012–2017), the urban areas of India are themselves suffering from overpopulation, congestion, slums, garbage dumps, burden on the existing infrastructure only to name a few.

Development is a complex process which is affected by both economic and non-economic factors. Development generally means the improvement of people's lifestyles through improved education, income, skill development and employment.

Development may mean different things to different people. It implies a change that is desirable. What is desirable at a particular time, place and in a particular culture may not be desirable at other places, or other times or culture. It refers to a better quality of life encompassing at least the following three components.

Self-sustenance. Providing the basic necessities of life including food, clothes, shelter, primary healthcare and security of life and property is a necessary condition. These facilities should be provided to the people.

Self-respect. Every person and every nation seeks some sort of self-respect. Absence or denial of self-respect indicates lack of development.

Freedom. Political freedom, economic freedom and freedom from social servitude are essential in life. As long as a society is bound by the servitude to ignorance, other men, institutions, and dogmatic beliefs, it cannot claim to have achieved the goal of 'development'.

Rural development means the utilization, protection, and enhancement of the natural, physical, and human resources needed to make long-term improvements in rural living conditions. It has to provide jobs and income opportunities, and enrich cultural life while maintaining and protecting the environment of rural areas. Ideally, rural development is accomplished through the coordinated use of available human, technical, financial, and natural resources in partnership with national, state, and local entities on initiatives for improving the conditions for citizens of rural areas.

The term Rural Development implies overall development of rural areas with a view to improve the quality of life of rural people. Rural development is a process in which typically a large number of stakeholders in different sectors of society are involved.

It aims to involve the community in finding solution to their problems. It ensures the poor people's participation in the process of development for complete utilization of physical and human resources for better living conditions. Thus, rural development means the process of improving living conditions, providing minimum needs, increasing productivity and employment opportunities and developing potentials of rural resources through integration of spatial, functional and temporal aspects.

The fundamental objectives of rural development are:

- to expand the range of economic and social choices available to individual and nation;
- to provide certain social goods and services in terms of social and economic infrastructure; and
- to raise level of living through the provision of more jobs and better education with greater attention to cultural and humanistic values.

1.6 INTEGRATED RURAL DEVELOPMENT

Integrated rural development is an ongoing process involving outside intervention and local aspirations; aiming to attain the betterment of groups of people living in rural areas and to sustain and improve rural values; through the redistribution of central resources, reducing comparative disadvantages for competition and finding new ways to reinforce and utilize rural resources. Integrated rural development systems are particular setups of central and local institutions (such as administration, knowledge, information and decision-making systems, social networks), working in coherence and so being able to achieve the ideas of integrated rural development.

1.7 APPROACHES TO RURAL DEVELOPMENT

Every country including India has a long history of experimenting with various approaches to rural development. Any approach of rural development has to start with the assessment of the current situation and the identification of existing bottlenecks. The checklist gives an idea of the internal and external factors to be considered.

1. Natural resources, agricultural and non-agricultural activities. Assessment of what is available and what needs to be done.
2. Human resources (quality and quantity). Some areas as against others are considered to be culturally rich and advanced specially if they have highly developed literature and arts along with adequate knowledge about the rest of the world. Some of the best examples of superior human quality in the Indian context can be seen in the villages of Kerala and West Bengal as against the inferior human quality in the villages of Mewat district in Haryana state.
3. Pattern of social organization (values, social stratification, social power structure, and land tenure system).
4. Economic structure (agricultural production structure, industry, market relations, etc.).
5. Technology in agriculture and non-agricultural sectors.
6. Infrastructure (physical and social infrastructure).
7. Institutions and organisations (administration, people's organisations, etc.).
8. Services (marketing, credit extension, social security).
9. Education and training (formal and informal).

Following are some of the important approaches to rural development:

(A) A Territorial Approach

A territorial, as opposed to the traditional sectoral (agriculture) approach to rural development, is the most important contribution of this new approach. This has materialized in decentralization towards state and rural entities. The unit over which territorial integration is achieved is often not appropriately defined. It should allow capturing economies of scale and internalizing externalities. Watershed management should thus include the downstream areas over which positive externalities are generated, unless there are interregional transfer mechanisms to pay for these services. Towns, with activities linked to agriculture and decentralized industries, are major loci of non-agricultural employment, and enhancing their dynamics is a fundamental dimension of successful regional development. A large effort is thus left to be done to seek integration of the dimensions of rural development at the regional level, and in coordinating programs with a comprehensive regional development strategy that integrates the roles of government, the private sector, and civil society.

(B) Integrated Rural Development Approach (IRDA)

IRDA aimed at transformation of existing structure. It started with the recognition that agriculture has a key role in overall economic growth through the provision of labour, capital, food, foreign exchange and a market in consumer goods for industrial sectors.

IRDA is called "top-down and blue-print approach". It was about the provision of infrastructure, training, services and inputs. It aimed at improving production and living conditions of small traditional farmers through multi-sectoral policies and agencies.

(C) Sustainable Development Approach

Sustainable development, as defined by the Brundtland Commission (1987), is "development that meets the needs of the present without compromising the ability of future generations to meet their own needs. It takes the impact of the environment into account and tries to minimize environmental damage. It emphasizes on sustainability which implies a greater concern for the future. The confluence of three preoccupations in sustainable development is: socially equitable, economically viable and environmentally bearable".

(D) Community-Driven Development (CDD) Approach

CDD is a relatively new approach to rural development, being used predominantly by the World Bank. CDD could be helpful for the sustainable livelihoods currently being developed by the Food and Agriculture Organization (FAO) and Department for International Development (DFID). A central feature of this approach is its attempts to place the community at the heart of the development process.

At each and every stage of the programme/project, community participation is ensured. All important decisions are taken by the community. People's organizations are formed to implement the project. The project staff extends the project facilitation support only but not decision making.

In the World Bank's (2003) definition, CDD is an approach that gives control over planning decisions and investment resources for local development projects to community groups.

The underlying assumption is that people are the best judges of how their livelihoods can be improved and, if given adequate support, resources, and access to information, they can organize themselves to provide for their immediate needs.

Main principles of CDD are:

- Placing control and resources in the hands of the community
- Viewing poor people as partners in development
- Building on existing institutions
- Emphasizing on local empowerment and capacity building within the community

Characteristics of CDD projects:

There are five possible defining characteristics of CDD projects.

1. Community focus
2. Participatory planning and design
3. Community control of resources
4. Community involvement in implementation
5. Community based monitoring and evaluation

Benefits of CDD approach:

The benefits of a CDD approach can be grouped into four categories.

1. Equity and Inclusiveness

CDD projects can do this in the following ways.

(i) Effective targeting
(ii) Putting resources in direct control of poor people
(iii) Inclusion of vulnerable and excluded groups

2. Efficiency

CDD can improve project efficiency and sustainability in the following ways:

(i) Demand-responsive allocation of resources
(ii) Reducing corruption and misuse of resources
(iii) Lower costs and better cost recovery
(iv) Better quality and maintenance
(iv) Greater utilization and willingness to pay

3. Governance

In CDD approach focus is on empowerment through the devolution of decision making and resources directly to communities which naturally affects power relations at the local level. Ideally, it makes local institutions more participatory, accountable, and responsive.

4. Human rights or Human-rights-based objectives

As the description of CDD shows, by giving communities the ability to make and implement their own development plans, CDD clearly embodies the spirit of the United Nation's "right to development".

Criticisms

There are some valid criticisms and inherent limitations associated with CDD.

Conceptually, CDD does not cater to problems that are beyond the capacity of local institutions. CDD by itself does not guarantee immunity from the risks of elite capture. Additional measuring may be needed to ensure effective participation of the poor. In the absence of careful selection criteria, the poorest communities with limited capacity are not included.

(E) Approach for New Opportunities

1. Opportunities offered by the "new agriculture"

While there is a serious profitability crisis in traditional agriculture due to falling international terms of trade, urbanization and increasing integration in international markets has opened new opportunities to increase farm incomes on a limited land basis, which characterizes the rural poor.

2. Industrialization of many rural areas

There has been an extraordinarily rapid increase in the importance of non-agricultural employment and incomes for rural areas, which finally lead to industrialization.

3. Rural areas are increasingly integrated economically with urban areas

Increasing integration between rural and urban markets is reflected in convergence between rural and urban wages.

4. There has been much progress towards decentralization of governance at the municipal level

As a consequence of the strategy of industrialization by import substitution used throughout Latin America from the 1950s to the mid-1980s, economic development has typically been highly centralized in a few mega-cities and a sector of large enterprises, leaving entire regions and productive sectors at the margin of the development dynamics. In the wake of limited success of structural adjustment policies with local economic and social development, strong demands for changes in this development pattern have emerged.

5. There has been much progress with local social capital formation, particularly the expansion of civil society organizations

Civil society is composed of the totality of voluntary civic and social organizations and institutions that form the basis of a functioning society. The London School of Economics, Centre for Civil Society's working definition is as follows: "Civil Society refers to the arena of uncoerced collected action around shared interests, purposes and values". It commonly embraces a diversity of spaces, actors and institutional forms, varying in their degree of formality, autonomy and power. Civil societies are often populated by organizations, such as registered charities, development non-governmental organizations, community groups, women's organizations, faith-based organizations, professional associations, trade unions, social movements, business associations, coalitions and advocacy groups. Civil society organizations over a period of time have increased rapidly, not only in India, but in innumerable countries of the world.

6. *There are increasing demands for the provision of environmental services*

CONCLUSION

It may be observed that all the above approaches are useful for the proper understanding of the subject of rural development and they are complementary to each other. Each approach has its own relevance and utility. In fact, no single approach can give us a complete view of the complex phenomenon of **rural development**.

CHAPTER 2

Socio-economic Structure of Rural India

CHAPTER OUTLINE

- Introduction
- Size, Growth and Distribution of Rural Population
    - National Picture
    - Picture in the Major States
    - Distribution and Density of Rural Population
- Sex Composition of Rural Population
    - Sex Ratio
    - Child Sex Ratio (0-6 Years)
- Age Composition of Rural Population
- Marital Status of Rural Population
- Fertility and Mortality Patterns
- Migration Patterns
- Size of Rural Settlements
- Literacy Rate
- Main Sources of Income in Rural India
- Overview of Socio-economic Structure of Rural India

2.1 INTRODUCTION

The basic objective of development is to improve the quality of life. We know that building a modern nation depends on the development of people and the organization of human activities. It is the development of human resources that unlocks the door to modernization and is one of the necessary conditions for all kinds of growth – social, political, cultural or economic. This principle applies to India as well, particularly as she is poised to emerge as a world political and economic power.

A country therefore plans for its people only. While planning for overall development and for providing services to the people, information regarding the size, growth, composition and quality of population plays an important role. Suppose schools or hospitals are to be opened in an area. To decide as to how many to set up, information regarding the total population of the area, their age and sex, is needed. It is in this context that the study of demography assumes significant importance.

Demographics can play a crucial role in understanding past trends and in preparing for future developments and policies. Furthermore, they believe that understanding demographic developments can provide important explanations of observed economic and social trends. Consequently, demography becomes an important ingredient in public policy analysis and development.

This chapter is aimed at familiarizing you with the population scenario of rural India. An attempt has been made to give you an overview of the rural population in our country, so that you may have a reasonable idea about its size, composition and growth as well as the related phenomena like migration and the size of rural settlements.

2.2 SIZE, GROWTH AND DISTRIBUTION OF RURAL POPULATION

2.2.1 National Picture

As per the Provisional Population Totals of Census of India, 2011, the total population of India is 1210.2 million. Of this, the rural population accounts for 833.1 million and the urban population 377.1 million. In absolute numbers, the rural population has increased by 90.47 million and the urban population by 91.00 million over the last decade. In percentage terms, the rural population formed 68.84% of the total population with the urban population constituting 31.16%. Even though nearly 70 per cent of the country's population still lives in rural areas but for the first time since independence, the overall growth rate of population has sharply declined, according to the latest Census.

Let us now look at the growth rate of rural population. The growth of population is often used to connote the change in the number of people living in a particular area during a specific period of time. It is positive if there is increase in population and negative if there is decrease in population between any two given points in time. During 2001 and 2011, the rate of growth of rural population has been 12.13 per cent. According to the report, the growth of the country's rural population has been steadily declining since 1991. Table 2.2 presents the growth of rural population in India over a period of six years.

Table 2.1: Rural population of India, 1901 –2011

Year	*Total Population*	*Rural Population*	*% of Rural Population*
1901	238,396,327	212,544,454	89.16
1911	252,093,390	226,151,757	89.71
1921	251,321,213	223,235,046	88.82
1931	278,977,238	245,521,249	88.01
1941	318,660,580	274,507,283	86.14
1951	361,088,090	298,644,156	82.71
1961	439,234,771	360,298,168	82.03
1971	548,159,652	439,045,675	80.09
1981	683,329,097	523,866,550	76.66
1991	846,387,888	628,836,076	74.30
2001	1,027,015,247	741,660,293	72.22
2011	1,21,05,69,573	83,34,63,448	68.84

Source: Census of India 1981, 1991, 2001 and 2011

Table 2.2: Growth of rural population 1951-2011

Year	*Rural Population*	*Decennial Variation in Population*	*% Decennial Variation*
1951	298,644,156	24136873	8.79
1961	360,298,168	61654012	20.64
1971	439,045,675	78747507	21.86
1981	523,866,550	84820875	19.32
1991	628,836,076	104969526	20.04
2001	741,660,293	112824217	17.94
2011	833,463,448	91803155	12.3

Source: Census of India 1981, 1991, 2001 and 2011.

By looking carefully at the above table, you will find that the population growth from 1951 to 1971 has witnessed a very high growth of rural population while from 1981 onwards there has been high growth with definite signs of slowing down.

2.2.2 Picture in the Major States

Rural poverty population growth needs to be viewed not only in the context of increase in numbers but also within the broader perspective of its patterns in the different states of India. An analysis of the population growth patterns at the state level in India will help in understanding the regional contrasts in the growth pattern. Table 2.3 presents the state-wise growth of rural population. During 2001-11, the rate of growth of rural population has been 12.18 per cent. According to the report, the growth of the country's rural population is steadily declining since 1991.The highest growth rate has been recorded by Meghalaya (27.2%) and the lowest Kerala (-25.90%). Of the 28 states in the country, as many as ten recorded growth rates higher than the national average (12.3%). From the table you may also note that the so-called four BIMARU (Bihar, Madhya Pradesh, Rajasthan, and Uttar Pradesh) states have recorded positive growth rates higher than the national average. The statistics reveal that the maximum number of people living in rural areas in a particular state is 15.5 crore in Uttar Pradesh thereby accounting for 18.0 per cent of the country's rural population. Though the growth rate of population in rural areas of Empowered Action Group (EAG) States is nearly three times that in rural areas in non EAG states, it is for the first time that significant fall of growth rate is seen in the rural areas of EAG states. The EAG states are Rajasthan, Uttar Pradesh, Uttarakhand, Bihar, Jharkhand, Madhya Pradesh, Chhattisgarh and Odisha. Four states that recorded a decline in the rural population during 2001-11 are Kerala (-25.90 %), Goa (-18.5%), Nagaland (-14.6%) and Sikkim (-5.5%).

Table 2.3: Growth of rural population 2001-2011

Sr. No.	*State/UT**	*Rural Population: growth per cent*		
		2001	*2011*	*2001-2011*
1.	Meghalaya	1853457	2371439	27.2
2.	Bihar	74199596	92341436	24.3
3.	Arunachal Pradesh	868429	1066358	22.6
4.	Puducherry#	325596	395200	21.3
5.	Jharkhand	20922731	25055073	19.6
6.	Jammu and Kashmir	7464608	9108060	19.4
7.	Rajasthan	43267678	51500352	19.0
8.	Madhya Pradesh	44282528	52557404	18.4
9.	Uttar Pradesh	1315402300	155317278	18.0
10.	Chhattisgarh	16620627	19607961	17.8
11.	Mizoram	450018	525435	17.4
12.	Assam	23248994	26807034	15.5

13.	Himachal Pradesh	5482367	6176050	12.7
14.	**INDIA**	**741660293**	**833463448**	**12.3**
15.	Uttarakhand	6309317	25055073	11.5
16.	Maharashtra	55732513	61556074	10.4
17.	Haryana	14968850	16509359	9.8
18.	Gujarat	31697615	34694609	9.3
19.	Manipur	1818224	1736236	9.1
20.	Punjab	16043740	17344192	7.8
21.	West Bengal	57734690	62183113	7.7
22.	D & N Haveli #	100740	183114	7.7
23.	Karnataka	34814100	37469335	7.4
24.	Tamil Nadu	34869286	37229590	6.6
25	Tripura	2648074	2712464	2.2
26.	Andhra Pradesh	55223944	56361702	1.7
27.	A & N Islands #	239588	237093	-1.2
28.	Sikkim	480488	456999	-5.5
29.	Nagaland	1635815	1407536	-14.6
30.	Goa	675129	551731	-18.5
31.	Kerala	23571484	17471135	-25.9
32.	Daman & Diu #	100740	60396	-40.1
33.	NCT of Delhi #	963215	419042	-55.6
34.	Lakshadweep #	33647	14141	-58.0
35.	Chandigarh #	92118	28991	-68.5

Source: Census of India 2001 & 2011.

Table 2.4 shows the total rural population, number of villages (rural), total number of rural households and percentage of rural households to total number of households for the year 2011 for selected states in the country. Data shows that Bihar has the highest percentage of rural households (88.52%), followed by Himachal Pradesh (88.52) and Odisha (87.23). 73.38% of total households are in rural India.

2.2.3 Distribution and Density of Rural Population

Now, you have a clear idea about the growth of rural population in the various states and union territories as well as the country as a whole. Why do some states have more population than some others? Let us address this question in some detail. It is the unevenness of distribution, which is a significant feature of India's rural population. The factors that have guided the distribution pattern of population are the availability of cultivable land, depth and fertility of soil, depth of the underground water table, availability of water for irrigation, etc. Depending on these factors, the density of population varies from place to place. As per the 2011 census, India has an average density of 324 persons per square kilometer, but the rural population density is 254, which has increased from 214 in 1991. Table 2.5 shows the density of population in some of the major states of India. Though there are variations in density, the overall increase in the density of population is a matter of great concern as it puts immense pressure on our natural resources.

Table 2.4: Total rural population, no. of villages and % of rural households of selected states (2011)

Sr. No.	*States/UT's*	*No. of Households*	*Total Rural Population*	*No. of Villages Rural*	*Total No. of Households Rural*	*% of Household in Rural*
	All India	**244626755**	**885581639**	**644648**	**179515446**	**73.38%**
1.	Jammu & Kashmir	2094081	8822753	6584	1601606	76.48
2.	Himachal Pradesh	1425559	5633636	20693	1261950	88.52
3.	Punjab	5032199	16864339	12645	3269467	64.97
4.	Haryana	4630959	16035620	6835	2969509	64.12
5.	Bihar	20074242	98552475	44935	17829066	88.82
6.	Jharkhand	6041931	27397111	32584	5044234	83.49
7.	Odisha	9884494	36286717	51442	8622210	87.23
8.	Rajasthan	13136591	54412400	44785	10223072	77.82
9.	Andhra Pradesh	12270141	36065361	17521	9344157	76.15
10.	Chhattisgarh	5712353	19575136	20133	4538557	79.45
11.	Madhya Pradesh	14723864	51674827	55011	11288946	76.67
12.	Uttar Pradesh	32475072	162777327	107040	26014883	80.11

Source: Census of India 2011.

Table 2.5: Density of rural population

States	*Density of Rural Population*	
	1991	*2001*
INDIA	214	255
Andhra Pradesh	180	205
Assam	257	300
Bihar *	441	436
Gujarat	142	166
Haryana	287	346
Karnataka	166	186
Kerala	603	664
MP**	117	102
Maharashtra	161	185
Orissa	179	204
Punjab	292	328
Rajasthan	101	128
Tamil Nadu	297	281
Uttar Pradesh***	386	455
West Bengal	576	674

* 1991 density includes both Bihar and Jharkhand while 2001 is only for Bihar and excludes Jharkhand

** 1991 density includes both Madhya Pradesh and Chhattisgarh while 2001 is only for Madhya Pradesh and excludes Chhattisgarh

*** 1991 density includes both Uttar Pradesh and Uttarakhand while 2001 is only for Uttar Pradesh and excludes Uttarakhand

2.3 SEX COMPOSITION OF RURAL POPULATION

This section provides details that should help you in understanding the various aspects of demographic dynamics, which influence the growth of population and its distribution. The most significant aspect of demographic dynamics is the sex ratio. It is an important social indicator to measure the extent of the prevailing equity between males and females in a society at a given point in time. It is an outcome mainly of the interplay of sex differentials in mortality, sex-selective migration, sex ratio at birth and at times the sex differential in population enumeration.

2.3.1 Sex Ratio

According to the 2011 Census, the sex ratio in India stands at 940 females per 1000 males, which is an improvement of 7 points over 933 recorded in the 2001 census. Though the overall female-to-male ratio has improved marginally as compared to the last census and since 1901 (see Table 2.6), it continues to be the lowest in the world. The survey shows that fewer girls were born than boys. Some of the important reasons for this declining trend, specific to our country, are: i) neglect of the girl child resulting in their higher mortality at younger ages, ii) high maternal mortality, iii) sex selective female abortions, and iv) female infanticide.

Table 2.6: Sex ratio in India 1901-2011

Year	*Combined*	*Rural*	*Urban*
1901	972	979	910
1911	964	975	872
1921	955	970	846
1931	950	966	838
1941	945	965	831
1951	946	965	860
1961	941	963	845
1971	930	949	858
1981	934	951	878
1991	927	948	935
2001	933	935	903
2011	940	947	926

Source: Census of India, 1991, 2001 and 2011

Viewed in its regional perspective there is a phenomenal diversity in the sex ratio (see Table 2.7) in India. The highest sex ratio (1048) has been reported in Kerala, mainly because Kerala has been experiencing male-selective out migration to other parts of the country for employment since long, and the high literacy rates contribute to a low female mortality rate. From the table below it can be seen that as many as 15 states have recorded a higher sex ratio than the national average (943). The states that display more or less balanced sex ratio include Uttarakhand (963), Tamil Nadu (996), Andhra Pradesh (993), Odisha (979), and Himachal Pradesh (972). From the table you may also note that the so-called four BIMARU states, i.e., Bihar (918), Madhya Pradesh (931), Rajasthan (928), Uttar Pradesh (912) have recorded a lower sex ratio than the national average. Haryana has reported the lowest sex ratio (879). It is so mainly because of the increasing trend of female fetal abortions guided by sex determination tests as well as a strong preference for the male child at the cost of the female child. The other states with fairly large paucity of females are Punjab (895), Sikkim (890) and Jammu & Kashmir (889). Daman and Diu has a sex ratio of 618, next only to Dadra and Nagar Haveli at 775.

The three major states of Jammu and Kashmir, Bihar and Gujarat have shown a decline in the sex ratio compared with the figures of Census 2001, while 29 States and Union Territories have shown an increase.

Table 2.7: State-wise sex ratio 2011

Sr. No.	*India/States/Union Territory*	*Total*	*Rural*	*Urban*
1.	Kerala	1048	1078	1091
2.	Puducherry #	1001	1028	1042
3.	Tamil Nadu	996	993	1000
4.	Andhra Pradesh	993	996	987
5.	Manipur	992	976	1026
6.	Chhattisgarh	991	1001	956
7.	Meghalaya	989	986	1001
8.	Odisha	979	989	932
9.	Mizoram	976	952	998
10.	Karnataka	973	979	963
11.	Goa	973	1003	956
12.	Himachal Pradesh	972	986	853
13.	Uttarakhand	963	1000	884
14.	Tripura	960	955	973
15.	Assam	958	960	946
16.	West Bengal	950	953	944
17.	Jharkhand	949	961	910
18.	Lakshadweep#	947	952	945
19.	INDIA	943	949	929
20.	Nagaland	931	940	909

Contd...

Contd...

21.	Madhya Pradesh	931	936	918
22.	Maharashtra	929	952	903
23.	Rajasthan	928	933	914
24.	Bihar	918	921	895
25.	Uttar Pradesh	912	918	894
26.	Punjab	895	907	875
27.	Sikkim	890	882	913
28.	Jammu & Kashmir	889	908	840
29.	Haryana	879	882	873
30.	A & N Islands #	876	877	874
31.	NCT of Delhi#	868	852	868
32.	Chandigarh#	818	690	822
33.	D & N Haveli #	774	863	682
34.	Daman & Diu #	618	864	551

Source: Census of India 2011

2.3.2 Child Sex Ratio

To understand the imbalances it is necessary to have an idea of the child sex ratio in India. As per the Census, 2011 the child sex ratio (0-6 years) has shown a decline from 927 females per thousand males in 2001 to 914 females per thousand males in 2011 and has reached its lowest levels since 1961. The increasing trend has been seen in Punjab, Haryana, Himachal Pradesh, Gujarat, Tamil Nadu, Mizoram and the Andaman and Nicobar Islands, while in all the remaining 27 states and union territories, the ratio has shown a decline. It was the highest in Mizoram at 971, closely followed by Meghalaya (970), while at the rock bottom was Haryana with 830 and Punjab with 846 (Table 2.8).

The child sex ratio has continued to display a healthier trend in rural areas of the country as compared to urban ones (See Table 2.8). Child sex ratio in rural areas according to the 2011 Census was 923 girls per 1000 boys while in urban areas it was a measly 905 which pulled down the nationwide ratio as well. The table shows that in 2011, Punjab, Haryana, Delhi and Chandigarh registered a child sex ratio below 900 in their rural areas. In the 2011 Census, Jammu & Kashmir, Rajasthan, Uttarakhand and Maharashtra in rural India were the new entrants in this category. The number of states recording a child sex ratio above one thousand has reduced from two to one.

Table 2.8: Child sex ratio (0-6 years): 1991 – 2011

Sr. No.	*India/States/UTs*	*Child Sex Ratio (0-6 Years)*					
		Rural			*Urban*		
		1991	2001	2011	1991	2001	2011
1.	India	948	934	923	935	903	905
2.	Jammu & Kashmir	NA	952	865	NA	872	850
3.	Haryana	877	824	835	884	809	
4.	Punjab	878	795	844	866	789	852
5.	Delhi	900	853	814	917	766	873
6.	Chandigarh	910	852	871	879	744	880
7.	Rajasthan	919	914	892	909	886	874
8.	Gujarat	925	905	914	908	827	852
9.	Uttar Pradesh	927	922	906	928	880	885
10.	Daman & Diu	933	920	932	996	935	894
11.	Madhya Pradesh	944	941	923	931	906	901
12.	Tamil Nadu	945	931	936	955	951	952
13.	Lakshadweep	951	1010	911	932	920	911
14.	Uttarakhand	952	914	899	936	874	868
15.	Bihar	953	940	938	949	924	912
16.	Maharashtra	953	923	890	934	908	899
17	Kerala	958	964	965	958	958	963
18.	Karnataka	963	954	950	951	939	946
19.	Puducherry	963	971	953	962	951	975
20.	Himachal Pradesh	966	900	912	904	858	881
21.	Sikkim	967	991	964	936	925	934
22.	Tripura	968	978	960	959	948	947
23.	West Bengal	969	967	959	955	948	947
24.	Odisha	969	954	946	949	927	913
25.	Goa	972	948	945	953	919	940
26.	Mizoram	973	978	966	965	961	974
27.	Andaman & Nicobar Islands	973	976	976	970	940	954
28.	Manipur	975	956	931	972	980	949
29.	Assam	977	967	964	955	931	944

Contd...

Contd...

30.	Andhra Pradesh	979	965	941	962	958	935
31.	Arunachal Pradesh	986	957	975	946	981	957
32.	Jharkhand	986	973	957	950	931	908
33.	Chhattisgarh	988	982	977	960	941	937
34.	Meghalaya	989	977	972	968	964	954
35.	Nagaland	1001	983	933	959	935	973
36.	Dadra & Nagar Haveli	1015	995	970	977	885	872

Note: The table excludes Jammu and Kashmir where census was not held in 1991

Source: Census of India 1991, 2001 and 2011

2.4 AGE COMPOSITION OF RURAL POPULATION

The age composition is another basic characteristic of a population. It not only influences the rate of growth but also enables us to determine the proportion of labour force in the total population as well as the dependency ratio. The usefulness of age data is more noticeable when it is cross classified by variables like marital status, literacy educational attainment, economic activity which vary with age in different patterns.

India has one of the largest proportions of population in the younger age groups in the world. 19.8% of the population of the rural country has been in the age group 0-10 years at the Census 2011. 41% of the population account for less than 18 years of age. 61% of the rural population of India is in the age group of 15-59 years. The proportion of young children in the age group 0-4 and also the proportion of population in the age group 0-14 are higher in rural areas than in urban areas both for males and females. A higher proportion of males and females in the working age group 15-59 live in urban areas as compared to rural areas.

Table 2.10 shows the age composition of the population in some of the major states of India. At the national level, 8.2 per cent population in urban areas constitutes below 5 years of age as against 10.3 per cent for rural area. Sex differences in the share of child population are negligible both in rural and urban areas. The share of male child population is about 1 per cent higher in rural areas of Kerala. Among the bigger states, the percentage of child population in rural areas varies from 7.5 in Kerala to 13.5 in Bihar. At the national level, 30.9 per cent of rural population in the year 2011 was below 15 years of age against 25.5 per cent for urban areas. Percentage of population below 15 years of age in rural areas varies from 23.3 in Kerala to 37.9 in Bihar. At the national level, the age group 15-59 contributes 61.0 per cent in rural areas and 66.6 per cent population in urban areas. In rural areas the percentage varies from 55.2 in Bihar to 65.6 in Andhra Pradesh. In urban areas the same varies from 61.1 in Bihar to 70.0 per cent in Jammu & Kashmir and Himachal Pradesh. At the national level, percentage of aged (60+) population is 8.0. Composition of 60+ aged female population is higher in all the bigger states except Assam, Bihar, Himachal Pradesh, Jammu & Kashmir and Jharkhand. In rural areas population in the age group 60+ constitutes 8.1 per cent of the total population and variation in aged population ranges from 5.4 per cent in Delhi to 12.6 per cent in Kerala. The urban proportion of aged population in most of the states is lower than the corresponding rural share except for Assam, Bihar, Delhi, Jammu & Kashmir, Jharkhand, Rajasthan, and West Bengal.

Table 2.9: Percentage distribution of population by broad age groups and residence, rural India, 2011

Sr. No.	*Age Group*	*Percentage*
1.	0-4	10.3
2.	5-9	9.5
3.	10-14	11.0
4.	15-59	61.0
5.	60+	8.1

Source: Census of India, 2011

2.5 MARITAL STATUS OF RURAL POPULATION

In India, one of the most important factors responsible for the high population growth is the persistence of markedly low level of age at marriage in many of the Indian states. In India, the Child Marriage Restraint Act 1978 has laid down 18 years as the minimum age at marriage for females. Yet, even today the age at marriage remains quite low—in certain cases below 15 years.

UNFPA reported that 47% of girls in India are married before the legal minimum age. Bihar has the highest incidence of child marriage at (68%), followed by Jharkhand (55.7%), Rajasthan (57.6%), Uttar Pradesh (54.9%), West Bengal (54.8%) and Madhya Pradesh (53.8%).

Table 2.10: State-wise distribution of population by age-group (rural/urban) (per cent) (2011)

States	*Rural*							*Urban*						
	Below 10	*10–19*	*20–39*	*40–59*	*60–79*	*80 and above*	*All*	*Below 10*	*10–19*	*20–39*	*40–59*	*60–79*	*80 and above*	*All*
Andhra Pradesh	15.8	18.3	34.6	21.9	8.9	0.7	100	15.5	16.6	36.1	24.7	6.7	0.4	100
Assam	21.2	21.9	34.0	16.9	5.6	0.5	100	15.4	17.3	38.8	22.0	6.1	0.5	100
Bihar	24.7	24.7	28.7	14.9	6.3	0.5	100	20.2	22.7	32.3	17.6	6.7	0.5	100
Chhattisgarh	21.6	19.7	33.0	18.4	6.9	0.4	100	17.5	19.3	36.2	20.7	6.0	0.4	100
Delhi	20.7	20.7	37.3	15.7	4.9	0.5	100	17.9	19.1	38.3	18.7	5.5	0.5	100
Gujarat	18.8	20.3	32.7	19.6	8.0	0.7	100	16.8	17.5	36.9	21.0	7.1	0.7	100
Haryana	19.5	21.6	34.4	17.3	6.5	0.8	100	18.3	19.6	35.9	19.7	6.1	0.6	100
Himachal Pradesh	16.7	18.4	33.2	21.2	9.1	1.4	100	13.2	17.0	34.6	26.5	7.8	0.9	100
Jammu & Kashmir	16.8	21.2	35.7	18.4	7.2	0.9	100	12.3	16.5	38.2	23.1	8.9	0.8	100
Jharkhand	21.9	24.4	31.0	16.3	6.1	0.5	100	17.7	20.8	35.2	19.2	6.4	0.5	100
Karnataka	17.0	19.1	34.3	20.8	8.1	0.7	100	16.3	17.4	37.5	21.4	6.9	0.6	100
Kerala	15.1	15.8	30.9	25.6	11.1	1.5	100	14.8	15.5	30.9	26.5	11.2	1.2	100

States	*Rural*							*Urban*						
	Below 10	*10–19*	*20–39*	*40–59*	*60–79*	*80 and above*	*All*	*Below 10*	*10–19*	*20–39*	*40–59*	*60–79*	*80 and above*	*All*
Madhya Pradesh	21.4	22.8	32.0	16.6	6.6	0.5	100	18.1	20.3	35.5	19.1	6.4	0.5	100
Maharashtra	18.9	19.4	31.5	19.7	9.4	1.0	100	16.6	17.1	37.3	21.0	7.2	0.6	100
Odisha	18.1	20.0	32.7	19.7	8.7	0.8	100	15.4	18.1	36.2	22.2	7.4	0.7	100
Punjab	16.5	19.2	34.4	19.9	8.7	1.3	100	16.9	17.4	35.2	21.7	8.0	0.8	100
Rajasthan	21.6	23.9	31.9	15.5	6.6	0.7	100	18.1	20.5	35.3	18.8	6.7	0.7	100
Tamil Nadu	15.7	16.4	33.9	23.0	10.0	1.0	100	14.8	15.2	36.1	23.9	9.2	0.9	100
Uttar Pradesh	22.0	25.3	30.9	14.9	6.4	0.6	100	18.3	22.4	35.3	17.4	5.9	0.5	100
West Bengal	17.4	20.4	34.8	19.9	7.0	0.6	100	12.8	15.4	36.3	25.3	9.3	1.0	100
All-India	**19.8**	**21.7**	**32.4**	**18.1**	**7.5**	**0.7**	**100**	**16.5**	**18.2**	**36.1**	**21.2**	**7.3**	**0.7**	**100**

Source: Sample Registration System (SRS) Statistical Report 2011, Census of India website (http://www.censusindia.gov.in/vital_statistics/SRS_Report/12SRS%20Statistical%20Report%20Table%20-%2020111.pdf.).

Child marriage is more common in rural areas (56%) than in urban areas (29%). Major factors influencing child marriage are economic considerations (poverty, marriage related expenses/dowry), gender norms and expectations, concerns about girl's safety and family honour, and lack of educational opportunities for girls. As per the latest DLHS (2007-2008) data, around 48% of currently married women in age group 20-24 years got married before 18 in rural areas compared to 29% in rural areas. Although the gap between urban and rural areas has almost halved from 30.2 percentage points in 1992-1993 (NFHS) to 18.6 percentage points in 2007-2008 (DHLS), currently married women in rural areas are twice more likely to be child brides than their urban counterparts.

Census 2011 data on marital status of persons show that at the national level, 60.0 per cent of females aged 10 years and more are married. The proportion of married females is higher in rural areas than that of urban areas in majority of the bigger states. However, the trend in the states of Andhra Pradesh, Assam, Gujarat, Haryana, Jammu & Kashmir, Karnataka, Kerala, Punjab and Tamil Nadu is otherwise. Among the bigger states the lowest percentage of married females is found to be in Jammu & Kashmir (52.0) and the highest in Andhra Pradesh (63.4). Percentage of never married female aged 10+ in the bigger states varies from 23.1 in Andhra Pradesh to 40.9 in Jammu & Kashmir.

At the national level, 68.6 per cent of married females are in age 15+ and 69.3 per cent comes under rural areas. Among the bigger states, percentage of such married females varies from 58.7 in Jammu & Kashmir to 73.0 in Bihar. The percentage of never married female varies from 14.5 in Andhra Pradesh to 33.3 in Jammu & Kashmir. The maximum percentage of widowed/divorced/separated females is in Karnataka (16.4) and the minimum 7.5 in Bihar

The percentage of females who got effectively married before reaching 18 years of age is 3.7 at the national level and varies from 0.3 in Haryana and Jammu & Kashmir to 7.8 in West Bengal. Percentage of females marrying at 21 years and above is 52.2 at the national level and varies from 35.5 in Chhattisgarh to 85.3 in Jammu & Kashmir. About half of the rural female, at the National level, marry between 18 and 20 years of age compared to about one-third in urban areas.

At the national level, the mean age of effective marriage for females in the year 2011 is 21.2 years and varies from 20.7 years in rural areas to 22.7 years in urban areas.

There is a clear trend of rising age of marriage in all the states. As expected the incidence of early marriages is much higher in the rural areas than in the urban areas. Only a few states like Kerala, Punjab, Himachal

Pradesh and Jammu & Kashmir are more homogenous in terms of lower incidences of marriage at younger ages. In these states early marriages are waning away in both the rural and the urban areas.

2.6 FERTILITY AND MORTALITY PATTERNS

(a) MORTALITY RATE

Mortality is one of the basic components of population change and related data is essential for demographic studies and public health administration. It is the principal ingredient for population projections and life tables. The various measures of mortality are Crude Death Rate (CDR), Under-five Mortality Rate (U5MR), Infant Mortality Rate (IMR) and its components, Age Specific Mortality Rates (ASMR), Still Birth Rate (SBR) and Perinatal Mortality Rate (PMR).

(b) CRUDE DEATH RATE (CDR)

Table 2.11 shows the percentage change in the level of crude death rate between the period 2000-02 and 2010-12 for India and bigger states. Crude death rate (Table 2.11) at the national level for 2012 is 7.0 per thousand population and it varies from 7.6 in rural areas to 5.6 in urban areas. Among the bigger states, it varies from 4.2 in Delhi to 8.5 in Odisha. The states having death rate higher than or equal to the national level are Andhra Pradesh (7.4), Assam (7.9), Chhattisgarh (7.9), Karnataka (7.1), Madhya Pradesh (8.1), Odisha (8.5), Uttar Pradesh (7.7) and Tamil Nadu (7.4).

During this period (2000-2012), CDR in India has declined by 14.6 per cent. Among the bigger states, decline in CDR varies from 22.2 per cent in Uttar Pradesh to 3.8 per cent in Tamil Nadu. In Kerala, average CDR had shows marginal increase during 2000-02 to 2010-12 period, which could be possibly due to the changes in age structure of the population (Table 2.11).

The table shows that the death rate has declined both in rural and urban areas with an improvement in the general health conditions but since the decline in the birth rate is more than that in the death rate, the rate of growth of population has shown a rapid increase. At the state level, however, the trend in the decline of vital rates shows a mixed pattern (see Tables 2.11 and 2.15). In the Hindi speaking heartland comprising Rajasthan, Himachal Pradesh, Haryana, Uttar Pradesh, Madhya Pradesh and Bihar, where about 44% of the population of the country lives, significant decline in the vital rates is still a far cry with the sole exception of Himachal Pradesh.

Table 2.11: Percent change in average crude death rate (CDR) between 2000-02 and 2010-2012, by residence, India and bigger states

India and bigger States	*Total*			*Rural*			*Urban*		
	2010-12	*2000-2002*	*% Change*	*2010-12*	*2000-2002*	*% Change*	*2010-12*	*2000-2002*	*% Change*
India	7.0	8.3	-14.6	7.6	9.0	-15.4	5.6	6.2	-8.9
Andhra Pradesh	7.4	8.2	-7.9	8.4	9.0	-5.2	5.1	5.6	-6.9
Assam	7.9	9.5	-15.0	8.3	9.8	-15.0	5.6	6.2	-9.1
Bihar	6.6	8.3	-18.5	7.0	8.6	-19.1	5.5	6.5	-16.9
Chhattisgarh	7.9	NA	NA	8.3	NA	NA	5.9	NA	NA
Delhi	4.2	NA	NA	4.6	8.5	NA	4.2	NA	NA
Gujarat	6.6	6.7	-12.9	7.3	7.6	-13.3	5.6	5.9	-5.9
Haryana	6.4	6.5	-12.2	6.9	7.4	-8.4	5.4	6.9	-18.4
Himachal Pradesh	6.7	6.8	-6.9	7.0	8.2	-4.5	3.6	5.3	-28.3
Jammu & Kashmir	5.4	NA	NA	5.7	NA	NA	4.6	NA	NA
Jharkhand	6.8	NA	NA	7.1	NA	NA	5.1	NA	NA
Karnataka	7.1	7.1	-5.8	8.1	8.2	-2.3	5.3	6.0	-9.6
Kerala	6.9	7.0	7.8	7.0	6.6	7.9	6.5	6.2	6.8

India and bigger States	*Total*			*Rural*			*Urban*		
	2010-12	*2000-2002*	*% Change*	*2010-12*	*2000-2002*	*% Change*	*2010-12*	*2000-2002*	*% Change*
Madhya Pradesh	8.1	8.0	-19.3	8.6	10.8	-19.8	6.1	7.3	-16.8
Maharashtra	6.3	6.4	-14.0	7.3	8.5	-13.3	5.0	5.8	-11.5
Odisha	8.5	8.6	-16.3	8.9	10.7	-16.8	6.4	6.7	-3.4
Punjab	6.8	6.8	-4.5	7.5	7.5	0.8	5.5	6.2	-8.4
Rajasthan	6.6	6.7	-17.5	6.9	8.4	-17.8	5.7	6.4	-8.8
Tamil Nadu	7.4	7.5	-3.8	8.2	8.6	-4.7	6.4	6.1	7.4
Uttar Pradesh	7.7	7.8	-22.2	8.1	10.5	-22.0	6.0	7.7	-21.5
West Bengal	6.3	6.2	-10.1	6.3	7.1	-14.0	6.6	6.5	-0.7

Source: Sample Registration System (SRS) Statistical Report 2011, Census of India website

(c) Under 5 Mortality Rate (U5MR)

According to the Census 2011, at national level, the U5MR for females is 56 and for males are 49. U5MR among females is higher in all the states compared to males. The female-male gap in U5MR is higher in rural areas (female: 62, male: 54) compared to urban areas (female: 34, male: 31). U5MR is higher in rural areas than urban areas at national level and in various states. At national level, it varies from 56 in rural areas to 32 in urban areas. As mentioned above, the rural-urban gap in U5MR at national level is 24 points and the gap varies among the bigger states, which is between 43 in Assam to 3 in Kerala.

(d) Infant Mortality Rate (IMR)

Infant Mortality Rate (IMR) is defined as the number of deaths of infants of age less than one year per thousand live births. According to the Family Welfare Statistics in India, 2011, at all India level, the rural-urban gap in IMR is 18 points (rural - 46, urban -28) in 2010. All the bigger states reported higher IMR in rural areas and the rural-urban gap in IMR varied between 4 points in Kerala to 25 points in Assam. Rural areas of Madhya Pradesh registered the highest IMR (72) followed by Odisha (68), Uttar Pradesh (66). Rural areas of Kerala recorded the lowest IMR (12) in the country. Uttar Pradesh and Chhattisgarh recorded highest IMR in urban areas. Kerala had the lowest IMR (11) in urban areas. Amongst the smaller states, rural and urban areas of Goa recorded lowest IMR in 2009. During 1990 to 2012, IMR of rural areas has declined from 86 to 48 whereas the decline in urban IMR was from 50 to 29. There is a decline of 46.51% in rural IMR and of 44% in urban IMR during this period (Table 2.12).

According to the latest bulletin of the Sample Registration System (SRS) released in 2011 shows that the IMR for rural areas has dropped by three points from 51 to 48 deaths per 1,000 live births while the urban rate now stands at 29 from the previous 31. Table 2.12 gives the infant mortality rates in India from 1994 to 2012.

The increase in medical attention to the pregnant women at the time of live births may have resulted in decline in IMR over the period. But in the rural areas, the medical attention is still on the lower side (Table 2.13).

Table 2.12: Infant mortality rates in India 1994-2011

Period	*Rural*	*Urban*	*Combined*
1994	**80**	52	74
1995	**80**	48	74
1996	**77**	48	72
1997	**77**	48	71
1998	**77**	45	72
1999	**75**	44	70
2000	**74**	43	68
2001	**72**	42	66
2002	**69**	40	63
2003	**66**	38	60
2004	**64**	40	58
2005	**64**	40	58
2006	**62**	39	57
2007	**61**	37	55
2008	**58**	36	53
2009	**55**	34	50
2010	**51**	31	47
2011	**48**	29	44

Source: SRS Bulletin - December 2011, Registrar General of India

Table 2.13: Per cent distribution of live births by type of medical attention received by the mother at delivery by residence—all India

Type of Medical Attention	*Year*	*Total*	*Rural*	*Urban*
Institutional (government + private hospital)	2005	34.5	**24.4**	70.4
	2006	34.9	**24.9**	71.0
	2007	38.6	**28.7**	74.5
	2008	47.1	**38.3**	78.5
	2009	57.7	**48.7**	87.1
Qualified professional (doctor, nurse or trained midwife) other than hospital.	2005	26.4	**29.4**	15.5
	2006	26.7	**29.7**	15.6
	2007	25.0	**27.8**	15.6
	2008	21.9	**24.2**	14.0
	2009	17.0	**19.7**	8.1

Contd...

Contd...

Untrained functionary and others	2005	39.2	**46.3**	14.0
	2006	38.4	**45.4**	13.3
	2007	36.4	**43.6**	10.4
	2008	30.9	**37.6**	7.5
	2009	25.1	**31.4**	4.7

Source: Sample Registration System, 2011

(e) Neonatal Mortality Rate (NNMR)

Neonatal mortality refers to the number of infants dying within one month. Neonatal health care is concerned with the condition of the newborn from birth to 4 weeks (28 days) of age. Neonatal survival is a sensitive indicator of population growth and socio-economic development. The survival rate of female infants correlates to subsequent population replacement. According to the Family Welfare Statistics in India, 2011, the NNMR is very high in rural areas (38 per 1000 live births) as compared to 21 in urban areas in 2009. The NNMR also varies considerably among the states: Madhya Pradesh (47), Uttar Pradesh (45), Odisha (43), Rajasthan (41), J&K (37), Himachal Pradesh (36), Haryana (35), Gujarat (34), Chhattisgarh (38) recorded higher NNMR as compared to national average. The NNMR is lowest in the Kerala (7). The significant feature is that, the NNMR came down or remained stagnant in 2009 as compared to 2008 except in the case of Haryana, Himachal Pradesh, Jharkhand and Karnataka.

(f) Post-Neonatal Mortality Rate (PNNMR)

This refers to the number of infant deaths at 28 days to one year of age per 1000 live births. According to the Family Welfare Statistics in India, 2011, the post-neonatal mortality rate came down to 16 in 2009 from 24 in 2002. The PNNMR is high in rural areas (17) as compared to urban areas.

(g) Perinatal Mortality Rate (PNMR)

This refers to the number of still births and deaths within the 1st week of delivery per 1000 live births. According to the Family Welfare Statistics in India, 2011, the PNMR varies in the range of 37 to 35 since 2001 and stood at 35 in 2009. It is high in rural areas (39) as compared to urban areas (23) during 2009.

(h) Child Mortality Rate (0-4)

Child mortality rate is measured in terms of number of deaths children (0-4 years) taking place per 1000 children (0-4 years age). As per SRS estimates, 2011, the Child mortality rate (CMR) has come down from 57.3 in 1972 to 26.5 in 1991 and 14.1 in 2009. The CMR is very high in rural areas (15.7) as compared to urban areas (8.7) in 2009 and this observation is relevant for almost all states uniformly. The highest CMR was recorded in Madhya Pradesh (21.4) closely followed by Uttar Pradesh (20.1) and Assam (19.0). Kerala with 2.6 CMR is the best performing state.

Table 2.14 shows the mortality indicators in India from the period 1998 to 2010. The table shows that there has been a considerable fall in infant mortality rate in rural India from 1998 (77.4) to 2009 (55.0). Same pattern can be also observed in case of NNMR and PNMR. No improvement is seen in case of still birth rate during this period.

Table 2.14: Mortality indicators in rural India 1998-2010

Years	*Crude Death Rate*	*Infant Mortality Rate*	*Neonatal Mortality Rate*	*Post-Natal Mortality Rate*	*Perinatal Mortality Rate*	*Still Birth Rate*
1998	9.7	77.4	49.0	28.4	45.2	8.9
1999	9.0	75.0	49.0	26.0	47.0	11.0
2000	9.3	74.0	49.0	25.0	44.0	9.0
2001	9.1	71.7	44.0	27.7	49.1	9.7
2002	8.7	69.0	NA	NA	NA	NA
2003	8.7	66.0	41.0	25.0	36.0	9.0
2004	8.2	64.0	41.0	22.0	39.0	10.0
2005	8.1	64.0	41.0	23.0	40.0	9.0
2006	8.1	62.0	41.0	22.0	41.0	9.0
2007	8.0	61.0	40.0	20.0	41.0	9.0
2008	8.0	58.0	39.0	19.0	39.0	9.0
2009	7.8	55.0	38.0	17.0	39.0	8.0
2010	7.7	51.0	36.0	NA	35.0	NA

Notes: 1. 1998 to & 2010: Excludes Jammu & Kashmir
2. 1998 to 2010: Excludes Mizoram
3. 1998 to 2010: Excludes Nagaland (Rural)
4. N.A. Not Available

Source: SRS Bulletin, January 2011 & December 2011, Statistical Report, 2009, Registrar General of India

(i) FERTILITY RATE

The three common measures of fertility are; (a) Crude Birth Rate (CBR), (b) Age-Specific Fertility Rates (ASFR), and (c) Total Fertility Rate (TFR).

(j) CRUDE BIRTH RATE (CBR)

Crude birth rate indicates the number of live births occurring during the year, per 1000 population estimated at mid-year. Data from the Sample Registration System, 2011, shows that the CBR in rural areas has declined from 30.9 in 1991 to 24.1 in 2009. The CBR is higher (24.1) in rural areas as compared to urban areas (18.3) (Table 2.15).

Table 2.15: Crude birth rate in rural and urban areas (1991-2009)

Year	*Rural*	*Urban*
1991	30.9	24.3
1992	30.9	23.1
1993	30.4	23.7
1994	30.5	23.1
1995	30.0	22.7
1996	29.3	21.6
1997	28.9	21.5
1998	28.0	21.1
1999	27.5	20.8
2000	27.6	20.7
2001	27.1	20.3
2002	26.6	20.0
2003	26.4	19.8
2004	26.9	19.0
2005	25.6	19.1
2006	25.2	18.8
2007	24.7	18.6
2008	24.4	18.5
2009	24.1	18.3

Source: Sample Registration System, 2009, Registrar General, India.

(k) Age Specific Fertility Rates (ASFR) & Age Specific Marital Fertility Rates (ASMFR)

ASFR is defined as the number of children born to women in the said age group per 1000 women in the same age group and ASMFR as the number of children born to married women in the said age group per 1000 women in the same age group. Throughout the period 2004-2009, the age group 20-24 continued to have peak fertility rates in rural and urban areas, but both these indicators are lower in urban areas as compared to rural areas. The ASMFR increased to 326 in 2009 from 303 in 2008 and the ASFR increased to 227.8 in 2009 from 218.6 in 2008 for the age group 20-24.

(l) Total Fertility Rate (TFR)

The TFR for the country increased from 2.6 in 2008 to 2.8 in 2010 with Bihar reporting the highest TFR at 3.8 followed by Madhya Pradesh (3.5) while Kerala and Tamil Nadu continued its outstanding performance with the lowest TFR of 1.8. Among the major states, the TFR level below 2.1 has been attained by Andhra Pradesh (1.9), Karnataka (2.0), Kerala (1.8), Maharashtra (2.0), Punjab (1.9), Tamil Nadu (1.8), Himachal Pradesh (1.9) and West Bengal (1.9) (Table 2.14). The rural women are having higher TFR (2.9) as compared to urban (2.0) women.

2.7 MIGRATION PATTERNS

According to some economists migration is considered to be a function of labour reallocation in response to market demands. Others explain it in terms of the push and pull caused by higher man-land ratio, underemployment at the place of origin and the pull of higher wages, opportunities for education and training, etc. Of the different streams of migration in India, rural to rural and rural to urban are important in the present context. Table 2.17 shows that according to NSS 64th Round 2007-2008, 92.6 per cent of the rural-rural migrants were females while only 12.2 per cent were males, who moved from one rural area to the other mostly due to marriages.

On the other hand, 52.8 per cent of the migrants who moved from one rural area to the other were males either for employment related reasons or movement of parents/earning member. The number of male migrants who moved from rural to urban areas was more and they moved mostly in search of jobs (60.9%). If you look at Table 2.17, the reasons for migration become very clear. It is not difficult to see that the lack of employment opportunities in rural areas is pushing more and more people to cities or towns resulting in the rise of slums and overall urban explosion.

Table 2.16: Total fertility rate by residence in India & major states 2010

India and Bigger States	*Rural*	*Urban*	*Total*
India	2.8	1.9	2.5
Andhra Pradesh	1.9	1.6	1.8
Assam	2.7	1.6	2.5
Bihar	3.8	2.7	3.7
Chhattisgarh	3.0	1.9	2.8
Delhi	2.1	1.9	1.9
Gujarat	2.7	2.1	2.5
Haryana	2.5	2.0	2.3
Himachal Pradesh	1.9	1.3	1.8
Jammu & Kashmir	2.2	1.4	2.0
Jharkhand	3.2	2.1	3.0
Karnataka	2.0	1.7	2.0
Kerala	1.8	1.8	1.8
Madhya Pradesh	3.5	2.2	3.2
Maharashtra	2.0	1.7	1.9
Odisha	2.4	1.6	2.3
Punjab	1.8	1.7	1.8
Rajasthan	3.3	2.4	3.1
Tamil Nadu	1.8	1.6	1.7
Uttar Pradesh	3.7	2.7	3.5
West Bengal	2.0	1.3	1.8

Source: SRS Statistical Report-2010 (Latest), Registrar General of India

Table 2.17: All-India proportion of internal migrants by reason for migration for rural-to-rural and rural-to-urban streams (per cent) (2007–08)

Reasons for migration	*Males*		*Females*	
	Rural-to-rural	*Rural-to-urban*	*Rural-to-rural*	*Rural-to-urban*
Employment-related reasons	29.1	60.9	0.5	2.6
Studies	10.5	7.8	0.5	2.5
Marriage	12.2	1.6	92.6	62.8
Movement of parents/earning member	23.7	22.8	3.6	28.2
Other reasons	24.4	6.9	2.9	4.0
All	100	100	100	100

Notes: Figures have been rounded off to 100;

Migrant: A household member whose last usual place of residence (UPR), anytime in the past, is different from the present place of enumeration is considered a migrant member in a household; UPR: UPR of a person is defined as a place (village/town) where the person has stayed continuously for a period of 6 months or more.

Source: NSS 64th Round, Report No. 533: Migration in India: July 2007–June 2008.

2.8 SIZE OF RURAL SETTLEMENTS

In the census, rural settlements have been divided into seven categories according to the population size of villages. These range from hamlets with less than 200 persons to large villages with more than 10,000 inhabitants.

Table 2.18: Inhabited villages classified by population size, 2001 & 2011

Size of Village in terms of Population	*Villages in the Size Group*			*Population living in those villages*		
	Number (2011)	*Percent*		*Number (2011)*	*Percent*	
		2011	*2001*		*2011*	*2001*
Less than 200	82151	13.74	36.90	8179551	0.98	7.16
200–499	114732	19.19		39685424	4.76	
500–999	141800	23.73	24.50	103321330	12.39	14.18
1,000–1,999	139164	23.29	21.90	197536058	23.69	24.69
2,000–4,999	96428	16.13	13.54	288773884	36.64	32.21
5,000–9,999	18652	3.12	2.49	123877458	14.86	13.21
10,000 and above	4681	0.78	0.67	72375147	8.68	8.55
All	597608	100	100	833748852	100	100

Source: Table A3, Census of India 2011, Part II A (i) General Population Tables

According to the 2011 Census more than 55 per cent of the rural population was concentrated in 40 per cent of the villages with populations ranging from 1000-4999 inhabitants (see Table 2.18). The corresponding figures for 2001 were 56% and 34% respectively. The inference is that population concentration in the larger villages is increasing while the number and the population of small villages and hamlets are decreasing. Also notice that in 2011 more than 60 per cent of the villages had less than 1000 inhabitants. This is a an important observation, because many rural development schemes do not reach such small villages where accessibility is a serious problem. Therefore, a consideration of the distribution of population is equally important in formulating plans and programmes for rural development.

Table 2.15 shows the average size of villages in major states. In Kerala the average size of the village is 17281 as per the 2001 Census while in Himachal Pradesh it is 273 and in Odisha 608. In such a situation particular rural development programmes launched on an all-India basis are bound to fail because of the problems of physical accessibility as well as cost-effectiveness, as generally the small villages tend to be in difficult and remote areas. Therefore, while planning for rural development adequate attention needs to be given to these factors.

2.9 LITERACY RATE

Literacy is an important driving force behind economic and social development and it is a powerful influence that tends to reduce the birth rate, thereby reducing the pressure of population. The Socio Economic and Caste Census 2011 (SECC) released in 2015 has found that 36 per cent of the 884 million people in rural India are illiterate. This is higher than the 32 per cent recorded by the Census of India 2011. Of the 64 per cent literate rural Indians, more than one fifth have not even completed primary school. Working in anything other than agriculture will be a tough ask, given the level of education – fewer than 10 per cent make it to higher secondary or above and just 3.41 per cent of households have a family member who is at least a graduate. The SECC also found that only 5.4 per cent of rural India has completed high school with a mere 3.4 per cent having graduated from college. This poor state of rural education is reflected in the fact that 23.5 per cent of rural households had no adults above the age of 25 who are literate – one of the categories of deprivation measured by the SECC, 2011.

The performance within states is hugely varied, with an alarming 47.6 per cent of rural Rajasthanis remaining illiterate followed by Madhya Pradesh (44.2), Bihar (44.0) compared to 9.3 per cent in Lakshadweep and 11.4 per cent in Kerala. Delhi performs the best when it comes to percentage of its rural population that has completed graduate studies – at 9.6 per cent; its performance is almost thrice as good as the national average.

Table 2.19: Highest education level completed (rural)

Sr. No.	*States/UT's*	*% of Illiterates*	*% of Literates but below Primary Level*	*% of Population completed Higher Education*	*% of Population completed Graduate Studies*
1.	India	35.0	13.9	5.4	3.4
2.	Jammu & Kashmir	39.52	10.1	6.0	3.5
3.	Himachal Pradesh	22.04	10.0	11.4	5.2
4.	Punjab	31.86	9.8	8.5	3.0
5.	Haryana	34.27	11.3	8.2	4.1
6.	Bihar	43.92	19.7	3.6	2.2
7.	West Bengal	35.58	13.2	3.4	2.6
8.	Odisha	39.29	15.5	3.8	2.1
9.	Jharkhand	39.26	13.7	3.6	2.7
10.	Rajasthan	47.58	14.6	3.8	2.9
11.	Gujarat	31.02	13.0	4.7	2.7
12.	Maharashtra	27.01	14.5	8.5	4.3
13.	AP	37.90	14.7	4..4	3.4
14.	Karnataka	31.54	11.3	6.2	3.6
15.	Kerala	11.38	7.9	11.3	7.7
16.	Tamil Nadu	26.39	8.4	7.1	6.6
17.	Uttarakhand	25.41	13.2	8.0	5.8
18.	Uttar Pradesh	38.15	15.2	5.2	3.5
19.	Chhattisgarh	39.55	16.4	4.8	2.1
20.	Madhya Pradesh	44.23	16.2	4.5	2.2
21.	Sikkim	20.12	19.2	5.2	4.0
24.	Assam	32.06	12.4	4.8	2.2
25.	NCT of Delhi	13.58	8.7	12.4	9.6

Source: Socio Economic and Caste Census (SECC), 2011

These numbers reiterate the poor quality of education being provided in rural India and the high drop-out rate, as brought up repeatedly by the Annual State of Education Report (ASER) in rural India by Pratham. According to ASER, 96 per cent of children aged 6-14 are enrolled in schools, but the fact that 36 per cent of rural Indians are illiterate points towards poor education quality, a high drop-out rate, or both.

According to NSSO survey (71st round), January to June 2014, literacy rate in rural areas was pegged at 71 per cent last year, compared to 86 per cent in urban areas, while among the age group of seven years and above, male literacy rate was found higher than the female literacy rate. Among the age group of seven years and above, the male literacy rate was registered at 83 per cent vis-a-vis the female literacy rate of 67 per cent. It was found that in the rural areas, nearly 4.5 per cent of males and 2.2 per cent of females completed education level of graduation and above, while in urban areas 17 per cent of males and 13 per cent of females completed this level of education.

In Rajasthan, Jumbish and Shiksha Karmi projects, and in Madhya Pradesh, the Education Guarantee Scheme, the District Primary Education Programme and programmes like Mahila Samakhaya have made some visible impact. In respect of female literacy, Bihar and Jharkhand are at the bottom. Even though the states with very low female literacy have made good progress in bridging the gender gap over the years, they require some more concerted efforts to reduce the gap further in the years to come. The enrolment and retention of girls in these states must increase and there should be more emphasis on adult literacy programmes for females.

2.10 MAIN SOURCE OF INCOME IN RURAL INDIA

Among the crucial findings of the SECC 2011, conducted by the Ministry of Rural Development, was that about 30 per cent of rural households are landless and derive a major part of their income from manual, casual labour. Another 30 per cent derive it from cultivation. The numbers also point to the subsistence level of farming that rural India currently practises. The countryside remains unable to find jobs that can pull families out of poverty. Just over 3 per cent of rural households have a family member who is a graduate, so skilled jobs are going to be hard to get. The eastern and central states of Chhattisgarh, Madhya Pradesh and Odisha have the poorest indicators. Even in the developed southern states of Kerala and Tamil Nadu, family incomes are low and dependence on casual manual labour is high. Female-headed households and Scheduled Caste and

Scheduled Tribe households are the worst off. There is a substantial difference in the standard of living of India's Scheduled Castes and Scheduled Tribes and "others". Fewer than five per cent of SC and ST households have a main earner who makes more than Rs 10,000 per month – for "others"; there are twice as many households.

Table 2.20 shows the main source of household income in Rural India of various selected states.

Table 2.20: Main source of household income (rural India)

Sr. No.	*States/UT's*	*% Cultivation*	*% Manual Casual Labour*
1.	All India	30.09	51.19
2.	Andhra Pradesh	22.47	58.90
3.	Bihar	18.24	70.88
4.	Chhattisgarh	40.15	52.13
5.	Haryana	33.08	42.70
6.	Jharkhand	29.28	51.69
7.	Kerala	10.26	50.61
8.	Madhya Pradesh	34.80	56.68
9.	Odisha	23.08	58.84
10.	Tamil Nadu	18.22	65.77
11.	Uttar Pradesh	40.24	45.64

Source: Socio Economic and Caste Census (SECC), 2011

According to the NSSO 68th Round, all-India estimate of average monthly per capita consumer expenditure (MPCE) was around Rs.1430 for rural India and about Rs. 2630 for urban India. Thus, average urban MPCE was about 84% higher than average rural MPCE for the country as a whole, though there were wide variations in this differential across states. For the average rural Indian, food accounted for 52.9% of the value of consumption during 2011-12. This included 10.8% for cereals and cereal substitutes, 8% for milk and milk products, 7.9% on beverages, refreshments and processed food, and 6.6% on vegetables. Among non-food item categories, fuel and light for household purposes (excluding transportation) accounted for 8%, clothing and footwear for 7%, medical expenses for 6.7%, education for 3.5%, conveyance for 4.2%, other consumer services (excl. conveyance) for 4%, and consumer durables for 4.5%.

A government survey on income and expenditure reveals that about 60 per cent of India's rural population lives on less than ₹ 35 a day and nearly as many in cities live on ₹ 66 a day. In terms of average per capita daily expenditure, it comes out to be about ₹ 35 in rural and ₹ 66 in urban India. About 60 per cent of the population lives with these expenditures or less in rural and urban areas.

2.11 OVERVIEW OF SOCIO-ECONOMIC STRUCTURE OF RURAL INDIA

Even though the proportion of rural population in our country has gradually declined over the years, from 82 per cent in 1951 to 68.84 per cent in 2011, there has been a considerable increase in the absolute number of people living in rural areas. This is indicated by the fact that the number of people living per square kilometre has increased from 214 in 1991 to 254 in 2011. The sex ratio in India is of great concern as it shows continuous decline both in the rural and the urban areas. The child sex ratio is particularly shocking as it reveals a strong preference for the mail child throughout the country and more so in the northwestern states. Coming to the age composition of population, not much difference has occurred. As of now the base is quite broad with the productive age group gradually swelling out with a tapering top. The only silver lining is that the age of marriage of females is rising, though very slowly, all over the country. This will perhaps be able to arrest the birth rate and hence the growth of population. Unfortunately, however, this positive change is not uniform and particularly in the Hindi speaking heartland the decline in vital rates is very slow which is adversely affecting the overall efforts for growth in this region. Analyzing the migration data, we have seen that rural to urban migration mostly for employment purposes is significant. This highlights the lack of employment opportunities in the villages. We can assume that the size of the villages also guides this process, as in comparison with large villages such as those in Kerala development is slow in small villages and hamlets, which are inaccessible. Development is directly related to awareness and it comes only through literacy as we have seen in Kerala. Though there are huge gaps between male and female literacy rates in both the rural and the urban areas, the gender gap has decreased as is indicated by the 2011 Census, which brings some hope for population stabilization and overall development.

CHAPTER 3

Development: Measurement and Policy

CHAPTER OUTLINE

- Bases of Development Measurement
- Measuring Development
    - Traditional Economic Measures
    - New Economic Measures
        - Income Distribution
        - Lorenz Curve
        - Gini's Coefficient
        - Absolute Poverty
    - Social Measures
    - Human Development Index (HDI)
    - Millennium Development Goals (MDGs)
- Development Policy

3.1 BASES OF DEVELOPMENT MEASUREMENT

There are several methods to ascertain the level of development of a country. Broadly, these can be divided under four main heads—economic, social, demographic and environmental.

Under **economic measures** are included GDP per capita, structure of the economy, access to raw materials, workers' productivity, availability of consumer goods and purchasing power parity. In order to estimate the total economic activity of a country or region, a variety of measures of national income and output are used including gross domestic product (GDP), gross national product (GNP), and net national income (NNI). Gross domestic product is defined as the value of all final goods and services produced in a country in one year. Gross National Product is defined as the market value of all goods and services produced in one year by labour and property supplied by the residents of a country. Net national income is GNP minus depreciation and net indirect taxes. Gross domestic product per capital is the main value of the output produced per person, which is also the mean income.

Social measures of development include literacy, education, health and welfare. All of these are intimately connected with economic development. A greater percentage of educated people are a pointer of economic development. Similarly, facilities for the improvement of health, their expansion and the quality of health services offered are also good indicators of economic development. The provision of safe drinking water and sanitation facilities are essential for maintenance of health. As such when these are not available to the citizens of a country, the situation is that of underdevelopment. Indicators of state of health are average life expectancy, calorie intake per person, number of doctors per thousand persons and the number of people per hospital bed.

The **demographic measures** of economic development are infant mortality rate, rate of natural increase (RNI), age structure and epidemiological transition. Infant mortality rate refers to the number of children who die before attaining the age of one year per thousand persons. A high infant mortality rate reflects poorly on the availability and state of health services. RNI is the crude birth rate minus the crude death rate of a population. Age structure can be defined as the relative number of individuals of each age in a population and is an indicator of fertility, mortality and migration patterns which further point towards the level of economic development of a country. Epidemiological transition refers to the transition from parasitic and infectious diseases to circulatory and degenerative diseases. (Epidemiology refers to the branch of medical sciences dealing with the transmission and control of diseases.)

Apart from the above, the World Bank and International Monetary Fund has come forward with 2 new measures of economic development. These are Purchasing Power Parity (PPP) and Human Development Index (HDI). **Purchasing power parity (PPP)** is a theory of long-term equilibrium exchange rates based on relative price levels of two countries. It measures the real purchasing power of economies as opposed to the prevailing exchange rate of currencies.

The **Human Development Index** (HDI) is a summary measure of human development that is published by the United Nations Development Programme (UNDP). The HDI provides an alternative to the common practice of evaluating a country's progress in development based on per capita Gross Domestic Product (GDP). The HDI is the signature trademark of the Human Development Report (HDR), an independent report commissioned by the UNDP that is written by a team of scholars, development practitioners and members of the Human Development Report Office of UNDP. The HDI has had a significant impact on drawing the attention of governments, corporations and international organizations to aspects of development that focus on the expansion of choices and freedoms, not just income.

The HDI is a summary composite index that measures a country's average achievements in three basic aspects of human development: longevity, knowledge, and a decent standard of living. Longevity is measured by life expectancy at birth; knowledge is measured by a combination of the adult literacy rate and the combined primary, secondary and tertiary gross enrolment ratio; and standard of living by GDP per capita (PPP US$).

The 2009 report which covers the period up to 2007 placed 38 countries (out of 182) in the top category of 'Very High Human Development' and refers to them as 'developed countries'—the top ten being Norway (0.971), Australia (0.970), Iceland (0.969), Canada (0.966), Ireland (0.965), Netherlands (0.964), Sweden (0.963), France (0.961), Switzerland (0.960) and Japan (0.960). The bottom ten in the category of least development countries and Niger (0.340), Afghanistan (0.352), Sierra Leone (0.365), Central African Republic (0.369), Mali (0.371), Burkina Faso (0.389), Democratic Republic of the Congo (0.389), Chad (0.392), Burundi (0.394) and Guinea-Bissau (0.396). India is at 134th position (0.612) in the category of medium human development. Because of the new methodology adopted since 2010 Human Development Report, the new reported HDI figures appear lower than the HDI figures in previous reports. There are 49 countries in the very high category according to the latest report (2015). From 50 to 105 are the countries which lie in the high category. Medium from 106 to 143, Low from 144 to 188. The position of India (0.609) is 130.

Of late some more related measures of economic development have come to the fore—Gender-related Development Index, Gender Empowerment Measure, Human Poverty Index and Physical Quality of Life Index. The gender-related development index (GDI) is a composite indicator that measures the average achievement of a population in the same dimensions as the HDI while adjusting for gender inequalities in the level of achievement in the three basic aspects of human development. It uses the same variables as the HDI, disaggregated by gender.

The gender empowerment measure (GEM) is a composite indicator that captures gender inequality in three key areas:

- Political participation and decision-making, as measured by women's and men's percentage of parliamentary representation.
- Economic participation and decision-making power, as measured by two indicators—women's and men's percentage shares of positions as legislators, senior officials and managers and women's and men's percentage shares of professional and technical positions.

- Power over economic resources, as measured by women's and men's estimated earned income (PPP US$).

Poverty has traditionally been measured as a lack of income—but this is far too narrow a definition. Human poverty is a concept that captures the many dimensions of poverty that exist in both poor and rich countries—it is the denial of choices and opportunities for living a life one has reason to value. The **HPI-1—human poverty index for developing countries**—measures human deprivations in the same three aspects of human development as the HDI (longevity, knowledge and a decent standard of living). **HPI-2—human poverty index for selected high-income OECD countries**—includes, in addition to the three dimensions in HPI-1, social exclusion.

The **Physical Quality of Life Index (PQLI)** is an attempt to measure the quality of life or well-being of a country. The value is the average of three statistics: basic literacy rate, infant mortality, and life expectancy at age one, all equally weighted on a 0 to 100 scale.

It was developed for the Overseas Development Council in the mid-1970s by Morris David Morris, as one of a number of measures created due to dissatisfaction with the use of GNP as an indicator of development. PQLI might be regarded as an improvement but shares the general problems of measuring quality of life in a quantitative way. It has also been criticized because there is considerable overlap between infant mortality and life expectancy.

Standard of living is usually measured by standards such as real (i.e., inflation adjusted) income per person and poverty rate. Other measures such as access and quality of healthcare, income growth inequality and educational standards are also used. Examples are access to certain goods (such as number of TV or cars per 1000 people), or measures of health such as life expectancy. "It is the ease by which people living in a time or place are able to satisfy their needs and/or wants."

The idea of a 'standard' may be contrasted with the quality of life, which takes into account not only the material standard of living, but also other more intangible aspects that make up human life, such as leisure, safety, cultural resources, social life, physical health, environmental quality issues, etc. More complex means of measuring well-being must be employed to make such judgments, and these are very often political, thus controversial. Even between two nations or societies that have similar material standards of living, quality of life factors may in fact make one of these places more attractive to a given individual or group.

3.2 MEASURING DEVELOPMENT

3.2.1 Traditional Economic Measures

In economic terms, development has traditionally been defined as the ability to generate and sustain economic growth. The annual increase in Gross National Product (GNP) and Gross Domestic Product (GDP) is used to measure economic growth. Per capita values are used to indicate whether or not overall economic growth is faster than population growth so we know whether the hypothetical average citizen of a country is better off. Furthermore, "real" figures that are adjusted for inflation are used to give an account of an average citizen's material well-being such as ***purchasing power parity*** values which are used to make better comparisons between different countries.

Measuring development in such terms reflects dominant strategies and approaches to development. Generally, economic development was seen as a planned alteration to the structure of production and employment so that agriculture's share of both declined and that of the manufacturing and services sector increased. This resulted in policies that tended to focus on industrialisation usually at the expense of agriculture and rural development. These economic measures of development were often supplemented by reference to non-economic social indicators such as literacy, health, life expectancy, etc.

Until the 1970s development was seen exclusively as an economic phenomenon where it was assumed that GNP growth would trickle down to the majority of people through jobs and other opportunities. Such ***trickle down*** was expected to a wider distribution of income and social benefits.

3.2.2 New Economic Measures

The 1970s witnessed a rising disillusionment with the pursuit of economic growth. In developed countries the environmental movement began to question the desirability of industrialisation that resulted in pollution and the depletion of natural resources. In developing countries the concern shifted to income distribution, employment and poverty eradication because, while the economies of developing countries were growing at historically fast rates, poverty and inequality were also rising.

As was seen in Singer's article (1989), the 1970s saw an attempt to *dethrone* GNP growth as the principal objective of development. The 1970s saw the emergence of both employment creation and income redistribution as priorities. Thus, issues of poverty and equality became the major themes of development. While much reference has been made to the ***dethronement*** of GNP in truth this did not mean that economic growth was regarded as irrelevant, but rather there was widespread acceptance that while economic growth was necessary for development, it alone was not sufficient to lift people out of poverty. Therefore, how economic growth was achieved and whom it benefited became more important.

The neo-classical counterrevolution of the 1980s and 1990s once again put economic growth at the forefront of policy making with restructuring the economy, making debt payments and stimulating economic growth taking precedence over efforts at reducing poverty and inequality. Ironically, this period was characterised by slow and even negative growth. Throughout this period poverty began to worsen as economies contracted under heavy debt burdens and IMF/World Bank structural adjustment programmes that disproportionately affected the poorest.

At the beginning of the millennium, although the neo-classical model continued to exist, the approach has softened somewhat. There is broader acceptance of the need to focus more on interventions that seek to reduce poverty, especially in the areas of developing human capital through the provision of social goods such as health and education. Such a change is exemplified by the promotion of Poverty Reduction Strategy Papers (PRSPs) by both the World Bank and the International Monetary Fund. Similarly, the international community endorsed the Millennium Development Goals (MDGs) as international targets to be achieved by 2015, which focuses development discourse on reducing poverty. However, economic growth as one of the principal indicators of development continues to dominate both in developed and developing countries. Indeed, some developing countries have voiced concerns and criticised donor conditionality on debt relief funds as being overly restricted to the provision of social services such as health and education, and not permitting sufficient flexibility to promote economic activity.

The pendulum of the debate therefore swings backwards and forwards between the relative importance of economic growth as the most effective way of tackling poverty, or whether interventions aimed at tackling poverty and inequality should be emphasised. In reality both approaches co-exist and there is acceptance that economic growth is an important measure to tackle poverty and inequality.

(a) Income Distribution

In economics, income distribution is how a nation's total economy is distributed amongst its population. Classical economists such as Adam

Smith, Thomas Malthus and David Ricardo were mainly concerned with factor income distribution, that is, the distribution of income among the main factors of production, land, labour and capital. But modern economists are more concerned with the distribution of income across individuals and households and importance is given to the relationship between income, inequality and economic growth.

Income distribution is a common method to look at the distribution of income between the rich and poor. It consists of dividing the population into quintiles (fifths) or deciles (tenths) and according to ascending income levels determining what proportion of the total income is received by each group. Table 3.1 presents data from a number of countries on the share of income accruing to the poorest and the richest 10% of the population. Taking India as an example you will see that the poorest 10% of the population receive 3.9% of national income while the richest 10% receive 27.4% of national income. Using this information an inequality measure can also be obtained by calculating the ratio of income received by the richest 10% of the population to that received by the poorest 10% of the population, and so forth. In the case of India it can be seen that the richest 10% of the population receives 7.0 times more income than the poorest 10%. According to Global Wealth Report 2016, compiled by Credit Suisse Research Centre, India is the second most unequal country in the world with the top one percent of the population owing nearly 60% of the total wealth.

Table 3.1: Income, equality and poverty measures for selected countries

	Share of Income (%)— Poorest 10%	*Share of Income (%)— Richest 10%*	*Inequality Measure Ratio of Richest 10% to poorest 10%*	*Gini Coefficient*	*% of Population on less than $1[a] day [a] 1990-2002[b]*	*GDP per Capita PPP US$ 2002*
India	3.9	27.4	7.0	32.5	34.7	2670
Pakistan	3.7	28.3	7.6	33.0	13.4	1940
Bangladesh	3.9	26.7	6.8	31.8	36.0	1700
Zambia	1.1	41.0	36.6	52.6	63.7	840
Niger	0.8	35.4	46.0	50.5	61.4	800
Ethiopia	3.9	25.5	6.6	30.0	26.3	780
Madagascar	1.9	36.6	19.2	47.5	49.1	740
Tanzania	2.8	30.1	10.8	38.2	19.9	580

(a) Data refer to the most recent year available during the period specified.

(b) Poverty line is equivalent to $1.08 (1993 PPP US$).

Source: Human Development Report 2004.

One can observe from Table 3.1 that using such information provides a more detailed picture of poverty than relying on per capita GDP income alone. For example, it can be seen that other countries in the sample, while having even slightly higher incomes than Ethiopia, have a much more unequal distribution of this income resulting in higher poverty levels. For that matter India with high GDP per capita income has similar poverty levels as compared to Bangladesh with less income. In the case of Niger the richest 10 per cent of the population receives 46 times more than the poorest 10 per cent and in Zambia the ratio is 36.

(b) Lorenz Curve

The Lorenz curve is another method that diagrammatically represents the degree of equality in the distribution of income amongst a given population. The cumulative percentage of population is plotted on the horizontal axis, and the cumulative percentage of income received by the population on the vertical axis. The diagonal line represents a perfectly equal distribution of income with 10% of the population receiving 10% of income, 20% of the population receiving 20% of income and so forth. The Lorenz curve

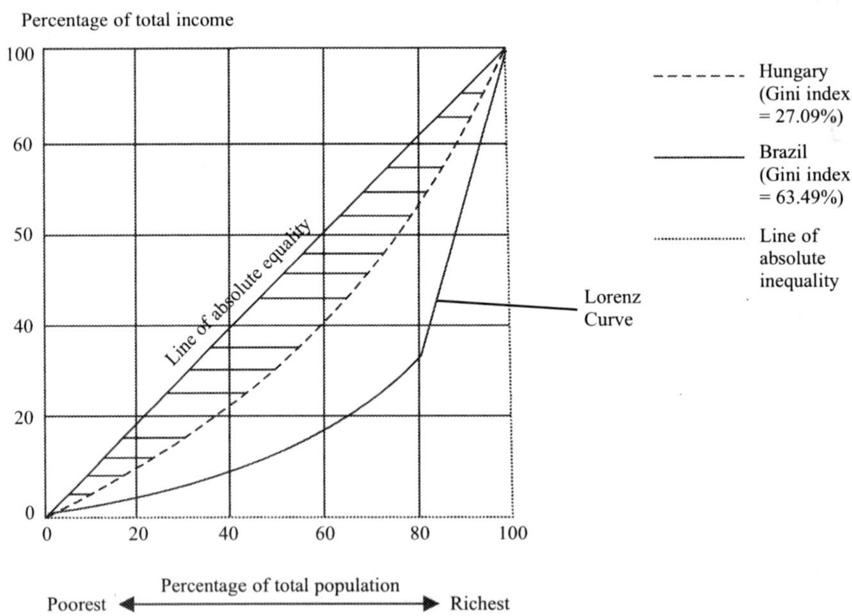

Fig. 3.1. Lorenz curve for selected countries

Source: World Bank 2000 Beyond Economic Growth: Meeting the Challenges of Global Development by Katherine Sheram, Tatyana P. Soubbotina World Bank Beyond Economic Growth.

shows the actual distribution of income amongst the population. The further away the Lorenz curve is from the diagonal line the greater the degree of inequality.

In Figure 3.1, the Lorenz Curve is drawn for both Hungary and Brazil. One can see that the curve for Brazil is much farther away from the diagonal line than the curve for Hungary, indicating that income is more unequally distributed in Brazil.

(c) Gini's Coefficient

The Gini coefficient or Gini index is a useful summary measure of income inequality, and is derived from the Lorenz Curve. The index is calculated as the area between a Lorenz curve and the line of absolute equality (the diagonal line), expressed as a percentage of the area of the 90° triangle under the line. A Gini coefficient of zero expresses perfect equality, where all values are the same (for examle, where everyone has the same income). Here Lorenz curve coincides with the straight line of a absolute equality. A Gini coefficient of one (or 100%) expresses maximum inequality among values (i.e., for a large number of people, where only one person has all the income or consumption, and all others have none, the Gini coefficient will be nearly one). Here the Lorenz curve concides with the x-axis. See the dotted line in Figure 3.1). In reality, neither perfect equality nor perfect inequality is possible. Thus, Gini indices are always greater than 0 per cent

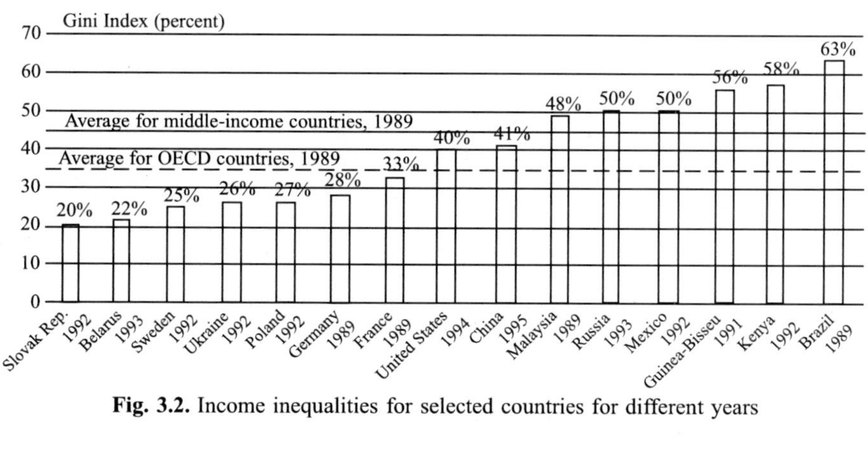

Fig. 3.2. Income inequalities for selected countries for different years

Note: An index value of a percent represents absolute equality In Income distribution: 100 per cent represents absolute inequality.

Source: World Bank 2000 Beyond Economic Growth: Meeting the Challenges of Global Development by Katherine Sheram, Tatyana P. Soubbotina World Bank Beyond Economic Growth.

but less than 100 per cent. (It should be noted that sometimes the Gini Coefficient, is expressed in decimal terms, on a scale of 0 to 1).

Looking at our sample of selected countries in Table 3.1 you will see that India's Gini Coefficient at 32.5% compares favourably with Zambia (52.6%) and Niger (50%). It also compares favourably when compared to those countries whose Gini Coefficients are plotted in Figure 3.2, being slightly less than the average for OECD countries. Therefore we can conclude that by international standards the distribution of income in India is relatively equal, particularly in comparison with many other developing countries.

(d) Absolute Poverty

Lastly, the poverty line is defined as the number of people who are unable to command sufficient resources to satisfy basic needs. It has been seen above that due to differences that exist between countries an international poverty line was established which counts anyone living on less than US$1 a day in PPP as being below the international poverty line. In 2008, the World Bank came out with a revised figure of $1.25 at 2005 purchasing power parity (PPP).

At a national level, countries determine their own poverty line, which is the threshold level of per capita income below which an individual is considered to be poor. This is usually based on a basic food basket. The quantity of the basket is determined in such a way that the given food basket meets a predetermined level of minimum calorie requirement. This basket is valued at nationally representative average prices to arrive at a consistent poverty line across regions and groups. Once this is done, an allowance is made for the nonfood component consistent with the spending patterns of the poor. This method yields a representative poverty line as it provides a monetary value of a poverty line that accounts for the food and nonfood components. As minimum subsistence levels vary from country to country and from region to region poverty lines that are constructed for individual countries may not facilitate an objective comparison between countries.

Poverty in India is widespread with the nation estimated to have a third of the world's poor. In 2012, the Indian Government stated 22% of its population is below its official poverty limit (RBI, 2012). The World Bank, in 2014 estimated 17.5% of Indian population or about 179.6 million people, lived below the new poverty line on purchasing power parity basis. According to UN's Millennium Development Goal; (MDG) programme 270 millions or 21.9% people out of 1.2 billion of Indians lived below poverty line of $1.25 in 2011-2012. According to the Modified Mixed Reference Period (MMRP) concept proposed by World Bank in 2015, India's poverty rate for period 2011-12 stood at 12.4% of total population, or about 172 million people; taking the revised poverty line as $1.90. The Asian Development Bank estimates Indian population to be at 1.28 billion with an average growth rate, from 2010-15, at 1.3%. In 2014, 49.9% of the population aged 15 years and above was employed. However, there are still 21.9% of the population who live below the national poverty line. Since the 1950s, the Indian government and non-governmental organizations have initiated several programmes to alleviate poverty, including subsidizing food and other necessities, increased access to loans, improving agricultural techniques and price supports, and promoting education and family planning. These measures have helped eliminate famines, cut absolute poverty levels by more than half, and reduced illiteracy and malnutrition.

3.2.3 Social measures

A number of problems are associated with using per capita GNP as a measure of development. Problems include its failure to include subsistence production and in incorporating welfare and income distribution considerations. Using GNP as a measure assumes that economic wealth equals development and takes no account of social, political and cultural dimensions. However, in addition a number of efforts have been made to develop indicators which could serve as complements or alternatives to this traditional measure. Such indicators seek to measure development in terms of interaction between social, political and economic factors or in terms of quality of life.

Early work by the United Nations Research Institute on Social Development (UNRISD) in 1970 developed a composite index of 16 core indicators consisting of 9 social indicators and 7 economic indicators. It found that ranking countries according to this index led to different results than rankings based on per capita GNP.

Another approach developed in the 1970s was the Physical Quality of Life Index (PQLI), which developed an index based on life expectancy at age 1, infant mortality and literacy. Comparison of this index to per capita GNP ranking showed that countries that tended to have high per capita GNPs tended to have high PQLIs and similarly those with low per capita GNPs had low PQLIs. However, it also showed that there were some countries that had high per capita GNPs but had low PQLIs and similarly other countries with low per capita GNPs but high PQLIs. This illustrated that improvements in the quality of life can be achieved without a huge rise in per capita GNP or alternatively higher levels of per capita GNP are not a guarantee of a better quality of life.

Methodologically similar to the PQLI, in 1990 the United Nations developed a Human Development Index (HDI) to provide a comparative indicator of socio-economic development for developed and developing countries.

3.2.4 Human Development Index (HDI)

The Human Development Index attempts to rank all countries on a scale of 0 (lowest human development) to 1 (highest human development) based on the following three goals of development:

(i) longevity as measured by life expectancy at birth;
(ii) knowledge as measured by a weighted average of adult literacy (two-thirds) and mean years of schooling (one-third); and
(iii) standard of living as measured by real per capita GDP adjusted for purchasing power parity (PPP) and an assumption of rapidly diminishing marginal utility above average world incomes.

Using these three measures of development HDI ranks all countries and classifies them according to three groups:

(i) low human development (0.0 to 0.50);
(ii) medium human development (0.50 to 0.79); and
(iii) high human development (0.80 to 1.0).

In a given year the HDI measure provides a relative measure of a country's human development compared to other countries. Also the HDI measures the *ends* of development (longetivity, knowledge and material choice) as opposed to the *means* of development as in the case of GDP. Table 3.2 shows the latest HDI Index Rankings from the UNDP's 2004 Human Development Report.

The HDI measures achievements in terms of life expectancy, educational attainment and adjusted real income.

Table 3.2: 2004 Human development index ranking

HDI rank		*HDI rank*				*HDI rank*	
High human development		*Medium human development*				*Low human development*	
1	Norway	56	Bulgaria	101	Iran	142	Pakistan
2	Sweden	57	Russian Federation	102	Occupied Palestinian	143	Togo

3	Australia	58	Libyan Arab Jamahiriya		Territories	144	Congo
4	Canada	59	Malaysia	103	El Salvador	145	Lesotho
5	Netherlands	60	Macedonia, TFYR	104	Guyana	146	Uganda
6	Belgium	61	Panama	105	Cape Verde	147	Zimbabwe
7	Iceland	62	Belarus	106	Syrian Arab Republic	148	Kenya
8	United Slates	63	Tonga	107	Uzbekistan	149	Yemen
9	Japan	64	Mauritius	108	Algeria	150	Madagascar
10	Ireland	65	Albania	109	Equatorial Guinea	151	Nigeria
11	Switzerland	66	Bosnia and Herzegovina	110	Kyrgyzstan	152	Mauritania
12	United Kingdom	67	Suriname	111	Indonesia	153	Haiti
13	Finland	68	Venezuela	112	Viet Nam	154	Djibouti
14	Austria	69	Romania	113	Moldova	155	Gambia
15	Luxembourg	70	Ukraine	114	Bolivia	156	Eritrea
16	France	71	Saint Lucia	115	Honduras	157	Senegal
17	Denmark	72	Brazil	116	Tajikistan	158	Timor-Leste
18	New Zealand	73	Colombia	117	Mongolia	159	Rwanda
19	Germany	74	Oman	118	Nicaragua	160	Guinea
20	Spain	75	Samroa (Western)	119	South Africa	151	Benin
21	Italy	76	Thailand	120	Egypt	162	Tanzania
22	Israel	77	Saudi Arabia	121	Guatemala	163	Cote d'lvoire
23	Hong Kong China (SAR)	78	Kazaklistan	122	Gabon	164	Zambia
24	Greece	79	Jamaica	123	Sao Tome and Principe	165	Malawi
25	Singapore	80	Lebanon	124	Solomon Islands	166	Angola

Contd...

HDI rank		*HDI rank*				*HDI rank*	
High human development		*Medium human development*				*Low human development*	
26	Portugal	81	Fiji	125	Morocco	167	Chad
27	Slovenia	82	Armenia	126	Namibia	168	Congo
28	Korea	83	Philippines	127	India	169	Central African Republic
29	Barbados	84	Maldives	128	Botswana	170	Ethiopia
30	Cyprus	85	Peru	129	Vanuatu	171	Mozambique
31	Malta	86	Turkmenistan	130	Cambodia	172	Guinea Bissau
32	Czech Republic	87	St. Vincent & the Grenadines	131	Ghana	173	Burundi
33	Brunei Darussalam	88	Turkey	132	Myanmar	174	Mali
34	Argentina	89	Paraguay	133	Papua New Guinea	175	Burkina Faso
35	Seychelles	90	Jordan	134	Bhutan	176	Niger
36	Estonia	91	Azerbaijan	135	Lao Peoples Dem. Rep.	177	Sierra Leone
37	Poland	92	Tunisia	136	Comoros		
38	Hungary	93	Grenada	137	Swaziland		
39	Saint Kitts and Nevis	94	China	138	Bangladesh		
40	Bahrain	95	Dominica	139	Sudan		
41	Lithuania	90	Sri Lanka	140	Nepal		
42	Slovakia	97	Georgia	141	Cameroon		

43	Chile	96	Dominican Republic				
44	Kuwait	99	Belize				
45	Costa Rica	100	Ecuador				
46	Uruguay						
47	Qatar						
48	Croatia						
49	United Arab Emirates						
50	Latvia						
51	Bahamas						
52	Cuba						
53	Mexico						
54	Trinidad and Tobago						
55	Antigua and Barbuda						

Source: Human Development Report 2004.

An important justification of using composite indicators that include social indicators is that they provide a better indication of development and allow for a better comparison of development achievements in different countries than ranking according to per capita incomes. Clearly,-if the rankings that emerge from using the HDI are similar to rankings based on per capita incomes then it could be said that ranking according to income provides a reasonable proxy for socio-economic development and there would be no need to include other social indicators.

However, ranking countries according to their HDI and GDP per capita gives different results. (Table 3.3) The column entitled GDP Rank minus HDI shows the differences in ranking between using the two measures: a positive number indicates how much a country's relative ranking increases by using the HDI instead of GDP per capita. Table 3.3 shows some interesting results. We can see that for some countries, e.g., Norway, Malaysia and Burundi, both rankings yield similar results. However, for other countries there are big differences; for example, Angola falls 38 places, Luxembourg 14 places and India 10 places when ranked by its human development index as opposed to income. In contrast Bulgaria's relative position improves by 10 places and Spain 5 places when ranked according to human development.

Table 3.3: HDI for selected countries

Country	*HDI Rank*	*GDP minus Rank*	*Rank HDI*	*GDP per Capita (PPP US$)*
High Human Development				
Norway	1	1	0.956	36,600
Luxembourg	19	–14	0.933	61,190
Spain	20	5	0.922	21,460
Medium Human Development				
Bulgaria	56	10	0.796	7,130
Malaysia	59	–2	0.793	9,120
India	127	–10	0.595	2670
Low Human Development				
Pakistan	142	–7	0.497	1940
Angola	166	–38	0.381	2,130
Burundi	173	0	0.339	630

Source: Generated from the UNDP Human Development Report 2004.

+ GDP per capita (PPP US$) rank minus HDI rank.

Generally, countries with higher HDIs tend to have higher per capita incomes. However, what is interesting to note is that some countries have higher HDIs and thus rank higher than other countries with similar per capita incomes. Countries with similar per capita incomes can have different levels of human development because of the way that income is used. (Table 3.4) For example Tajikistan has a considerably higher ranking than Burkina Faso though its income is less. One indication of this is the difference in literacy rates and life expectancy. Similarly, Mongolia too has a higher ranking than Pakistan though its income is less. And the difference in adult literacy is markedly different. This reinforces an earlier point made from Table 3.1 that per capita income by itself does not give a good indication of poverty or development in a country.

Table 3.4: HDI variations for countries with similar incomes

Country	*GDP per Capita*	*HDI Rank*	*Adult Literacy*	*Life Expectancy at Birth*
	(PPP US$)	*2004*	*(% ages 15 and above)*	*(Years)*
GDP per Capita from US$900 to US$1,100				
Tajikistan	980	116	99.5	68.8
Kenya	1,020	148	84.3	44.6
Burkina Faso	1,100	175	13	41.2
GDP per Capita from US$1,600 to US$ 1,800				
Mongolia	1,710	117	97.8	63.9
Bangladesh	1,700	138	41.1	61.4
Gambia	1,690	155	37.8	54.1
GDP per capita from US$ 1900–2700				
India	2670	127	61.3	63.7
Pakistan	1940	142	41.5	60.8
GDP per Capita from US $5,000 to US $5,300				
Cuba	5,259	52	96.1	76.7
Saint Lucia	5,300	71	94.8	72.5
Peru	5,010	85	85	69.8

Source: Generated from the UNDP Human Development Report 2004.

In addition to the widely used Human Development Index (HDI) the Human Development Report Office has been at the forefront of developing new human development measurements since its first report in 1990. Other composite indices have been developed over the years to address different aspects of human development and have been incorporated into the Human Development Report. Such indices include, for example, the gender related development index (GDI), the gender empowerment measure (GEM), the human poverty index (HPI), and the technological achievement index (TAI).

The Human Development Report Office has also been involved in developing both regional and national human development reports. The

HDI has made an important contribution to our understanding of what constitutes development, which countries are succeeding and how different groups and regions within countries are faring: it allows for a broader measure of development performance.

3.2.5 Millennium Development Goals (MDGs)

In September 2000, 189 nations, in the United Nations Millennium Declaration committed themselves to making the right to development a reality for everyone and to freeing the entire human race from want. They acknowledged that progress is based on sustainable economic growth, which must focus on the poor, with human rights at the centre. The objective of the Declaration is to promote *"a comprehensive approach and a coordinated strategy, tackling many problems simultaneously across a broad front"*.

The Declaration set out 8 goals for 2015. In summary these goals call for halving by the year 2015, the number of people who live on less than one dollar a day. This effort also involves finding solutions to hunger, malnutrition and disease, promoting gender equality and the empowerment of women, guaranteeing a basic education for everyone, and supporting the Agenda 21 principles of sustainable development. Direct support from the richer countries, in the form of aid, trade, debt relief and investment is to be provided to help the developing countries.

To help track progress, the UN Secretariat and the specialised agencies of the UN system, as well as representatives of IMF, the World Bank and OECD defined a set of time-bound and measurable goals and targets for combating poverty, hunger, disease, illiteracy, environmental degradation and discrimination against women. To monitor progress towards these goals and targets, 48 indicators have been identified to assess progress over the period from 1990 to 2015, when targets are expected to be met.

Increasingly, the 8 MDGs and the measurement of progress towards them are becoming important focus points in development discourse. For example the 2003 Human Development Report included tables outlining the position of each country in relation to the MDGs. The subsequent report in 2004 cross-references its tables in relation to the indicators linked to the MDGs. In order to help focus analysis and assessment of progress at the country level, the Millennium indicators and background data are presented by country in millennium country profiles.

Country-level monitoring is an indispensable element in assessing progress towards the MDGs and in mobilising resources to assist developing countries in meeting the targets. The United Nations Development Programme, assisted by other agencies and the UN Secretariat, is coordinating efforts and supporting the preparation of national monitoring reports in countries. The MDG Goals and Targets are presented in **Box 2.**

3.3 DEVELOPMENT POLICY

As development policy is the central theme of this book, it is worth reflecting on what is understood by it. Policy is difficult to define: a British civil servant once famously commented: "*Policy is rather like an elephant — you know it when you see it, but you cannot easily define it*". (Cunningham, 1963, cited in Keeley and Scoones 2003:23).

At its simplest, development policy can be regarded as giving expression to an underlying theory or set of beliefs about development. Development policy encompasses a conceptualisation of what development is, what it should achieve and how it should be achieved. It is a statement of intent or a framework for the implementation of actions to achieve this vision of development. It can be seen as a declaration of what those with decision-making powers intend to do with those powers. An example of a national development policy would be the introduction of Universal Primary Education (UPE) whereby every child is entitled to attend school free of charge.

The way that development policy is perceived is changing. Traditionally, policy has been associated with *public* policy, whose domain is seen as the national and international arena. Development policy has been considered a sequence of high-level formulation with subsequent top-down application, which is the exclusive domain of central governments, bilateral and multilateral donors. This static view and centralised view of development policy existed because of the close association between policy formulation,the resources and power to deliver policies, and the central role that the state played.

The 1980s marked a departure in the way development policy is viewed. The decade saw the breakdown of the consensus of the central role in development for an interventionist state. It witnessed an increasing role in policy debate and implementation for different thespians such as NGOs, aid agencies and the private sector. This expansion in the number of people involved in policy has resulted in policy becoming a contested field, indicating that more attention needs to be paid to the process of policy formulation and implementation, including issues such as: What are the motivations and common interests of their people?

And why do they come into conflict about policies?

How do groups influence policies? How policy is finally formulated as an outcome of the interaction of different stakeholders/actors?

To reflect these changes development policy has been broadly defined by Mackintosh (1992:1) "*as purposeful actions undertaken by the State (government and its employees) and other institutions (such as voluntary organisations) to promote a wider public objective such as social and economic development and not just private gain*".

Different perspectives on development are important determinants of development policy. As the conceptualisation of development is subject to debate, so too are the policies that give expression to any particular meaning of development. On the whole, **approaches to development could be characterised on a continuum with growth-centred development on one side, and people-centred development on the other side.**

Growth-centred development values economic growth above other criteria, while **people-centred development** has a relatively greater emphasis on social concerns. Between the two approaches there is a shifting middle ground that places varying degrees of emphasis on growth and human development. For example, the international predominance of growth-centred development in the 1980s favoured policies such as globalization, privatisation, market liberalization (LPG), and so forth, while the re-emergence of the human centred development in the late 1990s again emphasised increased provision of social services, especially health and education, as essential components of the ***war on poverty.***

Political processes and ideologies are other determinants of policies. Internationally, the shift to conservative governments in Western countries and the demise of the Soviet Union was instrumental in defining the structural adjustment agenda pursued by both the World Bank and IMF, which favoured privatisation, market liberalisation and so forth. Subsequent criticism of the social and human costs of structural adjustment and the re-emerging influence of international agencies promoting human development, such as the United National Development Programme, led to a softening of the growth-oriented approach.

Development policy is therefore a complex process involving a broad range of sectors, multiple levels of intervention and multiple actors. The term "development policy" tends to oversimplify the scope of what it involves. It suggests a rather limited area of action, whereas sectors covered by development policy can include economic, social and environmental areas. These, in turn, can be further divided into many different policy areas. The social sector includes policies linked to health, education, gender, urbanisation and so forth. The economic sector can cover agriculture, industrialisation, international aid, etc. Each of these sectors, in turn, can be further subdivided.

The people involved in influencing policy are extensive and include politicians, donor agencies, multi-lateral agencies, experts, local government officials, central government officials, academic institutions, citizen groups and local interest groups.

Viewing development policy as a process is useful as it leads to a greater appreciation of its complexities and leads to an understanding of why things may not work the way they are planned to. One can thus move away from looking at policy implementation in a rigid way to take a more multidimensional view of the interplay of multiple actors and sectors.

Box 1: Period 1990–2000

By the 1990s experience had led to disappointment with both the State and the market as institutions for driving development. In the 1980s State intervention was blamed for hindering development leading to a situation whereby no alternative to development outside a neo-liberal approach could be considered. However, by the 1990s this approach was becoming discredited as many countries, which had adhered to structural adjustment programmes and opened their economies were not reaping the benefits of their efforts. Similarly, the financial crisis of the Asian economies in 1998, which had been held as examples to other developing countries in the 1980s, called into question the validity of the assumption that the market could be the driving force of development.

The result is that, although the market and neo-liberal orthodoxy prevails, belief in this ideology is more nuanced and has evolved as a softer "market-friendly" orthodoxy, which sees the State as an enabler. Both the World Bank and the IMF retain their influence on development policy, but poverty reduction is once again receiving attention and being *championed* by these institutions. Poverty reduction is however receiving attention within the context that growth is the essential driver for poverty reduction and the role of the State is to enable this and to provide social services such as heath and education. The attention to poverty reduction is best encapsulated in the Poverty Reduction Strategy Papers (PRSPs) that are now common for many developing countries, being requisites for debt relief and concessional finance. Of importance is that poverty reduction remains central to the development agenda.

The end of the cold war in the late 1980s created great optimism that the peace dividend resulting from reduced military expenditure would be a great boost to development efforts. Unfortunately, the end of the cold war has resulted in lower aid flows as the geo-political imperative for aid flows has been removed from the equation. The UN target of developed countries providing 0.7% of their GNP in development assistance is still a far off aspiration. It seems that a unipolar world has brought its own problems in relation to international security. Indeed, the post-cold war period has been categorised by a high degree of international conflict and civil war. Increasingly, it seems that the "cold war" and the "communist threat" have been reincarnated as the "war on terror" and the "terrorist threat", and have assumed a similar role in geopolitical considerations.

Box 2: The MDG goals and targets

Goal 1. Eradicate extreme poverty and hunger
Halve, between 1990 and 2015, the proportion of people whose income is less than one dollar a day. Halve, between 1990 and 2015, the proportion of people who suffer from hunger

Goal 2. Achieve universal primary education
Ensure that, by 2015, children everywhere, boys and girls alike, will be able to complete a full course of primary schooling

Goal 3. Promote gender equality and empower women
Eliminate gender disparity in primary and secondary education, preferably by 2005, and in all levels of education no later than 2015

Goal 4. Reduce child mortality
Reduce by two-thirds, between 1990 and 2015, the under-five mortality rate

Goal 5. Improve maternal health
Reduce by three quarters, between 1990 and 2015, the maternal mortality ratio

Goal 6. Combat HIV/AIDS, malaria and other diseases
Have halted by 2015 and begun to reverse the spread of HIV/AIDS
Have halted by 2015 and begun to reverse the incidence of malaria and other major diseases

Goal 7. Ensure environmental sustainability
Integrate the principles of sustainable development into country policies and programmes and reverse the loss of environmental resources
Halve, by 2015, the proportion of people without sustainable access to safe drinking water and basic sanitation
By 2020, to have achieved a significant improvement in the lives of at least 100 million slum dwellers

Goal 8. Develop a global partnership for development
Develop further an open, rule-based, predictable, non-discriminatory trading and financial system. Includes a commitment to good governance, development and poverty reduction — both nationally and internationally
Address the special needs of the least developed countries. Includes: tariff and quota-free access for least developed countries' exports; enhanced programme of debt relief for heavily indebted poor countries (HIPC) and cancellation of official bilateral debt; and more generous ODA for countries committed to poverty reduction
Address the special needs of landlocked developing countries and Small Island

developing states (through the Programme of Action for the Sustainable Development of Small Island Developing States and the outcome of the twenty-second special session of the General Assembly)
Deal comprehensively with the debt problems of developing countries through national and international measures in order to make debt sustainable in the long term
In cooperation with developing countries, develop and implement strategies for decent and productive work for youth
In cooperation with pharmaceutical companies, provide access to affordable essential drugs in developing countries

Source: Human Development Report 2004.

CHAPTER 4

Theories of Rural Development

CHAPTER OUTLINE

- Introduction
- Rostov's 5 stages of Economic Growth
- The Dependency Theory
- Big Push Theory
- Theory of Minimum Critical Effort
- Lewis's Theory
- Human Capacity Development Theory
- The Uni-Modal Approach to Agricultural Development
- The Bi-Modal Approach to Agricultural Development
- Other Theories
    - Structural Change Models
    - Neo-classical/Neo-Liberal Counter Revolution
    - New Growth Theories
    - Theories from Information Economics

4.1 INTRODUCTION

In the 1950s and 1960s the linear stages approach prevailed which viewed development as a series of stages through which all countries must pass. It primarily advocated for the right mixture of savings, investment and foreign aid for developing countries to facilitate rapid economic growth. This approach was replaced in the 1970s by two competing theories. The first school, the structural change models, focused on changes that developing countries undergo to generate and sustain economic growth. The other school, the dependency theorists, viewed "underdevelopment" in terms of international and domestic power relations and emphasised policies to eradicate poverty create employment and reduce disparities. Subsequently, the 1980s saw the rise of neo-liberal economic theory, which promoted the liberalisation of markets and the privatisation of state enterprises. In the 1990s and 2000s, while the neo-liberal model is dominant, its approach has been softened somewhat and allows greater scope for "market friendly" intervention to promote the accumulation of human and physical capital.

4.2 ROSTOV'S STAGES OF ECONOMIC GROWTH

Rostov's Economic Growth Theory is also called **linear stage theory**. This theory was founded on two lines of thought.

Firstly, huge capital investments into the economies of Western Europe after World War II had allowed them to reconstruct their economies in a few years time.

Second was that developed countries had once been subsistence agrarian societies which overtime changed into industrial economies. Thus, the theory was based on identifying the changes that developed countries had undergone and advocating for increased capital flows to enable developing countries to advance through these stages rapidly. An American economist, Walt Rostow, developed the linear stages theory, in which he identified five stages that countries pass through in their development.

- Stage 1 **Traditional society**, characterised by stagnation, subsistence agriculture and a stratified society.
- Stage 2 **Pre-conditions for take-off**, characterised by change through external forces, infrastructure development, increasing exports, and a new social and political elite.
- Stage 3 **Take-off**, characterised by investment of greater than 10 per cent of GDP, high growth manufacturing sectors, and institutional change favouring high growth.
- Stage 4 **Drive to maturity**, characterised by self-sustaining growth, the impact of growth spreading to all areas, and decreasing social inequality.
- Stage 5 **High mass consumption** characterised by a shift in sectoral dominance to durable consumer industries and growth of the service sector and welfare capitalism.

It was argued that developing countries were at stages 1 and 2 while developed countries had passed stage 3. This model was complemented by the Harrod–Domar Growth Model which showed that the more an economy could save and invest the faster it grew. According to this theory a major obstacle to development was the low level of savings and investment in developing countries, which could be overcome by the transfer of capital (through foreign aid and private investment) and technical assistance to developing countries.

This simplistic approach to development was not always borne out in the evidence. While increased savings and investment are important for economic growth, by themselves they are not enough to guarantee economic growth. The theory assumed that the same conditions that existed in Western Europe existed in developing countries. Also, the theory did not take account of the integrated nature of the international system whereby external forces beyond a country's control can nullify the best efforts of a country. The influence of such external forces led to the development of dependency theory, which has been explained in the next section.

The main shortcomings of Rostov's theory are

(a) It assumes western technology which is developed in capital abundant economy is an appropriate technology for developing countries with shortage of capital and surplus of labour.
(b) American way of doing things is not the only way and American way of life is not the only destination of development. Manufacturing firms in Japan did follow traditional form of management and out-perform the American counterpart. So development is possible to be achieved in different value system and different way of doing things.
(c) Not Empirical: The empirical coverage of Rostov's analysis is narrow and inadequate. The data analysis by him relate to twelve countries experience over the past century. Even for the countries the key statistics have been highly unreliable till now. The generalizations drawn on such a narrow statistical base cannot be very reliable.
(d) It simply considers local institutions as fitters of development despite. The fact that they are indigenous remedies to both market and state failures. Actually, some of them are outdated due to community failures, but all of them are not out dated.
(e) Moreover, it does not recognize unsustainable nature of private sector derived growth over generations, without involvement of government to internalize unaccounted externalities.

4.3 THE DEPENDENCY THEORY

Dependency Theory gained popularity during the 1970s. It was especially popular amongst intellectuals of developing countries who were sceptical of both the linear stages and structural changes models. The theory is based on the premise that countries are linked by relationships of dependence and dominance. Within dependency theory there were three major streams of thought:

(1) the neo-colonial dependence model;
(2) the false-paradigm model; and
(3) the dualistic development model.

1. The neo-colonial dependence model attributes underdevelopment to the unequal power relationships in the international capitalist system between rich (centre) and poor (periphery) countries. This theory attributes underdevelopment and poverty to the industrial policies and international institutions dominated by developed countries which seek to perpetuate a capitalist system of inequality. (The elite in developing countries who benefit from the continued existence of the *status quo* and hinder attempts at reform facilitates this system.) This theory stresses that underdevelopment is attributable to external factors. This is in contrast with the linear stages and structural changes models which stressed internal constraints to development such as the lack of investment or lack of education and skills.

2. The false-paradigm model, a less radical stream of thought, attributes underdevelopment to the application of inappropriate policies that fail to take into account traditional social structures and institutions. The model claims that biases towards inappropriate models and policies are propagated in a number of different ways. One is through inappropriate advice by technical experts from bilateral and multilateral donor organisations. Another is through the administrative and intellectual elite within countries who have received training that has emphasised western concepts and models and who unwittingly perpetuate these models in their own countries.

3. The dualistic development model, highlights a world of dual societies. Here rich nations and poor nations and, within developing countries, rich and poor people, co-exist. The dualistic model looks at the existence and persistence of increasing divergences between rich and poor countries and between rich and poor people, so that even within a country development can co-exist alongside underdevelopment. It has four elements:

(i) the co-existence of different realities within a given space such as modern production techniques at the same time as traditional methods;
(ii) that this dualism is persistent rather than transitory;
(iii) the gap is widening between the two societies; and
(iv) the existence of a developed enclave does little to improve the plight of the undeveloped section.

In general terms the dependency school rejects the exclusive emphasis in western economic models on accelerating GNP growth as the principal aim of development. They also question the validity of the pattern of development as outlined by the structural changes model. This school of thought places more emphasis on institutional reform both domestic and international. Policies advocated by these theories prioritise eradication of poverty, creation of more diversified employment opportunities and reduction of income inequality. More radical proponents of the theory advocate public ownership of assets and a large role of the State as the most effective way of promoting development. However, most proponents believe that the most effective way of tackling underdevelopment is to accelerate economic growth through domestic and international reforms that are accompanied by a mixture of private and public economic activity.

Two criticisms have been levelled against the dependency theorists. One is that there is a lack of prescription of how regions/countries can undo dependency and initiate and sustain development. The second points to the negative experience of developing countries which have pursued industrial nationalisation and State-run production.

4.4 BIG PUSH THEORY

This theory as given by Paul Rosenstein Rodan in 1943 states that launching a country into self sustained growth is like getting an airplane off the ground. On both cases there is need for a minimum effort before it become airborne. Proceeding bit by bit will not add to total sum of a single bit. So a minimum amount of investment is necessary if not a sufficient condition for success. This is because of the existence of three indivisibilities related to production, demand and saving.

In order to create a reciprocal demand for a given interrelated bunch of industries there is need for simultaneous investment in industries which can produce wide varieties of consumer and capital goods, and this represents a special form of externalities. Moreover given the existence of internal economies within the same firm and external economies within the same industry and for other firm out of the industry, the success of the given industry will depend on simultaneous existence of other industries which can benefit from this firm's positive externality and which can create externality for the firm under consideration. Moreover if an economy experienced socially optimal production and faced a granted demand there will be sustainable rise in national income. This will have strong impact on the saving potential of the country, given the fact that income elasticity is much strong compared to the interest elasticity of saving.

Unfortunately, private investment motivated by profit will result on unbalanced growth with its demand bottlenecks. Moreover, the need to internalize the externalities need future foresight and appropriate planning, so the task of investment can't be left to the private sector which makes its decision based on past information. Even if his expectations are rational, his decision will be more based on private cost and benefit than the social counterpart so will be suboptimal. Moreover the need to invest on trailing of labour force and the building of infrastructure which must precede the investment will necessitate huge investment by the governments. So in this theory investment decisions have to be done by government which is supposed to have better capacity and information.

But the main weaknesses of this school are:

(a) The optimum size within the given industry could result on monopoly or oligopoly suppliers with their inefficiency side-effects. This is related to the fact that the domestic market of many LDC's is very limited.

(b) It assumes closed economy but the existence of exports can reduce the need for domestic balanced growth.

(c) It assumes LDC's which are characterized by shortage of capital, can launch into such massive industrialization.

(d) It assumes LDC's where the government failure is so pervasive, government can plan and execute such project.

(e) It neglects the importance of institutional and value changes needed for development.

(f) Neglects the role of agriculture in development thereby facing shortage of food and raw material (RM) resulting in lost push inflation. Moreover the huge investment on overhead and labour training will create demand related inflation pressure at least in short run. So rise in inflation will result in rise in wages, decline in profit and finally collapse of the national economy.

The main important contribution of this school is in explaining the synergy that exists among investments. And this was widely applied on integrated approach to rural development.

4.5 THEORY OF MINIMUM CRITICAL EFFORT

The critical minimum effort thesis was propounded by Harvey Leibenstein in his book *Economic Backwardness and Economic Growth*, 1957.

There are two critical assumptions of this theory. First there is biological limit to the positive relationship between family size and income per capita. Second, it assumes poor people who are normally earning subsistence income will fail to save and invest. This will result on stagnant income and will stay under poverty indefinitely. Given these facts this theory puts four hypotheses that are the core of the theory.

(a) A backward economy is in equilibrium system whose equilibrium state has a degree of quasi-stability with respect to per capita income.
(b) If equilibrium of backward economy is disturbed, forces or influences that tend to raise per capita income set in motion, directly and indirectly, forces that have the effect of depressing per capita income.
(c) In the disequilibrium state of backward economy, for at least low income levels which are above the equilibrium, the effect of income depressing forces are stronger than income raising forces.
(d) During any period there is absolute maximum to the effect of income depressing forces, but the absolute maximum (if there is one) of income augmenting forces is greater than that.

This can be easily understood if we consider the graph given below.

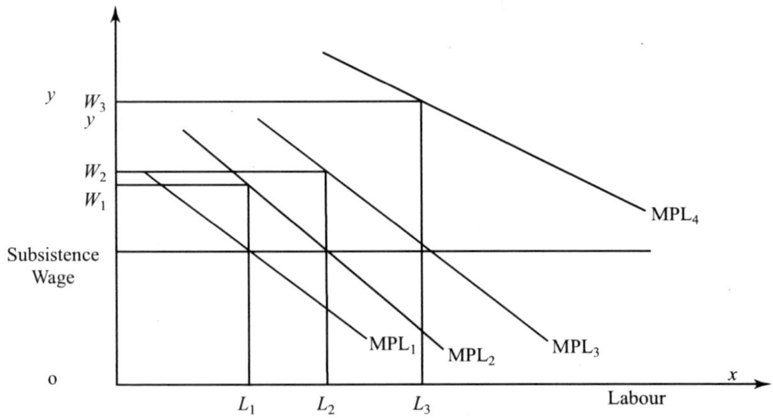

In subsistence wage it is assumed that there will be zero population growth and zero saving. Now let's us think that the technology is related to MPL_1 and they were earning with subsistence wage and labour force was L_0--(hypothesis (a)) Now assume that due to exogenous shock related to saving (investment)) or technology the marginal product is shifted to MPL_2 and under current labour force (L_0) the wage rate will rise to W_1. This will initiate population growth (hypothesis b), with each increase in population there will be increase in labour force which is getting lower wages due to declining marginal product of labour until the initial subsistence wage is reinstated at larger employment of (hypothesis (c) similar shift in to MPL_3 will also follow the same pattern. But if there is a critical minimum investment or technology growth which shifts the MPL_3 to MPL_4 resulting in increased income and population growth, but given the biological limit of population growth the initial level of subsistence will not be reinstated. Only then after income will be saved and reinvested, consistently, the economy will be in sustainable economic growth path.

Given this fact it insists in order to achieve the transition from stale of backwardness to the more developed state where we can expect steady secular growth, it is necessary though not always sufficient condition that at some point or during some period the economy should receive a stimulus to growth that is greater than a certain minimum size. Moreover, if there is need to change peoples' value system there is a need for minimum effort needed to generate substantial benefit and convince them that success must be gauged by market performance in which rational, rather than conventional or traditional considerations are the determinants of action.

In general, a minimum effort is needed to overcome internal diseconomies, external diseconomies, demand uncertainty, income depressing obstacles that can be generated by the stimulants of growth and by the need to generate sufficient momentum in the system so that the factors that stimulate growth continue to play their part. But it has its own shortcomings.

(a) The perfect relationship assumed between income, population (up to a limit) an investment is modified by different factors, so it is not that perfect.

(b) Even if the use of new technology or investment failed to raise per capita income, the skill and capital stock are changed so the old equilibrium will never be reinstated.

(c) Countries which experience up to 3% per capital income growth per annum and saving rate of 10 to 15% for many years did face downturn opposite to sustainable growth indefinitely.

The main contribution of this theory is that in addition to its implication of the need for minimum effort to achieve visible result, it makes it clear that there is some form of equilibrium in rural life. The current idea is different in which the insistence is on the utility maximization behaviour of farmer functioning in imperfect market and facing inefficient government.

4.6 LEWIS'S THEORY

In this theory the economy has two sectors. One sector is a backward agrarian sector using irreproducible capital – land under family institution in which every one earns the low average product and due to large population size the marginal product of labour is zero. And there is a modern capitalist sector in urban centres which operates under competitive situation paying labourers their marginal product and using reproducible capital. In rural areas there is surplus of disguisedly unemployed labour with zero marginal product and so does not affect agricultural production even if it is transferred to the modern sector. Moreover, given the existence of unlimited supply of labour, from rural area, the modern sector wage rate will be constant and equal to subsistence wage (average product) plus transfer allowance. The transfer allowance is important in order to encourage labourers to migrate from rural areas to urban centers in which they have to build new houses (rent), buy new commodities and face unaccustomed expenditures. Moreover, it also reflects the cost of training labourers by the capitalist or by themselves.

In the figure given below

OW_s — Average subsistence is wage in the agricultural sector

OW_m — Capitalist wage.

Now when capitalist invests and results in marginal product of labour as reflected in MPL_1 and given the W_m wage rate it will employ L_1 labour force where the marginal contribution of labour is equal to its cost. And by doing so the capitalist class will earn a profit of area *A* and this will be reinvested to shift the MPL_1 to MPL_2 which will result on employment of L_2 and the capitalist profit will increase by area *B*. And this will be reinvested to increase the employment to L_3. By this process of transferring the surplus labour in agriculture to industry, once backward agrarian economy will come out as industrialized modern economy.

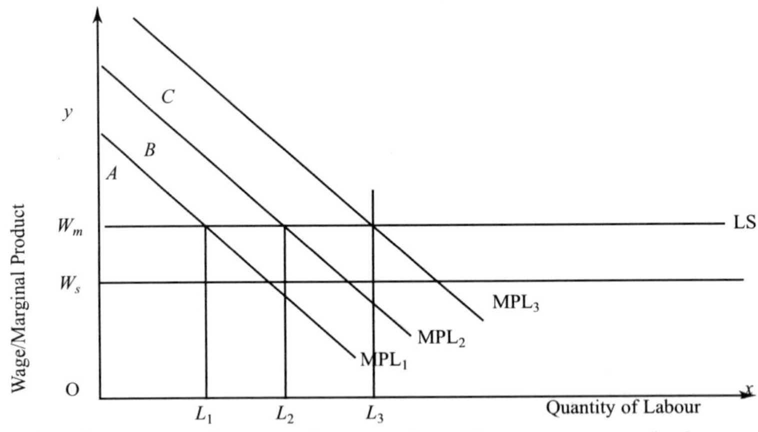

So this theory emphasises the transfer of income to reach the capitalist class which can save and invest and keep alive the dynamics of the economy toward modernization. And given zero marginal product of labour the transfer will not decrease total agricultural production.

The main shortcomings of this theory are as follows:

(a) Unrealistic Assumption: Schultz does not agree that MPL in overpopulated use is zero or negligible. If it were so, the subsistence wage would also be zero. The assumption of unlimited supply of labour in underdeveloped countries is not much relevant as it is not applicable to the countries like South America and South Africa.

(b) Adoption of Capital Intensive Techniques: There is no guarantee that capitalists will invest their profits in labour intensive technology. If they invest it in capital intensive as can be seen in graph given below— there will be no change in employment despite the increase in profit and change of MP_L from *yy* to *xx*. (Not applicable if capital accumulation is labour saving)

(c) Limited Supply of Skilled Labour: Although the theory assumes unskilled labour can easily be trained, skill formation was found to be a very complex and expensive task. (skilled labour not a temporary bottleneck as assumed by Lewis)

(d) Lack of Entrepreneurs: It assumes the existence of strong capitalist class despite the fact that one of the problems of developing economies is lack of strong entrepreneur class.

(e) Neglects Aggregrate Demand: It assumes assured demand which implies perfectly elastic export demand unless the failure to increase agricultural income will create demand bottlenecks.

(f) Unequal Distribution of Income: Due to much emphasis on growth and industrialization the income distribution will be very skewed where a few are earning and investing while the majority labour is under subsistence. And this is highly unrealistic given the existence of labour unions which oppose subsistence wage.

(g) One Sided Theory: The industrial expansion will face shortage of food and raw material due to agricultural underdevelopment. Lewis does not consider the possibility of progress in the agricultural sector.

(h) Employment Opportunity: Moreover experience shows that it is more practical and economical to create employment in rural areas than in urban areas but even that has not been found to be capable of providing jobs for the urban people.

The main contribution of this model is that it recognizes the low productivity of labour in rural areas and the use of family labour in production which is used intensively until $MP_L = 0$ given lower probability and finding alternative employment though the ruling wage rate is greater than zero.

4.7 HUMAN CAPACITY DEVELOPMENT THEORY

The early implicit recognition of intangible resource is to be found in Slow's analysis of labour and capital contribution to economic growth of USA.

He found that a significant variation in output (87 per cent) in the period of 1900 to 1949 cannot be explained by the traditional factors of production. This residual is thought to be measure of our ignorance or the contribution of technological progress as embodied in capital and labour.

And later Schultz by incorporating the investment in human development but using the same production function was able to explain a significant share of the Slow's residual. And he forcefully argued for the importance of human capital in development process by saying that "suppose there was an economy the land, physical reproducible capital including available techniques of production that we possess in the USA, but it attempted to function under the following restrictions: there would be no person available who had on-the-job experience, no one who had any schooling, no one who had information about the economy except of his locality, and the average span of life of the people will be only forty years, surely production will fall catastrophically. It is certain there will be lower output and extraordinary rigidity of economic organization until the capability of the people were raised by investing on them". This clearly shows that human capital is a precondition for efficient utilization of any means of production and general flexibility of the economic system. In general, any economic development effort which does not have human development as a critical input is destined to fail.

Based on these facts the human capacity theory of development emphasises the importance of human capital for achieving both economic and social developments. So the focus is on the totality of human potential and the need to harness it for the good of the people. In this viewpoint, human capital implies the mental and physical quality of people and this can be improved by education, training, healthcare or other spiritual methods like yoga.

And given most of the employment positions—that were once held by former colonial rulers were left open on the newly developing economies and given the huge shortage of skilled manpower observed in developing economies there was huge investment on education by developing economies/governments. And some of them insist that development is as simple as human development process. That is the more human development you have, the more effectively your economy can run, so for them development process was as simple process of human capital accumulation. And until recently no body dares to question such kind of thinking.

Criticisms of Human Capacity Developement Theory

The unnecessary emphasis on education without appropriate employment creation is found to lead to mass of educated but unemployed people without any real contribution to the economy but are fertile ground for any political disturbance and revolution. And the problem is going to get worst due to wrong kind of employment and promotion structure and politically motivated supply. Employment is related to educational achievement, the more educated get the job first and it does not matter if his/her education can add to the productivity. And promotion is done in the same manner. So when people get unemployed the only way they can find job in the formal sector is if they get more education. So shortage of demand will result on increase of supply of educated workers. Moreover, given the high government subsidy, individuals will pursue higher education until it is overcrowded and again they will have to search for higher level.

The point is, given the employment and promotion structure which is not related to productivity but educational achievement, the shortage of demand will create an increase than decrease of supply, intensifying the problem further. And this is made easy by high government subsidy given. Moreover, a youth which will work in manual employments will reject to work such kind of work once he/she gets educated so the marginal contribution of education to productivity could be zero if not negative. Moreover, the analysis that development is as simple as human development is falsified by the fact that despite many developing economies investment on education for many years, they remained poor. So once the minimum level of educational capacity is built which is critical to fill the gap left by the former colonial powers it would be wise if education supply was made to go inline with educational demand or observing capacity of the economy.

But the problem with such analysis is that education demand and supply does not work in perfectly competitive environment with perfect adjustment. You can't produce 1000 engineers when demand increases over given time. And normally investment decision which creates demand for educated labour force will be dependent on availability of educated human power, hard and soft infrastructure and conducive macroeconomic environment among other things. (So given the fact that in imperfect market of human development demand is influenced by supply the existence of educated labour force supply over current demand is very important.) But still cost and benefit analysis among those overheads which include education, health expenditure, hard and soft infrastructure will be unavoidable given the shortage of resources. And it is important to give due attention to quality of education rather than quantity of education.

In case of rural development the contribution of human development (related to education) are the following:

1. It will directly improve the productivity of agriculture.
2. It will improve the probability of getting off farm employment.
3. It will lead to improved family planning.
4. It can improve the health and nutrition of the people.
5. By widening the horizons of knowledge it can enable them to overcome ignorance and superstitions.
6. It can improve the risk taking and managerial capacity of the farmer.

4.8 THE UNI-MODAL APPROACH TO AGRICULTURAL DEVELOPMENT

The uni-modal approach to agricultural development questions the existence of production economies in farming. It is argued given the following.

1. **The preoccupation of farming with living things, high dependence on weather and season** — means you can't do different tasks at the same time and any time like manufacturing. You can do some agricultural tasks (say planting) at a given time in year (one or twice or three times in year) and in a given order (after plowing not before that or after weeding) will kill the capacity for labour specialization. Means one person can't weed or harvest all year round, and if he specialized he will be unemployed most of the time. By the same logic whatever machinery that you have will be ideal most of the time. So large scale farming will not only inefficiently use the scarce resource capital but also the most abundant resource will be replaced by the most scarce and under utilized capital. But small scale farms are not only endowed with family labour which is cheap and abundant but also their employment is flexible, they can perform different tasks. But more important in slug months they can work as urban or rural labourer.
2. **Management diseconomies in face of asymmetric information** — if you are hiring labour you are working not in perfect information labour market but in asymmetry information which resulted in both adverse selection and moral hazard problem. Even though it is not widely observed workers which are less efficient will be willing to work for lower wage. The problem is the most efficient workers which can produce more than their higher wage will be discouraged in participating in such lower paying jobs. The final outcome is that not

only the efficient part of the labour force is excluded but also most of your employees will be less skilled and less efficient ones. But far worst the worker once hired will lack incentive to work hard due to moral hazard problem (given wage is paid by hour not by productivity). So to avoid that you will need expensive screening and supervision cost which need to increase at an increasing rate with farm size. But small farms which are dependent on family workers do not need strong supervision. This is so given the fact that the institutional wage rate is average product of the farm, so family members have higher incentive to work to their best and improve their farming skill to the possible higher level.

3. **Labour market imperfection and family labour** — A rational economic agent will equalize his (his worker) value of marginal product and wage rate. The problem is the wage rate that is paid by the employer is not equal to the wage rate received by the worker if we make allowance for labour market imperfection and searching cost.

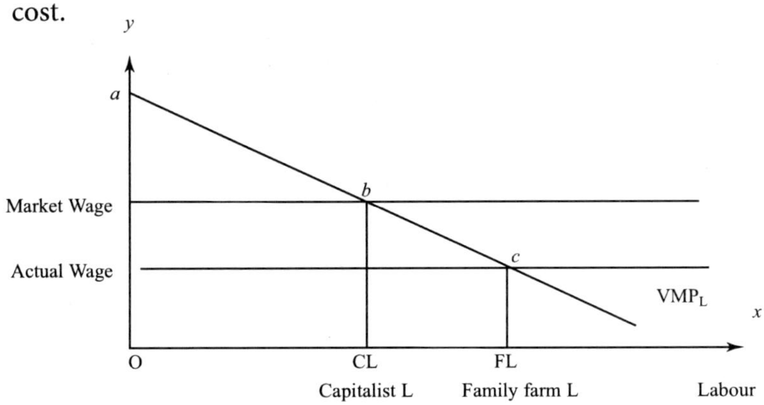

Second, there are monetary costs that he needs to spend when he is out there like eating expensive meal which can be prepared for a fraction of its value in home. So the actual wage rate (opportunity cost if he works in his own farm) that is paid to rural agricultural worker is much lower than the market wage rate.

In the above graph the capitalist will hire worker at a point where the market wage rate is equal to the value of marginal product of labour (VMP_L) or CL amount of labour. By doing so it will produce a total output of $abcL_0$. But family labour will equate high value of marginal product not to market wage rate but to his real opportunity cost in the market. So he will use labour intensively up to FL (which is higher than the capitalist sector employment CL) and will produce much higher level of output, $ac\text{FL}_0$. So small farmers not only produce more compared to large farmers but will make intensive use of the abundant factor of production labour and will save the scarce capital.

4. **Speculation on land and the use of land as reflection of prestige and wealth than economic input by large farms** — given ever increasing population size the market value of land will increase over time (remember Ricardo's extensive and intensive margin theory), so significant portion of land will be used for speculation while large portion of the population is without land. But far worst large scale farmers can use land as reflection of prestige while investing on scarce capital. This will result in not only unnecessary investment on scarce capital but also inefficient use of the abundant land and labour.

So if you allow for labour market and land market imperfection small farmers are more efficient and can produce more output, compared to large farms. And considering the preoccupation of farming with living things and seasonal pattern of employment the economic scale advantage is not relevant to agriculture as it is for other industries. But you can make the poor rural peasant engine of agricultural and rural development solving both growth and fair distribution goals at the same time. So by using small farmers with infusion of modern technology not only will be producing and using inputs in line with their shadow cost (you use intensively and extensively the more abundant and cheap factors of land and labour but also limit the use of the most expensive and scare factor of production) but also the observed growth will be egalitarian and fair to majority of the population. So the idea of uni-modal is based on using of one technology by all peasant farmers, to make them engine of growth without reducing them to landless agricultural labourers.

But small farmers lack access to credit and market; and whenever they do the transaction cost, the interest charged will be high. So uni-modal approach looks for institutional solution for such problems by using service than producer cooperatives to solve the marketing problem and using cooperative and MFI to solve the capital market diseconomies. The application of such modal was to be found in South Korea and Taiwan where green revolution was not effective on increasing output by manifold but also in making the observed growth fair and egalitarian.

From economic and social justice point of view uni-modal approach seems to be the most logical way. But all economists do not agree with this conclusion. The reservation evolves first in the idea of efficient land size. Empirical evidence shows that the relationship between productivity and land size is not downward sloping but inverted U shape.

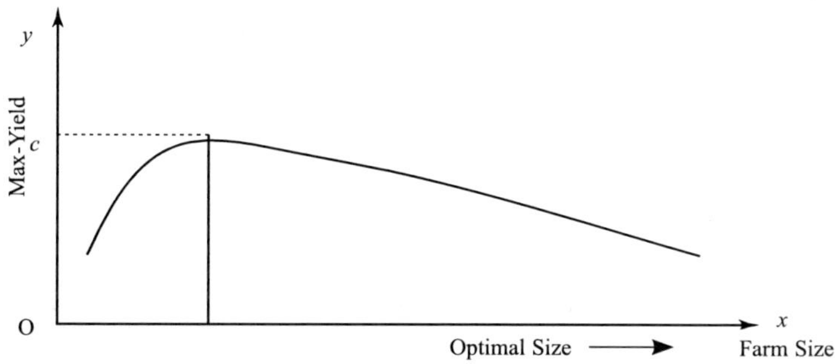

Means very small size is inefficient as very large farm size is due to diseconomies of scale. Means there is a minimum small land size which is needed in order to provide decent and full time employment for family members. And with the explosion of the population the peasant farm size is getting smaller and smaller in which not only it will fail to provide decent employment but also any output that is produced will be consumed within the family hindering urban and industrial development. But it was observed that land size of East Asian countries was mostly below one hectare when they introduced their green revolution (Table 4.1.)

Table 4.1: Land ownership in South Korea

Size of operational holdings (ha)	*Land distribution (%)*	
	1947	*1953*
Below 0.5	41.2	44.9
0.5-1.0	33.3	34.2
1.0-2.0	18.8	16.5
2.0-3.0	8.3	4.3
Above 3.0	1.4	0.1

Source: Ebert and Kajander (2006).

Even though land size in South Korea was much smaller (or similar) compared to many developing countries there was high irrigation investment done by colonial Japan and their government, so the effective land size per family per year was much larger compared to many African countries. So it is not sure if their experience can be replicated without working around water management and multiple farming through irrigation (Hayami, 1997). The second reservation revolves around the effect of irrigation and given revolution in reducing the impact of imperfect labour market and seasonal pattern of production. The high increase in output due to green technology did make the use of machinery (which avoids labour supervision cost) possible this, coupled with improvement in irrigation (which reduce the ideal time of machinery through multiple cropping) did improve the relative disadvantage of large farms. When the marketing and credit economies were considered, some studies did found that the inverted U shape relation between labour productivity and land size did disappear.

4.9 THE BI-MODAL APPROACH TO AGRICULTURAL DEVELOPMENT

"The bi-modal approach to agricultural and rural development evolves around the idea that large farms are more efficient compared to small farms. This is due to the existence of production, marketing and credit economics which results in lower cost of production". However, the uni-modal approach to rural development contests the production economics in agriculture operating in imperfect input market, and devises a way to deal with both capital market and output market indivisibility. In short, the central disagreement among both approaches is on the fact that if peasant farming system can be engine of agricultural and rural development or if it needs to be integrated into capitalist, mode of production.

According to advocates of **bi-modal** approach large scale farms have strong advantage over small scale farms. These advantages are related to technical, financial, and marketing economies of large scale farming. And, in general, it is assumed that all advantages that can accrue to small scale farming would occur to large scale, but not the *vise versa*. Production economies is related to the following:

1. **The use of up-to-date and most automatic machines.** Given the fact that most automatic machines need high fixed initial cost, they will need large scale production in order to break even with fixed cost. Moreover, the large scale farmers are web capitalized, informed and well connected to benefit from most up-to-date automatic machines. Imagine how much animal power is needed to do what a tractor can do in half an hour but for small farmer who owns less than one hectare purchasing tractor (to use it for half an hour per year) is not only un-economic but also it is behind its financial means.
2. **Benefit from high level labour specialization.** Adam Smith stated centuries ago that specialization in one task not only improves the dexterity of workers but also the time wasted in jumping from one job to another will be avoided and this will result in significant improvement in labour productivity. But most importantly if job is

divided into small and elementary pieces automatic machines can be used which can significantly reduce cost of production. So it is assumed that large farms by allowing specialization of labour in some routine jobs like plowing, planting, weeding, harvesting and so on can improve productivity of labour. But the use of modern and efficient machines will be possible if task is simplified by specialization.

3. **Better utilize by-products.** Farm by-products which are wasted in the farm are given to animals uneconomically. These can be efficiently used in large farms either by using as input in manufacturing or in providing feed to modern animal husbandry.
4. **Repair and maintenance economies.** It is not only machinery that needs a high initial fixed cost but also machinery repair, too. If you have few or one farm machinery it does not pay you to use your own repair machines how imperfect the repair industry and how uncompetitive its price are. But large farms can establish their own repair workshop and can significantly reduce their repair and maintain expenditure. And even if they did not own one, they can strongly negotiate for fair price due to their large business.
5. **Advantage of research and development.** R&D needs a lot of fixed cost (to cover, research expenditure) and risk taking (because all innovations does not pay back and some researches do fail to give result), which can be easily afforded by large capital farm's. But it is behind the means of small farmers. Means large farms are not only able to use most updated and cost effective means of production and product, but also can develop their own better ways. But far important in ever changing and dynamic global market is that they can easily adopt to changing global and national market priorities (consumer values).

The above listed production related advantages can be enjoyed, if the farm is large in both size of land and capital employed. Means considering cost of production in their static or dynamic sense large farms are at comparative advantage compared to small farms. Moreover large farms also benefit from both marketing and capital mark economies.

1. **Transport economics.** Large farmers can lower the transportation cost if they put inputs in bulk and sell their output in bulk too. For example if the cost of transporting a gunny bag of rice from Rohtak to Delhi is ₹100, then the cost of transporting 100 bags should be ₹10000, but because of transport economics it may only be ₹5000.
2. **Storage economics.** This is related to the fact that the area of storage increase with volume but cost of storage increase with area. If you

have storage with 3 metre width 3 metre height and 3 metre base the area will be 27m^3 but if you increase each by metre each area will jump to 64 m^3. Just compare the cost of construction which is increasing by less than 100 per cent and the 400 per cent increase in storage space. Means it is cheaper to store large amount of input and output than small input and output.

3. **Economics of scale information accusation and capacity to build social capital.** When markets are working in imperfect information environment large farms can spend on information which can help them to take informed decisions and rational price expectations. But when markets fail, social networks are important on provision of information and given high association between financial and social capital they are the well informed and well connected agents in market (and information is power all the time)
4. **Capacity to bargain for fair price.** In both input and output market they can bargain for fair price because first they have higher market power (due to bulk purchase and sale), they are well informed and last, but not least they are not participating under stress as many small farmers do.

Thus, large farms, according to the bi-modal approach to rural development, are not only efficient in production but also in marketing their product and purchasing inputs. And their advantage comes in triple form; i.e., production, marketing and capital market economics. This is because large size farm owners can easily access external capital at lower interest rate to finance their expenditure which is not possible for small farms. But far important large farm owners can finance their own expenditure and do not need external finance unless for big projects. Small farmers can't provide viable collateral for their demand for capital is limited which, unfortunately needs the same administration and supervision cost, and far worse they deal in agriculture which is highly dependent on nature so formal banks will fail to lend them at reasonable interest rate. So they have to depend on informal sources which charge a high interest rate.

So according to the bi-modal approach large farms are more efficient compared to small farms and thus over time large farms will overtake the peasant farming by purchasing their land and they will provide employment to the agricultural labourer currently peasant population. So the inefficient peasant farming will be replaced by more efficient capitalist farming.

Given the high productivity and efficiency the resource allocation will be efficient; the peasant will be able to enjoy fruit of his labour and the much needed agricultural surplus will not only be consumed by the inefficient peasant family, but most of it will be marketed which is needed for fast urbanization and industrial development. Even if labour is replaced by machinery given the tremendous achievement in productivity and cost reduction it can be addressed by targeted poverty reduction strategy once efficient and fast economic growth is achieved. So in the mean time two (bi) technologies will be used, one efficient large scale farming which will dominate the inefficient small scale farming over time.

Application of such model can be found in the Indian green revolution. Given the Indian government focus of achieving national food sufficiency at least cost in terms of money and time, they direct the government mechanism to encouragement of large scale farming on high potential areas. Furthermore, they did encourage and promote the adoption of modern technology by large farms; in addition to supply necessary infrastructure and irrigation facility. And to avoid price uncertainty a stabilized and fixed (sometimes above long run average) price is given like minimum support price (MSP), procurement price (PP), etc., to their output to keep the incentive (profit) level high. And cooperatives of large farmers are used to ease the problem: caused by market and state failures. Large farms were able to benefit from scale advantage and resulted on large scale eviction of landlessness and inter-personal and inter-regional inequality; but with tremendous improvement in productivity of both wheat and rice production. To the above technocratic way of thinking a radical solution was given by using collective farming in Tanzania and China with the idea that if large scale is efficient why not consolidate the large farms into single efficient economic entity to avoid the distribution consequence of large scale capitalist farming. But due to incentive and management diseconomies almost all collective farmings ended in failure. But the success of Taiwan and South Korea using small scale farmers led to the strong questioning of the arguments for large scale farming and resulted in uni-modal approach to agricultural development.

4.10 OTHER THEORIES

4.10.1 Structural Changes Models

Structural changes theory emerged in the 1970s. It encompasses a number of different models but the focus of the theory is that there is a sequential process through which economic, industrial and institutional structures of an underdeveloped economy are transformed over time to permit new industries and services to replace traditional agriculture as the engine of growth. As such development is an identifiable process with familiar features in all regions. This approach was more sophisticated than the linear stages model in that it acknowledged that increased investment alone, while necessary, was not sufficient for economic growth, and that structural changes involved a wide range of economic functions. Some of the features of the development process under this model were the shift from agriculture to industrial production, the accumulation of human and physical capital, the change in consumer demand from food items to manufactured goods, urbanisation, and a decline in population growth.

While the theory contends that development is an identifiable process of growth and change whose main features are similar in all countries, it allowed for the pattern and pace of development to vary according to domestic (resource endowments, size, etc.) and international factors (access to external capital, technology and trade). Overall, this theory of development is optimistic that correct policies can promote development. However, it can be criticised similarly to the linear stages model as seeing development as a linear process that follows a predefined route.

4.10.2 Neo-classical/Neo-liberal Counterrevolution

The 1980s saw conservative governments coming to power in the large western economies of the United States, Britain and West Germany. These governments favoured neo-classical economic policies such as opening markets, increasing competition and privatising State enterprises. This favourable environment for the neo-liberal policy agenda led to a questioning of the interventionist arguments of the dependency theorists. Central to the neo-liberal discourse was that underdevelopment was caused by poor resource allocation due to incorrect pricing policies and too much State intervention. Proponents of neo-liberal discourse argued that allowing competitive free markets to flourish, privatising State-owned enterprises, opening markets to free trade and investment, reducing the size of the State and removing State regulations would promote economic growth and efficiency.

In contrast to the dependency theorists, countries are undeveloped not because of predatory activities of developed countries, but because of bureaucracy, corruption and inefficiency. Advocates of the approach stressed the success of the "Asian Tigers" (for example South Korea and Taiwan) in the 1980s compared to the poor growth of the economies in Latin America where the State was playing an active role.

Within the neo-classical counterrevolution there is a continuum of approaches. The free market approach advocates that governments should not interfere in the economy, as it is counterproductive. The public choice approach goes further and claims that governments can do nothing right and therefore minimal government is best. The market-friendly approach, the most recent variant, recognises that there are many imperfections in developing country markets and so government does have a role in facilitating the operation of the market through market-friendly intervention and investing in social and physical infrastructure such as health facilities and education. It also recognises that government intervention may be necessary to secure environmental outcomes.

Disenchantment with the neo-classical/neo-liberal approach began to emerge in the late 1980s and early 1990s. It was expected that the free market reforms imposed on heavily indebted countries by the World Bank and the International Monetary Fund (IMF) would have prompted higher investment, productivity and growth, yet many countries experienced little or no growth, failed to attract foreign investment or stop the flight of domestic capital.

A difficulty of the neo-liberal proposal, that free markets and less government are necessary ingredients for development, is that many developing country economies are so different from Western economies that the assumptions and policy prescriptions are often not appropriate. Given the institutional, political and cultural structures of developing countries, formulating policies based on either the market or public intervention is very difficult. It is not therefore a case of either/or, but of assessing the individual realities of a country and identifying what mix may be most appropriate to the circumstances.

4.10.3 New Growth Theories

New growth theory emerged from the neo-classical school and involves modifying existing growth theories to incorporate the reality that some regions/countries fail to develop while others develop rapidly. While the traditional neo-classical model predicts that capital would flow to poor countries where it would have a higher return, the new growth theory models help explain anomalous international flows of capital from developing countries to developed countries that itensifies the wealth disparities between countries.

The theory permits that potential higher returns from investment in developing countries are eroded by lower levels of complementary investments in human capital (education), infrastructure, or research and development. The theory also allows that in a free market situation it is possible that countries will not automatically accumulate their optimal level of complementary capital. This model therefore suggests an active role for public policy in promoting direct and indirect investments in human capital and encouraging foreign investments in knowledge-intensive industries.

As the theory is rooted in neo-classical theory it faces the same limitations in that it assumes Western-style institutions and values in developing countries.

4.10.4 Theories from Information Economics

Under its assumptions of perfect and cost-free information, perfect mobility of factors of production, given technology, large number buyer and sellers and homogenous product among other things; market economy (purely completive economy) will result to the most possible efficiency in terms of providing maximum welfare at least cost. Economists know that some of the assumptions like perfect mobility in factor of production, perfect and cost free information and others are unrealistic. But they hold the view that if we include the cost of information and factor immobility, market economies are constrained optimal. Means the cost of providing welfare will increase by information collection and factor immobility but still market economy will provide the most possible higher welfare that can be generated from given resources. But information economist like Stiglitz insist that "the perfect competition — model was not robust — even slight departures from the underlying assumption of perfect information had large consequences".

Information imperfection will be created if someone has more information than the other. In such case not only the final outcome of market allocation can be effected but also action of agents (lender will reject to lend, employer will pay lower wage for efficient worker in order to hide the productivity of the employee) and the market can fail to exist if agents recognize there is asymmetric information to their disadvantage (bank insurance, future markets will fail to exist). But far worse economic agents can increase their marketing power by creating asymmetric information in the market, so asymmetric is also created by the market it-self. Think like this if a trader knows that price in capital city is increasing but no body knows, he can buy out of the market but his extensive purchase will convey information to the public of some expectations on price rise. So he will fail to benefit from his investment in information, so the only way he can benefit from the information is if he does it in disguise and if he is able to give conflicting signal to the market. So his need for market power will create information asymmetry.

Following are the methods to solve this problem.

1. **Improving information disclosure.** If the more productive worker, the less risk borrower or insurance purchaser can convince the employer, the bank and the insurance, respectively, about his true status then the asymmetric information problem will be avoided. But if information is costly and if the worker, borrower and insurance purchaser can't be trusted the other agents employee, bank or insurance have to collect information. But if they collect information it is at their best advantage to make it secret. Why does employer, bank or insurance advertise the performance of his worker, borrower or insurance company to let others bid him off? But far worse is expecting that their action will convey information about their expectation (information) will alter their behaviour. A firm will reject to pay higher wage for employee who is much productive because his wage rate will convey information about his capacity to other bidders and this will lead the firm to lose the worker. The same analysis can be said about the insurance and the bank. So "the fact that actions convey information leads people to alter their behaviour, and changes how markets function. This is why information imperfections have such profound effects".
2. **By visible hand of the state.** If there is imperfect information which can be covered by spending on information the market will be constrained, optimal means cost will increase by information cost but still it will be the best possible allocation allowing for information cost. But this conclusion assumes there are perfect and complete markets for goods and services, insurance, credit and so on. But still given public good nature of information, both perfect information disclosure and action will not pay the collector so even if markets are complete and working good, market economy with imperfect information will not be, constrained optimal means visible hand of government not only can improve distribution but also allocation, or some people can be made better without making others worse using visible hand of the state. But is not the case that the government will face similar information problems as market? Yes but it can use the link between markets to achieve efficient outcome. Government faces asymmetric information that is faced in insurance for example, it can increase tax in cigarette and related products to internalize the risk of insurance which is not possible for normal economic agents.
3. **Public investment on information and/or enacting of disclosure laws.** The third possible solution is to increase the availability of

information through public spending. These include the broadcasting of forecasted and historic prices, output, interest rates and so on, and to enforce disclosure laws. By doing this, not only information as public good will be provided at optimal level but also the incentive problem of economic agents which lead to distorted information and action (behaviour) can be avoided.

Some applications of imperfect information (and imperfect markets) in rural areas

1. **Sharecropping.** Landowner can hire a worker, but he needs a higher cost of supervising and monitoring to avoid moral hazard. (it refers to a situation where one side of the market can't observe the actions of the other. For this reason, it is sometimes called a hidden action problem) on part of the worker. This can hinder the landowner from using hired labour. But if a worker needs a land in such case he can't buy or rent one due to imperfect or non-existence capital markets despite the existence of ideal land which can produce more than the interest and wage rate. And this is hindered by the fact that risk (output and price related) will be observed by landowner if uses hired worker or the landless of he wants to rent or buy it. So the market failures (It is necessary for a market to be an efficient market because in an efficient market, we have not only the competitve price but market also serves the buyer properly. If the price is not a competitive then buyers are not served properly, i.e., an incompetent market and it is MARKET FAILURE. Whenever a market is not a competitive market, 4 factors are responsible for this: (i) Incomplete Information and Moral Hazard, (ii) Market Power, (iii) Externalities, (iv) Public goods) related to insurance and capital market coupled with asymmetric information and related moral hazard will result in inefficient allocation of resource. Both land and labour, which are abundant, will be underutilized. But the use of sharecropping which allow the worker to have a given per cent of the output will not only avoid the need for monitoring but also it will allow the sharing of risk by both landlord and tenant and the use of landlords capital on the land. So share cropping by linking the labour, land, capital and insurance market in to one will somehow improve the efficiency of rural areas working in imperfect market and imperfect information.
2. **Rural insurance.** The insurance market faces asymmetric information problems which will lead to both moral hazard and adverse selection problems. If a farmer knows better about his risk relative to the insurance company, the more risky farmers will be willing to pay a

higher premium and uninformed insurance company could end up with high portfolio risky farmers. This is commonly known as adverse selection. But far worse an insured farmer may do little in improving his productivity given he is granted by the insurer (moral hazard problem). Insurance companies can invest in monitoring and screening but this is too costly in rural areas where the population is widely spruced. To avoid this area level insurance is proposed in which individuals are paid compensation if the average product of the area is below acceptable level. In such case a farmer will have higher incentive to produce more than the area average. But it will fail to cover farmers from specific risk and it is not clear if farmers are willing to participate in such insurance.

3. **Rural banking.** The same asymmetric information on the credit worthiness of the borrower and use of fund will result on adverse selection (the borrower with higher risk project will offer higher interest so will be picked first) and moral hazard (given he is trading with banks money will tend to use it in risky project). To avoid these problems which increase the portfolio of risky asset banks can use screening and monitoring, but in rural areas where the majority of the population is widely dispersed the cost can be much higher to lead to missing credit markets. To deal with this problem of asymmetric information rural social capital in the form of group pressure is used to screen and monitor borrowers.
4. **Rural markets.** In rural areas where the trader is more informed compared to market not only leads to information secrecy by trader but also manipulative behaviour to avoid the disclosure of information by his action. This will not only lead to inefficient resource allocation but also wrong signal creation. This is behind the idea of public broadcast of price, output and other market related trends.

In this chapter we have discussed at a number of competing theories and approaches to economic development. While these diverge in terms of ideology and each have its own merits and weaknesses, a number of insights can be extracted from each theory. For example, the linear stages approach emphasizes the role that savings and investment play in long-term development. The structural changes models underline the importance of looking at the linkages between traditional agriculture and modern industry as well as factors involved in structural changes. The dependency school highlights how the structures of the international economy and policies of developed countries affect people living in the developing world as well as the roles of elites in the domestic economy. Many of the propositions of the neo-classical school related to the inefficiency of State-owned enterprise, the failures of development planning and the harmful effect of price distortions have also become widely accepted. However, the unquestioning faith in free markets, open economies and a limited role for the State in promoting development is open to challenge. The new growth theories, while closely associated with the neo-classical theory, allows for a more positive role for policy in promoting growth and development.

CHAPTER 5

Global Poverty Alleviation Strategies

CHAPTER OUTLINE

- What is Poverty?
- Who Are the Rural Poor?
- Poverty in Rural Areas
  - Rural Areas
  - Distribution of Poverty
  - Why poverty is a Primarily Rural Phenomenon?
- Other Dimensions of Poverty
  - Better Social Services in Urban Areas
  - Poverty and Gender
  - Poverty and Vulnerability
- Rural Poverty Reduction Through Rural Development
  - Rural Poverty Reduction vis-a-vis Urban Poverty Reduction
  - Quality of Life
  - Poverty Reduction Through Sustainable Agricultural Development

5.1 WHAT IS POVERTY?

> *Eighty percent of our global population has 20 per cent of the world's income .... Some 800 million people ... go to bed hungry every night, majority of them in rural areas. Indeed, 70 per cent of the poor of our globe are in rural areas ... why is it that this year in the demand for World Bank loans, we're almost at an all-time low in terms of the proportion of our lending for rural and agricultural purposes ...?*
>
> —JAMES D. WOLFENSOHN
> *President, The World Bank Group*

In this chapter we will examine the dimensions of rural poverty. While defining both *poverty* and *rural* poses difficulties. The majority of the world's poor still live in rural areas. This reality indicates that efforts to reduce poverty and meet the Millennium Goals must focus significantly on rural areas. Ironically, however, this is the sector that is being increasingly neglected.

As hunger is one of the principal manifestations of extreme poverty, its dimensions, and progress towards meeting the Millennium Development Target of halving the number going hungry by 2015, will be looked at. And then look at the differences between urban and rural areas in the provision of services. Subsequently, explore both the vulnerability and gender aspects of poverty. Finally, see how aid and support to the rural sector has been declining.

Defining poverty

Poverty has been discussed in broad terms in chapter 1 of this book. Now it is imperative, to return to definitions of poverty in more detail, since poverty is reduction is a key objective of rural development.

Some of the questions we need to consider include:

- What exactly is poverty?
- What is the meaning of mass poverty?
- How can we say whether a person or household is poor or not?
- How do we *define* poverty?

Although there are many different definitions of poverty. First, it's worth pointing out one of the basic distinctions made in discussions of poverty is the distinction between absolute poverty and relative poverty.

Absolute Poverty: "...a condition characterised by severe deprivation of basic human needs, including food, safe drinking water, sanitation facilities, health, shelter, education and information. It depends not only on income but also on access to services." [UN World Summit on Social Development, 1995].

Relative Poverty: "People are living in poverty, if their income and resources (material, cultural and social) are so inadequate as to preclude them from having a standard of living which is regarded as acceptable within their own society generally. As a result of inadequate income and resources people may be excluded and marginalised from participating in activities which are considered the norm for other people in society." [adapted from Ireland's National Anti-Poverty Strategy, 1997].

When discussing poverty, it is often said that absolute poverty is the type of poverty found in *developing countries,* while poverty in *developed countries* is more usually described as relative poverty. Gordon (2002), suggested that absolute poverty is also experienced in some developed countries, while relative poverty — which is partly related to the distribution of income — could be said to exist in any country with high levels of income inequality.

However, the definition of absolute poverty describes a condition where a person or household does not have enough to meet the most basic requirements for a decent life. What is it that the household does not have enough of — income? food? land? or shelter? All of these are important, and at least the first two are considered to be fundamental.

There is a tendency to measure poverty in terms of people's income. This is because income gives people the means to gain access to basic resources, which they need for their livelihood. If, on the other hand, poverty is measured in terms of the availability of food, this is more accurately a measure of food security. Whichever measure is used, it is often done in the form of a poverty line — this means, an amount of income (or food) is defined, which is required to avoid being in poverty. Those people (or households) who do not possess at least the target income (food) are then defined as being in poverty.

Table 5.1: Ethiopia (one of the poorest country of the world): different poverty measures

Poverty Measure	*Poverty line*	*% of poor*
Absolute poverty using adult equivalents	Birr 30-60	27
Absolute poverty using per capita consumption	Birr 30-60	34
Calorie poverty using calorie data	2200 kcal	39
Food poverty using food expenditure for minimum calories	Birr 46	42
Poverty as <2/3 mean per capita consumption	Birr 58	47
Poverty as <US$1 per day per person	Birr 150	85

Source: Dercon and Krishnan 1996

(Birr is the currency of Ethiopia)

Key points of poverty measures:

- If we use the common international standard of measuring absolute poverty by those who have <US$ 1.25 per day, most (42 per cent) Indians fall into this category. In 1981 it was as high as 60 per cent. According to the Planning Commission of India, 27.5 per cent of population live belows poverty line in 2004-2005 which has decreased from 51.3 per cent in 1977–78. And according to NSSO (1999-2000) poverty line is ₹327 per month per capita for rural India and ₹454 per capita for urban India. That's not surprising since the GDP per capita (PPP US$) for 2002 in India was estimated to be about 2670.

- The poverty lines used for most of the measures are based on monthly expenditures, and are generally estimated from a minimum list of food and non-food items which a poor household would consume, and the cost of obtaining these items. It should be noted that the poverty lines calculated in this way are much less than the poverty line using the US$1.25 per day criterion. According to NCAER (2009) of the 222 million households in India, the absolutely poor households (annual income below ₹45,000) accounted for 15.6%. But according to National Sample Survey Organisation's (NSSO) 55th round of survey conducted in 1999–2000 states that the poverty ratio came down from 36% in 1993–94 to 26% in 1999–2000.
- For the poorest households, most of their consumption and expenditure is likely to be on food items — therefore, an alternative to calculating the cost of obtaining a minimum list of items is to find out how much and what type of food is consumed directly, and calculate the calorific value of that consumption, comparing it to the minimum calorific intake of 2200 kcal per adult, which is the minimum needed for an adult to perform normal daily tasks, according to the World Health Organisation. According to the 55th round of National Sample Survey 87% of the population has a per capita intake of less than 2400 kcal a day and is thus below the poverty line. But it is to be noted that in many states of India even the rich do not consume 2400 calories per day due to dietary habits.

It was noted earlier that these measures of material well-being (also known as consumption measures) have been improved over time to take account of distributional issues and more accurately identify those suffering from material deprivation. More recently, the increasing use of the Human Development Index/Human Poverty Index, which includes social factors, allows for a broader definition of development to be reflected in measures, but these tend to be used more for international comparisons than within a country. What is important to note is that such approaches only provide a partial view of poverty. However, they are valuable to quantify the extent and depth of poverty and difference between areas and changes over time.

A multidimensional conceptualisation of poverty that includes physical, social and psychological dimensions is increasingly being accepted, as time passes. For example, in the World Development Report 1990, the World Bank defined poverty as encompassing material deprivation and low achievement in health and education, while the World Development Report

2001-2002 broadened this definition to include concepts such as vulnerability, exposure to risks, voicelessness and powerlessness. Similarly, one recent analysis of poverty suggests that it encompasses not just economic issues and capabilities, but also human capabilities (education, health, etc.), political rights, social and cultural rights, and security/vulnerability (OECD 2002). Gender and environmental sustainability cut across all of these dimensions.

Therefore, although the conceptualisation of poverty varies among different people, in general terms it is now universally associated with material deprivation, low levels of health and education, inequality, vulnerability, powerlessness and social exclusion. However, difficulties in measuring non-economic aspects of poverty result in material well-being/consumption aspects of poverty being more widely used and focused on.

Robert Chambers (1983), one of the leading writers and practitioners in rural development, provides a framework for looking at the multidimensional nature of rural poverty. As can be seen in Figure 5.1 he outlines five interacting factors that are both manifestations and causes of poverty. This representation of rural poverty, in addition to looking at the material struggle for survival, highlights how isolation, vulnerability and powerlessness both reinforce and are reinforced by material deprivation.

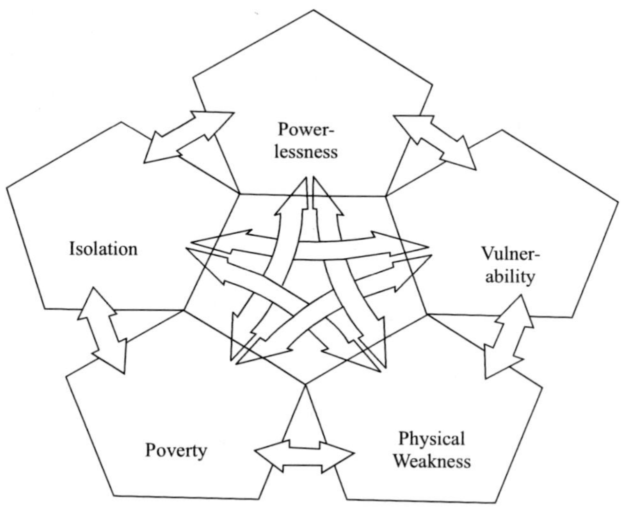

Fig. 5.1 Poverty trap

5.2 WHO ARE THE RURAL POOR?

Rural Poor By Region

Knowing and understanding the poor is as important as understanding poverty. Who are they, and where do they live? How do they get and use income? What are the barriers to their progress, especially in terms of inadequate health, schooling, land and other assets? How these characteristics differ across regions, and whether they help in resolving an issue crucial for policy: are these characteristics causes or effects of poverty?

IFAD's categorisation of the rural poor in its regions of operation provides an overview of the location and the types of poor people. Wage labourers, especially landless or casually employed farm-workers, are almost everywhere among those most likely to be poor.

Poverty incidence amongst children is everywhere much higher than amongst adults. Female headed households are more often found in Latin America and the Caribbean (LAC) Asia and the Pacific (AP), and Near East and North Africa (NENA). In most of West and Central Africa and East and Southern Africa they are not much more likely to be consumption-poor than male headed households. In Near East and North Africa (NENA), a high proportion of the rural poor are women, children and the elderly due to high out migration of prime-age males in the region.

Region	*Rainfed farmers*	*Small-holder farmers*	*Pastora-lists*	*Artisanal fisher-men*	*Wage labourers/ landless*	*Indige-nous people; scheduled castes/tribes*	*Female-headed house-holds*	*Dis-placed people*
WCA		√						
ESA		√		√	√			
AP		√	√	√	√	√	√	√
LAC	√	√	√	√	√	√	√	√
NENA	√		√	√	√	√	√	√

WCA: West and Central Africa: ESA East and Southern Africa: AP: Asia and the Pacific: LAC: Latin America and the Caribbean: NENA: Near East and North Africa

Source: IFAD (2001) pp. 20–22

5.3 POVERTY IN RURAL AREAS

Even a cursory look at developing countries, (Chapter 3, Tables 3.1 to 3.4) it is possible to identify a number of characteristics that these countries share. Similarly, the rural poor too share a number of these characteristics. (Table 5.2)

Table 5.2: Characteristics of the rural poor

Landless/little land	Poor access to services
Large number of dependents	Isolated geographically and socially
Poor health	Vulnerable to contingencies
Poor education	Powerless in exercising their rights
Low incomes	Marginalised socially and economically
Malnutrition	Poor housing

5.3.1 Rural Areas

Looking at rural development it is important to understand what is meant by rural. Again this is more difficult than it would seem from the outset. There is much debate about what are defined as rural and urban areas. Countries vary considerably in their definitions of urban and rural areas. For example, India[1] identifies the borderline between rural and urban areas based on a population of 5000 while Nigeria uses 10,000 as the borderline. Other countries such as China and Brazil do not base the distinction on population but on factors such as the availability of services and legal or political status.

On the one hand, it could be argued that trying to develop a universal definition of what is rural and urban is irrelevant and such a distinction is best considered on a case-by-case basis depending on local conditions. Also, distinguishing between rural and urban areas can be artificial and risks overlooking the important linkages between the two sectors. On the

1. In the Census of India 2001, the definition of urbans area adopted is as follows: (a) All Statutory places with a municipality, corporation, cantonment board or notified town area committee, etc. (b) A place satisfying the following three criteria simultaneously:
   (i) a minimum population of 5000.
   (ii) at least 75 per cent of male working population engaged in non-agricultural pursuits, and
   (iii) a density of population of at least 400 per sq. km (1000 per sq. mile)

other hand, the International Fund for Agricultural Development (IFAD 2001) argues the case for establishing an international definition of *rural* so that international comparisons can be made between countries.

However, since the definition of rural and urban areas within a country is likely to remain stable over a relatively long period of time this allows for better comparisons of differences between rural and urban areas within a country over time.

For practical purpose it can be said that rural areas have two common characteristics as outlined by IFAD (2001):

- They consist of individual dwellings or villages separated by farmland, scrub or forest with populations of between 5000 and 10,000.
- The majority of the population spends their working time in agriculture.

While this defines the rural sector based on the number of residents and primary activity it is important not to lose sight of the movement between the countryside and urban areas, both permanent and seasonal. Other important factors in rural development include the connections between urban and rural areas.

5.3.2 Distribution of Poverty

It is clear from Table 5.1 that many different poverty lines can be developed to measure poverty, depending on what is regarded as the minimum level of consumption required to be on the margin of poverty. Obviously, that minimum level of consumption will differ countries. In fact, in a large country like India the minimum level of consumption can even vary within the country.

Since minimum needs differ, it is difficult to compare poverty levels between countries –that is why the poverty line of US$1.25 per person per day is conventionally used. This is not a totally satisfactory poverty line, because we know that the cost of living varies among different countries. On the other hand, by any standard an income of US$1.25 per day is very low, so it gives the first estimate of the numbers in absolute poverty, and it allows us to gain an insight into the extent and geographical distribution of poverty.

It is a well known fact that global poverty is concentrated in rural areas, and within countries rural areas are typically at a disadvantage to urban areas. Thus, in the following section, an attempt has been made to find out the extent and distribution of poverty and rural poverty globally.

5.3.3 Why Poverty is Primarily a Rural Phenomenon?

The majority of the world's population lives in rural areas in developing countries and will continue to do so for the foreseeable future. Sub-Saharan Africa, South Asia and East Asia have a large percentage of their populations living in rural areas, upwards of 60%. Indeed some countries such as Ethiopia, Eritrea, Uganda, Thailand, Cambodia and Laos have rural populations in excess of 80 per cent. In contrast, developed countries' rural populations typically account for between 20–40 per cent of the overall population. Currently, over 50 per cent of the world population lives in rural areas.

While the percentage of the population living in rural areas is declining, a significant proportion will continue to live in rural areas in the near future. Figure 5.2 shows the percentage of the population living (and projected to live) in rural areas over the period 1975–2015 for various regions. In developing countries the vast majority of people will continue to live in rural areas in 2015. In case of Least Developed Countries 67% will be living in rural areas while it will be 66% in South Asia and 58% in Sub-Saharan Africa.

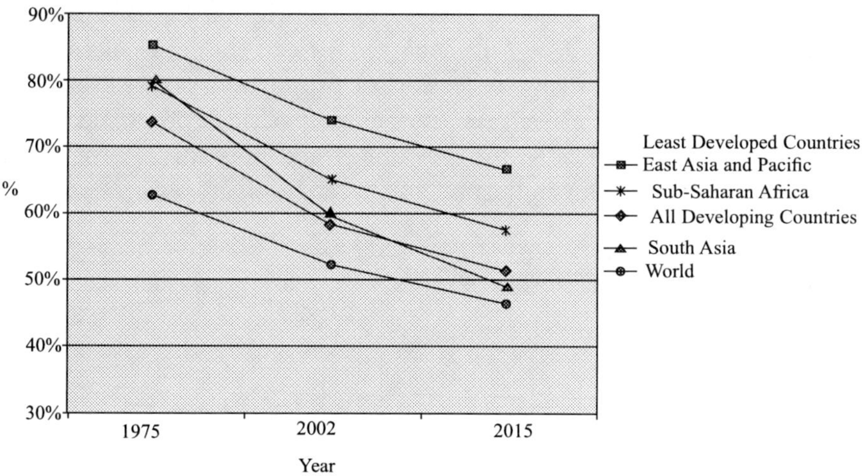

Fig. 5.2 Trends in rural population 1975–2015

The percentage of the population living below the international poverty line of US$1 for countries for which data is available, shows that Sub-Saharan Africa is the poorest region accounting for most of the countries that register over 50 per cent of their population living below the US$1 a day poverty line.

Table 5.3 shows the proportion of people living below the US$1 per day line in the major regions of the world.

Table 5.3: Share of population living on less than $1 per day

Region	*1987*	*1990*	*1993*	*1996*	*1998*
East Asia and Pacific	26.6	27.6	25.2	14.9	15.3
	23.9	18.5	15.9	10.0	11.3
Europe and Central Asia	0.2	1.6	4.0	5.1	5.1
Latin America and Caribbean	15.3	16.8	15.3	15.6	15.6
Middle East and North Africa	4.3	2.4	1.9	1.8	1.9
South Asia	44.9	44.0	42.4	42.3	40.0
Sub-Saharan Africa	46.6	47.7	49.7	48.5	46.3
Total	28.3	29.0	28.1	24.5	24.0
Excluding China	28.5	28.1	27.7		

Source: World Bank, 2001

It can be seen from Figure 5.3 that overall rural areas account for 75% of global poverty. In absolute terms the majority of the rural poor are found in Asia followed by Sub-Saharan Africa. The large quantity of rural poor in Asia is also a reflection of proportion of the world's population living in Asia (53%). As Sub-Saharan Africa's proportion of the world population is 11.2%, the fact that it accounts for 24% of the world's rural poor gives an indication of the widespread poverty in its rural areas.

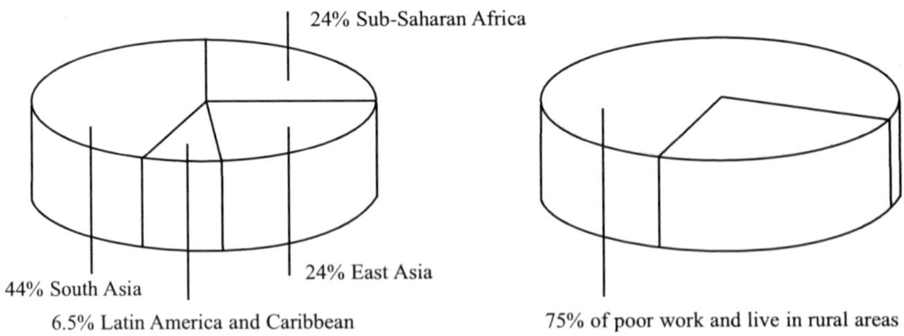

Fig. 5.3 Global distribution of rural poverty

This fact is clear that poor live in rural areas. The next question is the type of rural area they live in, that is, favoured or marginal areas? The geographical distribution of rural population is given in Table 5.4.

Table 5.4: Geographic distribution of rural population and the rural poor in developing countries

Region (number of countries)	*Total population*	*Total rural population*	*Rural population on favoured lands*	*Rural population on marginal lands*	*Rural poor on marginal lands*	*Average rural poverty on marginal lands*
Sub-Saharan Africa (40)	530	375	101	274	176	64
Asia (20)	2840	2044	755	1289	375	29
Central and S. America (26)	430	117	40	77	48	61
W. Asia and N. Africa (40)	345	156	37	119	35	19
Total (105)	4145	2693	933	1759	633	36

Source: CGIAR 1997.

One important point to note from Table 5.4 is that, in all the regions for which data are given, the rural population on marginal lands is much greater than the rural population of "favoured" lands. This is highly significant in terms of strategies to address rural poverty, and rural and agricultural development. Why? Because sometimes it is assumed that rural poverty can be eradicated by just focussing on *favoured* lands, sometimes known as high-potential areas.

Many developing country governments have developed agricultural strategies on this basis. The agricultural development approach known as the *Green Revolution,* which was pioneered in parts of India, Mexico, the Philippines and other countries from the 1960s onwards, primarily focused on high-potential areas.

However, examining the data on rural poverty in marginal lands, it is obvious that any strategy that focuses only on high-potential areas is neglecting the majority of the rural poor.

There is another important and related point — the strategies, which might be appropriate in high-potential areas, will probably not be appropriate in marginal areas. The reasons for this are many, and include the following:

- Strategies in high-potential areas tend to focus on maximising increases in agricultural output, usually through intensifying the use of farm inputs including purchased inputs (improved seed, inorganic fertilisers and pesticides). By contrast, in marginal areas, soil conditions and land quality usually do not allow for the safe application of significant quantities of purchased inputs.
- Cropping patterns tend to differ between high-potential and marginal areas: there may be a greater tendency towards monoculture in high-potential areas, whereas in marginal areas farmers may be more likely to grow a wider range of crops, for reasons of risk-spreading.
- Also, given that farmers in high-potential areas will usually be more market-oriented, market infrastructure and credit facilities are more likely to develop through market processes; in addition, farmers are more likely to be able to finance input purchase and other market requirements themselves. In contrast, in marginal areas the infrastructure to allow for market-orientation and specialisation is generally not well developed, and farmers have less cash to support increased production.
- The optimal strategy for agricultural development and livelihood sustainability in high-potential areas may be specialisation and intensification, but in marginal areas the optimal strategy may be diversification, including involvement in non-farm activities.

The fact that poverty tends to be located in rural areas is borne out by looking at individual countries as well. In Table 5.5 the percentage of households below the poverty line for individual countries in both urban and rural areas are presented. It is clear that making comparisons among countries based on their individual poverty lines is difficult because each country has a different standard. Notwithstanding this, what is important to note is that poverty is higher in rural areas. Also, to the extent that a high proportion of a country's population lives in rural areas, this indicates that rural areas have a high number of poor people in absolute terms. For example, in the case of India, 27% of the rural population lives below the poverty line compared with 26% in urban areas tends to mask the absolute number of people in the respective areas living below the poverty line. With 72.2% of the population living in rural areas and 27.8% in urban areas, based on the respective poverty lines the numbers living below the poverty line would be approximately 200 million in rural areas and 11 million in urban areas. (2001 Census)

Table 5.5: Percentage of population living below the poverty line in urban and rural areas (2000)

Country	*Urban Poverty*	*Rural Poverty*
India	26	27
Kenya	49	53
Bolivia	53	95
Honduras	37	75

Source: Country PRSPs

In summary, the argument to focus on rural areas can be made on the basis that the majority of people living in poverty live in rural areas, that poverty is more acute in rural areas than urban areas and that for the foreseeable future the majority of the poor will continue to live in rural areas. The concentration of rural poverty is particularly high in India. A study by the Oxford Poverty and Human Development Initiative using a Multi-dimensional Poverty Index (MPI) found that there are 421 million poor living under the MPI in eight north Indian states of Bihar, Chhattisgarh, Jharkhand, Madhya Pradesh, Odisha, Rajasthan, Uttar Pradesh and West Bengal. This number is higher than the 410 million poor living in the 26 poorest African nations. A 2007 report by the state-run National Commission for Entreprises in the Unorganised Sector (NCEUS) found that 77% of India, or 836 million people, lived on less than 20 rupees per day. And obviously as stated before, poverty is a rural phenomena. As one of the targets of the first goal of the MDGs is to halve the portion of people living in poverty between 1990 and 2015, its achievement requires reducing poverty particularly in rural areas.

5.4 OTHER DIMENSIONS OF POVERTY

5.4.1 Better Social Services in Urban Areas

We have seen that poverty tends to be concentrated in rural areas. As may be expected this is also reflected by the fact that rural areas are at a disadvantage in relation to the provision of services. The position of India when compared to other countries is not good at all as far as access to health and sanitation is concerned. This point is very clear when we observe Table 5.6(a). Now if we observe the rural, urban differences then one can very well understand how poverty tends to be more prevalent in rural areas. Table 5.6(a) shows that generally rural areas have less access than urban areas to safe water, adequate sanitation and health services.

Table 5.6(a): Access to water and sanitation in India

Contents	*% Urban*	*% Rural*	*% Total*
Access to improved source of water (2008)[1]	96	84	88
Access to improved sanitation (2008)[1]	54	21	31

1. *UNICEF/WHO estimate for 2007 based on the 2006 Demographic and Health Survey and the 2001 census.*

Table 5.6(b): Access to health and sanitation for selected countries

HDI	*Country*	*Health Expenditure*			*Populati-on with sunstain-able access to afford-able essenti-al drugs (%)*	*Populati-on with sustain-able access to im-proved sanitation (%)*	*Population with sustainable access to an improved water source (%)*
		Public (% of GDP) 2001	*Private (% of GDP) 2001*	*Per Capita (PPP US$) 2001*			
1	Norway	6.9	1.2	2920	95-100	100	100
2	Sweden	7.5	1.3	2270	95-100	100	100
96	Sri Lanka	1.8	1.9	122	95-100	94	77
127	India	0.9	4.2	80	0-49	28	84
142	Pakistan	1.0	3.0	85	50-79	62	90
177	Sierra Leone	2.6	1.7	26	0-49	66	57

Source: Generated from Human Development Report 2004

Table 5.6(b) shows that in India less than 21 per cent of the rural population had access to adequate sanitation compared to 54 per cent in urban areas. Additionally, in the case of India the following differences in access to services have been noted in the *Sustainable Development and Poverty Reduction Programme:*

- 62% in rural areas did not access medical facilities compared to 38% in urban areas (of those who reported to be ill);
- the literacy rate in urban areas is 80.30% compared to 59.4% in rural areas; and

- the net primary enrolment rate is 74.5% in urban areas compared to 28% in rural areas.

5.4.2 Poverty and Gender

Poverty has a critical gender dimension. While studies do not suggest that women suffer more from consumption poverty than men; women tend not to do as well in other areas such as empowerment and participation. Generally, women tend to have less access to and control of assets and services such as land, credit, technology, technical assistance, education and healthcare. Discrimination and marginalisation are common features of poverty as experienced by women.

In relation to consumption poverty, in the case of India, according to Table 5.5, the percentage of people living below the poverty line in rural areas is almost identical for both males and females. However, in urban areas, females are more likely to suffer higher levels of poverty. In looking at various indicators of nutrition amongst children, females also tended to compare unfavourably to their male counterparts.

Gender inequality in education is notable amongst regions and within countries. Countries having high human development like Norway, Sweden, Australia, Canada, etc. have 100% literacy, both for male and female. But in developing countries the scene is different. India's female literacy 46.4 and male 69.0. Bangladesh (31.4 and 50.3) and Pakistan (28.5 and 53.4). (Human Development Report, 2004). Thus, regional variation is also obvious. Overall, in developing countries female literacy is 88% of their male counterparts and 79% in Sub-Saharan Africa. In the case of India, Table 5.7(a) outlines differences in literacy rates between males and females and between urban and rural areas according to Census of India 2001. It can be seen that while overall rural dwellers fare particularly badly compared to their urban counterparts, female rural dwellers are at a particular disadvantage with a literacy rate of only 46.70%.

Table 5.7(a): Literacy rates (%) according to residency and gender in India

	Urban	*Rural*	*National*
Male	86.70	71.40	75.85
Female	73.20	46.70	54.16
Total	80.30	59.4	65.38

Source: Census of India 2001.

Another area where there is a marked difference between men and women in urban and rural areas is the burden of work they shoulder. A study of selected countries in the Human Development Report has shown that on an average women spend 20% more time working than men in rural areas. According to Hussain and Tahir (2010) women put in much more time to work as compared to men. Men in India have much more free time when compared to men belonging to developed countries (Table 5.7b).

Table 5.7(b): Gender inequality in work time in selected countries

HDI	*Country*	*Burden of work, total work time (minutes per day)*	
		Women	*Men*
4	Canada	420	429
17	Denmark	449	458
117	Mongolia	545	501
127	India	457	391
138	Nepal (Rural)	641	547
140	Bangladesh (Rural)	545	496
83	Philippines (Rural)	546	452

Source: Generated from Human Development Report 2004.

It must be noted that some aspects of poverty that most affect women tend to be difficult to detect statistically. However, from the perspective of designing support for rural poverty alleviation it is important that gender differences in access and ownership of assets and the multiple roles women play, both productive and reproductive, are taken into account when designing interventions.

5.4.3 Poverty and Vulnerability

The poor, particularly the rural poor, are at risk from climatic factors such as droughts and floods; natural disasters such as earthquakes and landslides; man-made disasters such as war and civil unrest as well as epidemics of diseases. Poverty means that people do not have the necessary buffer to absorb these shocks, which leaves them poorer. For the rural people, vulnerability can be further compounded by remoteness, which makes access to public services to deal with crises and delivery of aid more difficult.

On the positive side the rural poor tend to have better community and family links, which assists them in dealing with emergencies more than their urban counterparts.

IFAD (2000) has identified two patterns that make people in rural areas particularly vulnerable. One is the high rate of births and child deaths in chronically poor families. Rural women tend to have one to three children more than urban women and the gap is bigger for the poor. The other pattern is sharp reduction in incomes during bad times, such as drought, the inability to build up assets, reliance on casual labour and residence in unreliably watered areas. IFAD points out that tackling rural poverty has been positive in reducing vulnerability. For example, reducing child mortality has after a number of years resulted in reduced fertility and a lower dependency ratio thus reducing vulnerability.

HIV/AIDS has become a major source of vulnerability especially in Africa. Some 34 million are now infected, with about two-thirds of them in Africa. Initially, an urban problem, it is increasingly affecting the rural poor. In Africa, deaths have particularly affected women aged 15–30 which has resulted in a growing number of orphans and particular difficulties in agriculture. As HIV/AIDS affects the productive age group it has been cruelly effective in pushing people further into poverty by reducing their capacity to meet their needs through producing food, earning income at a time when their needs become greater. Areas of particular vulnerability to HIV/AIDS in rural areas have been along truck routes, areas where there is much rural-urban migration or seasonal migration and where there has been civil turmoil.

Poverty reduction requires a serious commitment from developed countries to work in partnership with developing countries, especially the poorest. This is recognised explicitly in the MDGs. However, it can be seen here that development assistance has been declining, that least developed countries have suffered most from this and also that development assistance to the rural sector has fallen dramatically.

To achieve the MDGs a minimum of an additional $50 billion in Official Development Assistance (ODA) will be required from donors – or almost the same as is currently spent on ODA ($56.5 billion). However, in the ten years from 1992 to 2002, ODA declined in real terms by almost 12%.

Total ODA in 2001 represented a decrease from 0.33% of their Gross National Income (GNI) in 1990 to 0.22% in 2000. Only five countries currently meet the UN target of spending 0.7% of GNI on aid. Funding to the poorest countries fell most dramatically with the share of ODA going to least developed countries falling from 26% in 1990 to 22% in 2000. (Table 5.8)

Table 5.8: Trends in ODA

	22 OECD Donors	
	1990	*2000*
ODA as % of GNI	0.33	0.22
ODA as per capita of donor country	$78	$67
ODA to least developed countries (as % of total)	26	22

Source: International Development Association (2007).

5.5 RURAL POVERTY REDUCTION THROUGH RURAL DEVELOPMENT

5.5.1 Rural Poverty Reduction vis-a-vis Urban Poverty Reduction

In addition to the fact that the greater incidence and depth of poverty encountered in rural areas justifies intervention. IFAD (2001) argues that investment in rural poverty reduction is more effective and efficient than investment in urban poverty reduction. IFAD's argument is based on four pillars:

(i) Resources spent on rural poverty reduction are cost-effective
(ii) Rural urban interactions
(iii) Reduction in rural to urban migration
(iv) Growth effects of rural poverty reduction

(i) **Resources spent on rural poverty reduction are cost-effective.** The basis of this argument has three components. First, since the outlay per head is less in rural areas, such as in providing health and education, then increased spending in rural areas should yield higher outcomes than similar increases in urban areas.
Secondly, anti-poverty expenditure in rural areas tends to focus on increasing the productivity of the poor, whereas in urban areas it tends to focus on providing services, such as sanitation and shelter, therefore it is likely that rural expenditure will be more effective over the long run in reducing poverty.
Thirdly, since few economies of scale exist in agriculture, it is likely to be more efficient. However, it needs to be noted that because of the high dispersion of rural public action, the associated high management costs could offset the advantages of rural public spending.

(ii) **Rural urban interactions.** Here it is argued that policies aimed at reducing urban poverty may leave urban poverty unchanged as it would attract more people to urban centres leading to further congestion, and could cause urban wages to fall as more people move to the cities. Also, increased supply of cheaper food due to reduced non-labour costs of food production, facilitated by increasing rural productivity, would result in a better-off urban and rural poor.

(iii) **Reduction in Rural to Urban Migration.** The argument here is that reducing rural poverty reduces the incentive for rural to urban migration.

(iv) **Growth effects of rural poverty reduction.** Firstly, urban-rural inequalities due to differences in schools, clinics, prices and technology are likely to affect growth because they create barriers to the advancement of capable people.
Secondly, since anti poverty expenditure in rural areas is consistent with small-scale, labour-intensive production, and as few economies of scale exist in agriculture, it is likely to promote both efficiency and equality.

5.5.2 Quality of Life

Till now the issue of rural development in terms of reduction of poverty has been discussed. However, it also needs to be recognised that rural development also refers to the broad development of rural areas, in a way that provides a good quality of life to rural dwellers.

The term *quality of life* directs attention to the holistic nature of what constitutes a livelihood. It can be regarded as a first step that people have enough to eat, but what about their access to schools, health facilities, clean water, shelter? Do they have access to electricity and to markets? Do they have access to affordable fuel for cooking and heating? Are they safe from conflict? Do they have a *voice* in terms of access to sources of political influence and a role in decision-making? Are women's rights respected in the area? All of these issues need to be addressed in a broader development perspective.

In addition, there are unique roles of rural areas in relation to urban areas, as recognised by three categories of rural-urban interaction:

(i) **The positive contribution of rural areas to urban areas.** Rural areas supply food, fuel (fuelwood, hydro-electricity) and often water to urban areas — although there can be questions about the environmental sustainability of some of these activities. Rural areas provide markets (demand) for the products of urban areas.

(ii) **The avoidance of negative effects.** When rural areas develop, rural-urban migration can be reduced: if rural areas stagnate, rural-urban migration can become excessive and result in major problems of unplanned urban growth, congestion, and an increase in urban poverty.

(iii) **The *psychic* effects of positive rural development.** In more *developed* countries, the positive contribution of thriving rural areas to urban populations has been increasingly recognised. This has been seen in areas such as tourism, recognition of the increased value put on the protection of cultures and landscape, and so on. In other words, people living in urban areas show increased interest in the sustainable development of rural areas, because of the unique attributes of rural areas, which, almost by definition, urban areas lack.

However, it is not reasonable for these attributes to be protected or preserved because they are valued by urban populations if this is done *at the expense of* rural populations: the principle of rural-urban equity has to be enshrined in any rural development strategy. What does this mean? It means that characteristics of rural areas that might be valued by urban populations (or foreign tourists, for example), such as *traditional cultures,* or areas of high wildlife value, should not be preserved in an unchanged state if this means the marginalisation of those who are living the *traditional culture;* or if people living in areas of high wildlife value are forced out of such areas because of the creation of wildlife parks for tourists — as has happened in many countries.

Therefore, rural development is not just about the eradication of poverty amongst people who live in rural areas; it is also about the sustainable improvement of livelihoods in rural areas in a way that contributes to a balanced overall process of development.

5.5.3 Poverty Reduction Through Sustainable Agricultural Development

The 1990s led to poverty reduction once again being placed centre stage. Since the majority of the poor live in rural areas there was renewed interest in agriculture and rural development. However, unlike the large integrated rural development and government interventionist programmes of the 1970s, this time there was more interest in smaller market-led rural credit programmes and demand-led agricultural extension services. In relation to production, sustainable agriculture gained prominence. Debt relief also created a greater incentive for increased social investments in areas such as health and education.

Sustainable Agricultural Development

Sustainable agriculture also needs to be viewed within the broader context of concerns to promote sustainable development, as formally laid down at the United National Conference on Environment and Development (UNCED) in 1992 and in the resulting programme for action, *Agenda 21*.

Sustainable development as a goal has many dimensions, and given the continued importance of agriculture as a source of livelihood for a majority of people in a majority of developing countries, there are many ways in which agriculture and sustainable development interact.

One element of the *Agenda 21* programme is a broad range of actions for conservation and management of resources for development, including promoting sustainable agriculture and rural development, and actions for the management of fragile ecosystems, combating deforestation and rational management and use of fisheries resources. All of these areas are relevant to agricultural development, broadly defined, and are essentially concerned with the sound management of natural resources in ways that: (a) contribute to livelihoods; and (b) do not deplete the underlying resource base.

Box 1: Relationships between agricultural growth, poverty alleviation and environmental sustainability

Hazell (1999) notes that there is a continued need for agricultural growth in developing countries which must be equitable — to alleviate poverty and address food insecurity issues — and must sustain the natural resource base. These triple aims are not necessarily complementary, but are more likely to be so when agricultural development is (a) broad based, involving small and medium farmers, (b) market driven, (c) participatory and decentralised, and (d) driven by technological changes which enhance factor productivity but does not degrade the resource base. Hazell proposes some key points to address each of the three key issues:

Agricultural growth

Conventional development thinking on the requirements for agricultural "transformation" focussed on the five I's, which are still seen as relevant:

1. Innovation – through agricultural research and extension
2. Infrastructure
3. Inputs
4. Institutions
5. Incentives.

Poverty reduction

In terms of the ways in which agricultural development can contribute to poverty reduction, Hazell terms these the "equity modifiers":

- Promote broad-based agricultural development, with priority given to small and medium farms in terms of publicly-funded agricultural research and extension,

Contd...

Contd...

and in marketing, credit and input supplies undertake land reforms where necessary
- Invest in human capital (e.g. education, clean water, health care and nutrition, support to family planning services, etc.)
- Ensure all agricultural supports as well as human capital programmes reach rural women
- Involve all rural stakeholders in setting priorities for public investments
- Actively encourage the rural non-farm economy.

Environmental sustainability

In order for equity-oriented agricultural development to be environmentally sustainable, Hazell proposes the following *environmental modifiers:*
- Give higher priority to less favoured ("low potential") areas even though they may be resource-poor
- Pay more attention in agricultural research to sustainability aspects of recommended technologies, to broader natural resource management issues (e.g., at watershed level), and to specific problems of resource-poor areas
- Ensure that farmers have secure property rights (which can be based on indigenous tenure systems)
- Strengthen community management systems on common property resources (or privatise if there are no negative externalities or equity factors involved in doing so)
- Address externality problems through a variety of instruments
- Improve the performance of relevant public institutions involved in managing and regulating natural resources, and devolve management to resource users where possible
- Correct price distortions which encourage excessive use of modern inputs in intensive agriculture, for example, by removing subsidies on fertiliser and pesticide use (fertiliser subsidies might still be justified in low-productivity areas)
- Establish resource monitoring systems and environmental education programmes.

Source: Hazell (1999).

The link between sustainable livelihoods and sustainable resource management, and the possibilities for developments addressing both issues simultaneously, is one of the key areas of focus of current development policy and practice, essentially because it addresses the two key development priorities of alleviating poverty and reversing environmental degradation. In fact there is a broad consensus on the need to focus on the "critical triangle" (Scherr, 1999) of the poverty-agriculture-environment nexus, although that still leaves many questions open on how to proceed and prioritise. Hazell (1999) gives his approach in terms of agricultural growth, poverty alleviation and environmental sustainability (Box 1).

CHAPTER 6

Institutions and Organisations for Rural Development

CHAPTER OUTLINE

- Institutions and Organisations
- Difference between Institutions and Organisations
- Economic Importance of Institutions and Organisations
- State as Development Institution
- Market as Development Institution
- Evolution of Alternative Institutions
- Service Co-operatives
- Value Chain and Contract Farming
- Micro-finance Institutions
- Warehouses
- Commodity Exchange
- Social Capital
- Civic Societies and Non-governmental Organisations (NGOs)

6.1 INSTITUTIONS AND ORGANISATIONS

Development, and rural development specifically, is a long-term process, which often involves profound social and economic changes, and a change in the institutional structure of the society. Part of the process of development, in fact, is building of institutions that are suitable for the more complex transactions which tend to arise as development proceeds. For example, as farmers shift from producing mostly for themselves, and their family, towards greater production for the market, a whole set of supporting institutions and organisations need to develop to provide for market exchanges. Institutions such as a legal structure to deal with commercial contracts, and organisations such as farmers' co-operatives, are likely to arise to facilitate such trade.

It is important to have an understanding of the role of institutions and organisations in rural development. For much of the 1980s there was a strong tendency in development debates to discuss institutional arrangements in terms of a simple dichotomy between *state* and *market*. This dichotomy is still used to some extent, and in the period of economic liberalisation and structural adjustment there has tended to be a dominant viewpoint that, for developing countries to develop, they needed to rely more on the market and reduce the role of the State. During the 1980s there was much criticism of the *predatory State*, where the State was seen as operating for the benefit of certain vested interests, rather than for the good of the population as a whole. One of the policy consequences of this mode of thinking was the move towards large-scale privatisation of state companies and abolition of quasi-State institutions such as state marketing boards. It was claimed that *the market* would be more effective in carrying out such activities, and that if the country is liberalised, the market would respond in a way that would provide the optimum benefits.

As a consequence of these policy prescriptions, many countries have liberalised their economies, privatised State enterprises, and reduced the role of the State in many areas. However, the outcome of these measures has been mixed: in some countries such as Zambia, for example, most human development indicators have deteriorated as liberalisation has proceeded. There has therefore been a wider recognition that the market will not, by itself, deliver sustainable and equitable development.

Partly as a result of the ambiguous results of *pure* forms of liberalisation, there has been a greater recognition of the importance of institutions and organisations in development, and also greater recognition in general of the preconditions for effective operation of markets. This has resulted in attempts to redefine the legitimate role of the State, and also has led to greater recognition of the broad role of a wide range of institutions and organisations which are *neither State nor market*, but which are part of wider civil society.

Specifically, with regard to agricultural production and food security, it is now widely accepted that there are many areas of necessary public sector intervention. Jayne (1997) notes that there is a need for:

> "*Refocusing the debate from economic liberalisation to economic development within a market-oriented system [which] will require increased attention to the institutional details of the political economy*".

Jayne suggests a range of broad areas of development activity which would be required alongside liberalisation to ensure that market-oriented development is effective and sustainable. These areas include:

- Improved physical infrastructure (road, rail, port and communications)
- Invest more in market-oriented agricultural research
- Modify remaining parastatal pricing policies and change external trade policies to promote regional trade
- Invest more to develop political, legal and economic foundations of private marketing systems
- Co-ordinate policies and investments to gain complementary benefits from higher-valued cash and food crop production
- Increase business skills training and related support for farmer organizations
- Invest in local analytical and policy-making capacity.

To these areas of activity, some of which also have food security benefits, could be added a wide range of more direct food security-related actions for food deficit areas. For example, in relation to research for enhanced production and livelihood security in vulnerable environments, support for seasonal labour-intensive rural works, support for the development of targeted micro-credit programmes, development of emergency/early warning capabilities, etc., all would be beneficial. The key point is the need for a variety of well-grounded actions appropriate to a particular set of circumstances, which will in almost all circumstances combine public, private, and civil society actions. This is in contrast to uniform application of standard prescriptions derived from ideological viewpoints.

Box 1: North's analysis of institutions

Douglass North is one of the leading academic writers on the role of institutions in economic development. His work has influenced much of the subsequent thinking on the subject [North 1990].

North refers to institutions as *the rules of the game* in a society. These rules guide human interaction. Institutions may be either formal or informal. Formal institutions include laws and policies, while informal institutions include social customs, which might be more deeply embedded in culture, and are therefore more resistant to change.

An interesting issue here is that when formal institutions are changing rapidly, informal institutions may not change at the same pace, and may in fact pull in an opposite direction to that of the formal institutions. A good example of this is the outcome for the management of natural resources of land reforms in Ethiopia since the Derg period. Whereas in many parts of Ethiopia natural resource use was regulated through local organisations and their sets of rules, when land was declared State property – a change in the formal institutional arrangements governing land ownership , one effect was to disable the local sets of rules — the informal institutions. Local sets of rules were replaced with State rules, which, however, could not be

Contd...

Contd...

effectively enforced. The result has been very widespread and degradation and deforestation.

Organisations are regarded by North as the *players* in the game — these might include particular government departments, community groups, trading enterprises, and so on.

North brought attention to the importance of *transaction costs* in economic developments, which are essentially the costs of engaging in exchange. He noted that transaction costs in *traditional* village communities tend to be low, because of the closeness of relationships and the existence of traditional mechanisms for resolving conflicts. However, part of the process of economic development is the expansion of long-distance transactions in more distant markets. This allows more specialisation, but also increases transaction costs. If these costs are too high trade will not take place. The challenge of economic development therefore is to reduce the transaction costs associated with more complex types of exchange, and this is done by developing appropriate institutions.

Developing new institutions is partly a matter of political economy. North suggests that it is usually the powerful in society who determine the institutional framework, usually for their interest — but this may not always be the case.

An early analysis of the constraints to enhancing agriculture in Sub-Saharan Africa (Beynon 1990) similarly provides strong support for the role of the State in easing structural constraints to production. During the 1980s the implementation of structural adjustment programmes in many countries was accompanied by a call to *get the prices right*. It was argued that there was price discrimination against farmers in many Sub-Saharan African countries as a result of government policies which, for example, forced farmers to deliver produce to monopoly State marketing boards at below-market prices, and which maintained overvalued currencies, as a result of which producers of export crops received less than they *should* have done if exchange rates were determined by the market. Two policy prescriptions, which were followed by most governments, were

- to abolish State marketing boards and the compulsory supply to them, allowing domestic prices to be set by the market; and
- to allow foreign exchange rates to be set by the market — this generally meant a devaluation of the currency.

But were these measures sufficient to bring about clear improvement in farmers' conditions, and in food security?

Beynon's analysis, although conducted using data from the 1970s and 1980s, suggests that the aggregate supply response of farmers to price increases is relatively low.

Box 2: Agricultural supply response
A note on agricultural supply response

The analysis of agricultural supply response examines the extent to which farmers will change production as a response to a change in prices. The calculation of crop supply elasticities is a measure of the proportionate (per cent) change in output as a response to a given proportionate (per cent) change in price. For example, if the price of wheat increased by 10 per cent and wheat output increased by 5 per cent, the supply elasticity would be 0.5.

Beynon observes that individual crop supply elasticities in Sub-Saharan Africa are quite high. This indicates that farmers are responsive to changes in relative prices: in other words, if the price of maize increases by 20 per cent and the price of wheat falls by 20 per cent, farmers are quite likely to shift to growing more maize.

But the key issue for agricultural development is aggregate supply response i.e., the increase in production in the agricultural sector as a whole. It is more difficult to calculate supply elasticities in aggregate, because of the different trends in prices, different forms of measurement, etc., but Beynons analysis suggests that aggregate supply elasticities tend to be rather low, and that this is largely because of a range of structural constraints which hinder farmers in their efforts to increase output.

Beynon listed eight external constraints that particularly affected agriculture in Sub-Saharan Africa:

- Markets are imperfect
- Lack of consumer goods
- Low levels of human capital
- Land constraints
- Labour constraints
- Technological limitations
- Capital constraints
- Inadequate rural infrastructure

(i) **Markets are imperfect.** Many markets are fragmented, making the price mechanism relatively ineffective. Many markets are *missing*, for example, the limited development of insurance markets in developing countries contributes to the fact that farmers tend to be risk-averse in their selection of crops, tending to produce for domestic consumption first, even when production for the market might give them greater returns.

(ii) **Lack of consumer goods.** This may be less of an issue now than in previous decades, but years of economic stagnation in many African countries resulted in a lack of consumer goods in the market, and therefore limited farm demand for such goods. Partly as a result there was little incentive for farmers to produce more.

(iii) **Low levels of human capital.** Bad health affects the ability of farmers to work longer to respond to increased prices. The HIV/AIDS pandemic has had a huge negative impact in this respect in many countries.

(iv) **Land constraints.** The increasing problems of land degradation, limited access to irrigation, and poor soil quality in many areas, all limit the capacity of farmers to increase production.

(v) **Labour constraints.** Many households suffer labour constraints, particularly female-headed households, and households where the adult males migrate for long periods to urban areas to earn money. In addition, the concentration of peak labour periods at certain times means that genuine labour shortages are experienced.

(vi) **Technological limitations.** *Traditional* agriculture has tended to use rather rudimentary agricultural technology, which does not allow for easy expansion in production. This is particularly the case where hoes or other manual implements are used, but where draught animals are used, there are other problems, for example lack of feed resources, which constrain the ability to expand production. The use of inorganic inputs is also significantly less than in other developing countries.

(vii) **Capital constraints.** Limited availability of credit seriously reduces the ability of farmers to expand even if they wanted to. In addition, lack of clarity on land ownership limits the access of farmers to sources of credit due to lack of acceptable collateral.

(viii) **Inadequate rural infrastructure.** Inadequate rural infrastructure includes a whole range of services which are required in support of production, including transport, communications, power, water supply, storage, effective agricultural research and extension services, credit institutions, marketing facilities, distribution outlets for agricultural inputs, etc.

This long list of structural factors indicates the extent of the challenge facing countries trying to promote agricultural and rural development. It also indicates that this is not a process that can be completed in the short run, but needs long-term investment. Without such investments, farmers are less likely to respond even when output prices increase significantly.

Beynon (1990) therefore notes that

"*...to the extent that roads, irrigation, new technology, research and extension and measures of human capital are either public goods or involve significant indivisibilities and economies of scale, this only serves to emphasise the role of the State. The lower the absolute level of development, the less likely it is* *that the private sector will be able to invest in response to higher price incentives."*

A more recent discussion of the rationale for the reform of agricultural markets in Africa (Kherallah et al., 2002) points to the variety of factors *internal and external, national and international,* which led to reforms which:

> "*...consisted mainly of the abandoning of price controls, allowing private sector entry into agricultural trading activities, eliminating or easing trade restrictions, and removing or reducing the State role in marketing*".

Kherallah (et al.) examine outcomes of agricultural market reform in terms of impacts on:

(i) the nature and efficiency of the market itself;
(ii) the broader impact on agricultural production; and
(iii) impacts on equity, food security and income growth.

There is also the broader impact on the provision of public goods, which is an issue of particular and broader relevance in the context of rural development, since public goods are conventionally seen as a key area of State activity.

In short, according to Burns and Admassie (1994), "*...the institution consists of a system of authority and power*".

6.2 DIFFERENCE BETWEEN INSTITUTIONS AND ORGANISATIONS

In much of the general discussion of institutions, especially formal institutions, "*the system of authority and power*" is often taken to be the Government. But it is possible to also have local, self-governing institutions, such as those involved in the management of common property resources, which are the immediate system of authority and power with respect to the use of natural resources.

Important questions to be answered in relation to institutions: (1) What is the distinction between *institutions* and *organisations*? (2) Why the institutional framework at one level may shift, while organisations reflecting a different framework may persist at another level, with indeterminate effects? (iii) What is the concept of *social capital*?

(i) The distinction between *institutions,* and *organisations.* If institutions are defined in part by sets of rules, organisations are those entities which implement actions according to those sets of rules.

Thus, for example, the existence of rules governing the use of a water course for irrigation denotes the existence of an institutional framework limiting individual use of the water, and imposing sanctions for non-compliance; a water users organisation is the specific entity which organises water sharing according to these institutional rules, and which implements specific sanctions (say, fining a farmer for over-use of water, or forcing them to miss the next water allocation) according to the institutional "order" laid down.

Uphoff brings out the differences (and similarities) between institutions and organisations as follows:

> "*Institutions, whether organisations or not, are complexes of norms and behaviours that persist over time by serving collectively valued purposes, while organisations, whether institutions or not, are structures of recognised and accepted roles*". (Uphoff, 1993).

The key difference here, is that institutions refer to social norms (rules) and behaviours which tend to persist, whereas organisations are structures, which may or may not have a long existence. Uphoff cites, for example, *the law* as an institution which is not an organisation. The Supreme Court as an example of an institution which is also an organisation, and a specific law practice as an organisation which is not an institution. The importance of this distinction lies primarily in the point that, as Uphoff notes, "*...the process of institutionalisation is an essential aspect of development.*" (1993). Institutions such as the market, the State, and the law, are fundamental elements of complex developed societies, while the specific organisational structures which exist within that institutional framework may vary widely.

(ii) The institutional framework at one level may shift, while organisations reflecting a different framework may persist at another level, with indeterminate effects. The Dessa'e forest in Tigray Region provides an example. In the mid-1990s the State changed the rules governing the management of the forest in favour of State management, while the *rist*-based organisations implementing local-level management continued to exist, but were undermined by the State's actions.

(iii) There has been considerable recent interest in the concept of *social capital* (Putnam 1993; Dasgupta and Serageldin (eds.) 2000).

However, the meaning of social capital is sometimes unclear, as to whether it denotes the existence of social norms and behaviours which predispose a community towards collective action, and or whether it denotes the existence of organisations which can bring about such collective action. If social norms do not exist, are weak, or are even predisposed to individualistic behaviour, a major issue for development is whether organisations can be created through community development work to enable collective action to take place.

6.3 ECONOMIC IMPORTANCE OF INSTITUTIONS AND ORGANIZATIONS

Institutions are laws, social norms, traditions, religious beliefs and values, which determine the relationship between economic agents (individuals, households, firms, countries and so on) and economic agents and their environment. Institutions are sanctioned by community, by state or/and by other economic agents to coordinate the effort of each and every agent toward specific goal. Institutions can be formal, as sanctioned by law, or informal, as sanctioned by social norms. It is always important to remember that informal institutions are as important as formal institutions. This is so, given the fact that "rules that contradict the moral of the people would not be sanctioned socially and, if stipulated formally, would not function effectively" (Hayami, 1997). This is because socially rejected institutions will demand huge enforcement cost to be practical. Let's see the following institutions as example.

Table 6.1: Example of formal and informal institutions

Institutions	*Nature*	*Effect on economy*
Private property will have protection under the law	Formal	It will promote capital accumulation, entrepreneurship, innovation, self development, risk taking and so on
It is not right to steal any body's property	Informal	It will make the formal rules that protect private property very effectively; if formal rules are absent it will substitute them
Exchange of private property has to be by free will of each party involved	Formal	It will improve market efficiency by making reward proportional or equal to effort and will make exchange win-win situation
It is not right to force some one to trade his personal possession	Informal	It will make the formal rules that protect private property very effectively; if formal rules are absent it will substitute them
Every person has obligation to pay tax	Formal	It will improve the provision of public goods by promoting the supply of public goods
It is wrong to evade income tax	Informal	It will make tax enforcement very effective
Children have to supply the basic needs of their senior parents	Informal	It will generate social security for old age

In simple words, institutions are needed to organize diverse economic agents into functional body, called organization. The organization can be family, firm, ministry, market, state and so on. Organization is a functional body or group organized to act for specific purpose. The two important organizations, for economics, are market and state. Market will organize the self motivated act of economic agents toward maximization of social welfare, using the invisible hand of competition. Producers are producing to maximize profit, individuals are trying to maximize utility, workers are trying to have better paying job with better working environment. Countries are trying to have more foreign income and more inflow of foreign investment and so on. Basically, market is built from matrix of rules (institutions), which coordinate the self-promoting act of individuals toward social welfare maximization. This is done by competition using prices as shooting star to guide agents toward the need direction. When people need more bread, they will pay more for it. As result price of bread will increase. Producers in order to maximize profit, will start producing more bread at least cost possible. If they are not using the least cost combination of inputs and technology, competition will force them out of market. As result more bread, which is demanded by the society, will be produced in least cost possible. This will result in maximum welfare possible, given the limited resources at society's disposal. However, viewed from a different angle market is a complex matrix of institutions too.

The optimality of these institutions is what determines the optimality of the market as organization. If private property is not having legal protection and exchange is not based on free will, how can we assume the baker will waste most of his/her time and resource to produce the best quality bread, using the least cost combination of inputs? Why not steal it from some one else?

If institutions are well defined and enforced, they will provide optimal signals to coordinate egocentric action of individuals to make it compatible with maximization of social welfare. Not only institutions will guide agents' effort in the right direction, but also will introduce certainty on future outcome of current action. A farmer will only crop his land optimally, if and only if he/she is assured that he/she is the sole owner of his/her effort. People will be willing to save and lend to somebody, if and only if they know that they will be paid pack with interest. In general, institution of private property will make, both, saving and production socially optimal, by providing assured rules, which govern the relationship between agents and agents and their environment.

Efficiency of market as organization, which is the main focus of main stream economics, is result of its institutional efficiency. In simple words market is both organization and institution. Similarly, state is an institution with set of rules for governance. At the same time, state is an organization built out of three organizations classified as administrative body, legislative body and judicial body. Normally, state will have its own social objectives. To achieve these objectives, it will need to coordinate action of its people and its own parts toward predetermined objective. This is done by fixing different formal institutions or laws. How much tax people have to pay, what service people can expect from government, how people elect their political leaders, how people monitor the elected officials and so on; will determine the efficiency of the state.

Organizations are built of economic agents and the relationship between economic agents within the organization and economic agents and the organization is defined by institutions. Moreover, the relationship of that organization with wider economic system is also specified by the institutions, which define the ownership right of resource and the distribution of wealth among people. Jamia Millia Islamia University is built of students, teachers, administration and supporting staff. The relationship between these different agents of the University is defined by university's formal and informal rules and regulations, which define the relationship of each agent with each other and the University. Moreover, the relationship between Jamia Millia Islamia University and the overall economic (national) system[2] is defined by wider national institutions. If these institutions are of a right kind Jamia Millia Islamia University will achieve its objectives.

In general, organization is a functional body organized by set of rules and institutions are set of rules, which organize a group of economic agents into functional body. Institutions will provide necessary signal and expectation to coordinate the activity of individuals. Right incentives and signals provided by the right institutions will achieve efficient resource utilization by the mass. But, if institutions are of a wrong kind, egocentric act of individuals can possibly result in disastrous outcome to everyone. Just think about private property. If it is appropriately enforced, it will grant fruit of own labour to the owner, which can provide positive signal for hard working rational individuals. Unfortunately, if it was not properly enforced some people will prefer to share the output of others than produce their own output. As as result national output will decline by amount which can be produced by those who prefer to be a free rider. Far worst even those who prefer to work, after observing that their output is shared by others, will work less hard or will be free riders. This will have a devastating impact on economic efficiency. A good example for the above prediction is 1990s Somalia starvation, which is caused by lack of private property on agricultural products. Note that everybody is acting rationally to maximize its own welfare. But, the final outcome of such rational action will depend on the existence of institutions, which promote efficiency. In this case, the right institution is private property of own output.

As can be shown below, if market is perfect, as assumed in mainstream economics, it is the only institution needed to coordinate the rural development effort, in specific, and general development effort, in general.

6.4 STATE AS DEVELOPMENT INSTITUTION

Due to market failures and missing markets, market allocation will not result in the best possible resource allocation, in other words, market forces alone will not result in best possible rural development. That is why we need alternative institutions to give complementary signal to coordinate diverse activities of many agents, with diverse and personal objective, toward achievement of fast and sustainable development.

Market will coordinate the action of egocentric economic agents to ward maximization of social welfare using the invisible hand of competition with incentive provided by prices. In other words, market allocation under its assumptions will result in best possible resource allocation, because it uses efficient institutions which guide individuals toward maximization of social welfare. The three fundamental institutions among the diverse matrix of market institutions are:

1. **Private property will have protection under the law.** Means you can't take somebody's property and output without his/her consent. You can't take the baker's bread without his/her will. If not the baker will not have proper incentive to produce the best bread at least cost, to save, to invest and to be innovative in his management. It also means the baker can't take other peoples' money without their consent.
2. **Exchange has to be by consent of all parties involved.** This is an extension of the above market institution. If private property is respected, it can be exchanged only by full consent of everybody involved. When you buy bread, you are exchanging your private property on your money to have private property on the bread.
3. **Freely agreed contract has to be enforced by state or other third party.** Once people freely sign a contract, it has to be enforced. If

not, it will increase uncertainty for agents and this will increase production risk, to limit their efficiency.

Based on these three fundamental market institutions, there will be a complex matrix of formal and informal institutions that are used to coordinate action of egocentric economic agents toward maximization of social welfare. These institutions will deal with how long labour have to work, how labour efficiency has to be assessed, how much is the minimum acceptable wage rate, whether purchased goods and services can be returned or not and so on. However, when market is imperfect, the above conclusion is not necessarily true. This is why we need alternative institutions to complement market forces. The next most important institution is the state. Market institutions are based on free exchange of property. But state institutions are based on coercive power and mandatory transfer of property. Under some conditions, market failures and missing markets, such institutions can do better than free will based market institutions. The role of state in rural development as complementary to market and its rationales are given below.

1. **Provision of public goods and services.** It is already shown that for public goods and services market will result in suboptimal supply of public goods. If the choice to pay for public goods and services is left to the free will of the people, the supply of public goods and services will be sub-optimal. This is so since people have more incentive to get things free than to pay for public goods and services. That is why, expecting people to pay for roads, schools, defense, public administration and so on by will, they will face mandatory taxation. Using the tax revenue, that state is expected to supply optimal public goods and services. In simple words, in order to supply the critically needed public goods for development, instead of coercive power free will based market exchange should be used to improve the market allocation.
2. **Solves problem of negative externality.** If market demand is the same as social marginal benefit and if market supply is the same as social marginal cost, market forces will result in the best possible resource allocation—assuming if other market failures do not exist. However, when there is negative externality, social marginal cost will be higher than private marginal cost, as a result market institutions will oversupply the goods or the services. That is why mandatory tax has to be laid to make the private marginal cost equal to social marginal cost. When mandatory taxes are laid in production, market forces will result in efficient and optimal production of the goods or

the services. A factory may produce more goods and services to maximize private profit, ignoring the negative cost exerted on society in terms of river pollution, air pollution and others. By laying taxes, to increase cost of production, it is possible to reduce the production of the good or service. Moreover, the tax revenue can be used to compensate economic agents affected by the externality.

Thus education, healthcare, sanitation and other social goods do exert positive externality on society's welfare. In other words, the marginal social benefit is higher than private marginal benefit. As a result, market forces will supply less than optimal social goods. That is why state has to subsidize the supply of education, healthcare, sanitation and other social goods in order to enable people to be more educated and healthy.

3. **State investment on collection and dissemination of information.** Given rural areas are highly dependent on farming and farming is dependent on random natural events, there will be high level of risk in rural areas. As stated above, given information, insurance, financial intermediation and future markets are either missing or highly imperfect, market forces will result on Pareto[1] suboptimal resource allocation. That is why state intervention in the form of price stabilization, safety net, drought relief and other forms can have productive impact on rural development. Moreover, given public nature of information, state investment on collection and dissemination of information is critical for efficient allocation of resources by market forces. States can work either in reduction of risk faced by economic agents or creation of risk management capability within economic agents or both. A classic example for the first one is oil price stabilization through a buffer fund as implemented in Ethiopia. Drought relief, safety net and income diversification efforts are good examples for the second one. Moreover, state intervention to improve the functionality of financial intermediaries and risk management institutions (like insurance companies) is an example of risk management capacity building.
4. **Creation of egalitarian society.** Even if markets are efficient, in which you can't make someone better off without making somebody worse off, the final distribution of benefits may not be egalitarian. If the initial distribution of capabilities (education, wealth, asset, social

[1]Italian sociologist and economist whose theories influenced the development of fascism in Italy (1848–1923).

network and soon) is unfair, the final distribution of economic benefits will not be fair. Such distribution of quality of life may not be acceptable to society, given the fact that the social value of the poor persons' benefit can overweigh the social loss of the rich.

If market is working under perfect conditions, its distribution is neutral. As a result, it does not matter if land, labour, capital and other resources are owned by X or Y, if you have land, the value of the land for you is the market price. When you use the land for production purpose, the opportunity cost that you are facing is equal to the price of the land. And if you buy it from others the cost of the land is equal to its price. So the cost of production will not be affected by distribution of resources, if markets are perfect. One method is to tax the rich and spend that money on improving the capabilities of the poor. And the second method is to tax the rich in order to subsidize the poor.[2] Means, even if markets are working perfectly, there is role for government to distribute capability and consumption.

If markets are imperfect, skewed distribution of wealth and living standard could result from market power of the better off than from its contribution to social good. In such a case redistribution of wealth is advocated, even by those who accept market allocation of wealth and living standard as legit and moral[3]. If there is efficient but land constrained farmer, in otherwise perfect market, he/she can buy or rent land at existing market price. So whether he/she owns land or not will not make any difference in cost of production. Under imperfect market, however, he/she may not have access to land at the existing market price. Under such reality, redistribution of land to favour him/her can improve efficiency and redistribution which disfavours him/her can reduce efficiency. So redistribution under imperfect market can lead to more or less efficiency depending on local conditions.

5. **Creation of rural urban balance.** Missing markets, missing public goods (services) and missing administrative services are common reality of rural areas within developing economies. These facts coupled

[2]The first one is like giving a tractor to the poor farmer, so he can cultivate his land, which can make himself self-sufficient in the long run. The second one is giving food to the poor farmer. The second option can create serious dependency problem.

[3]Those who believe that market allocation by marginal productivity is justified but if market failures like monopoly lead to skewed income distribution government should correct it through lump sum tax and transfer (which are less distortional).

with low organizational capital of rural population, can make development highly urban biased phenomena. To solve this challenge, state intervention to organize rural population into functional political body and to improve the provision of goods and services is critically needed in rural areas.

6. **State's capability to shorten the period of development:** The important point about market is that it will tend to solve its own failures in the long run. Not only market forces will self-perfect in the long run, but also complementary local institutions will spontaneously emerge to solve the problem of market failures. Means, market forces if are left for themselves, in the long run can solve their own problems and can lead to economic development. Unfortunately, the implication is that we have to wait 200 to 300 years in order to achieve the level of development attained by developed economies.

With appropriate and selective use of the visible hand of the state, government can possibly shorten the gestation period of development in to maximum of 50 years (as was the case in Japan) or to minimum of 20 to 30 years (as was the case in East Asian countries). In developing countries like India, where majority of the population is living in rural areas, any jump ignoring rural set-up may not be so beneficial. The need for such a jump will call for optimal government intervention in rural areas, where series of market failures and missing markets are widely observed.

STATE FAILURE

Following are the reasons for state failure.

1. **Information asymmetry and managerial diseconomies from the state side.** If state produces goods and services by itself, as was/is the case in Communist countries, it will face series managerial diseconomies and asymmetric information problem related to demand dynamics. In market economy demand dynamics is communicated to producers through dynamics in market prices. When market and its prices are eliminated, the state will normally face asymmetric information related to demand dynamics. As a result, state will fail to organize production to meet every changing customer demand.

State engaged in production of diverse goods and services will face managerial diseconomies, too.

But even within a mixed economy, where the state is concentrating on solving externality and public goods (service) problems, state will face series information asymmetry related to economic agents actual income, wealth and use of public goods (services). If the state lacks adequate information on income, expenditure, wealth and demand for public goods (services), it can't fix optimal tax to supply optimal public goods (services). The reason why state in developing economies is highly dependent on indirect than direct tax is because it has better information related to indirect tax base than direct tax base. Under such reality, state intervention to avoid free riders in the allocation of public goods (services) will fail to tax all individuals either according to their ability or their benefit. Means some public goods and services will not be supplied, because the state needs high administrative cost to enforce tax laws under asymmetric information.

Lack of information about the occurrence and extent of externality will destroy state capacity to internalize externality. Since the state does not have all necessary information needed in order to internalize externality, it will face more administrative cost. If the administrative cost is higher than the benefit of solving the externality problem, it would be rational for state to ignore the externality problem.

2. **Information asymmetry from public side.** In democratic system, where there is higher accountability of government to the people's choice, asymmetric information faced by voting population will result on suboptimal state policy. If public choice, about government action is reflected by peoples' capacity to vote into office individuals who do their wish, they need to know the application of each and every policy and their possible outcomes. Unfortunately, due to need for state secrecy, there will be imperfect disclosure of state policy and actions. This will give higher freedom for politicians to divert from their electoral choice and stay in office. Even if, each and every, information is made public, voters will not have the capacity to understand the net impact of all state policies. When economists can't even agree on the net impact of any policy, how is a layman can do better? This is why state intervention is not granted to be productive.

3. **The failure of voting to consider intensity of want.** In democratic system every person is given equal voting right. If 10 people are expected to lose 100 birreach, due to proposed new policy, social welfare will decline by 1000 birr. But if 500 people are going to benefit 1 birr each, the expected social gain is 500 birr. Given the fact that 500 people are for the new policy and only 10 are against the policy, the new policy will be implemented with support birr significant majority. This is despite the fact that total welfare will decrease by such action. Means voting, which does not consider intensity of want, can't necessarily lead to maximum social welfare.

4. **Lack of incentive and high inefficiency in public sector.** The bureaucratic system, which is used in public offices, is less flexible to changing conditions and the incentive system used in public sector is loosely linked to efficiency. That is why development, which needs dynamic, efficient and flexible decision making, faces rigid bottlenecks from the public sector.

First, decisions will take longer time and such bureaucratic rigidity will negatively affect efficiency of the public sector. Second, the public sector facing highly asymmetric information will have less capable workers, which normally work less than their full capacity.

There is a tendency for states to pay lower salary, everywhere in the world, which creates adverse selection problem. Only option is less workers, who can't find alternative employment, will be employed at low paying public sector. Most often, these people are the less productive part of the labor force[7]. To make things worst, since reward in public sector is not directly related to productivity, there will be a series moral hazard problem among the civil servants. Means there is no adequate incentive for civil servants to be as efficient as private sector employees. Even if there are exceptional workers within the public sector, social capital among civil servants will be used to ostracize the efficient ones. If everyone is producing 5 units per day and a new one is producing 10 units per day, it will signal to the state that others are either incapable or unwillful to be efficient enough. As a result they will use their social capital to discourage productivity by ostracizing efficient workers[8]. Means, both economic and social institutions, found within the public sector, will not promote efficiency of civil servants. Observing that civil servants are inefficient, the state has a rational base to pay low salary, keeping the vicious circle ongoing![9]

In general, state can solve some market failures, but is not a magic institution that can solve every market failure problem, everywhere. Means, state is a critical institution for rural development, but is not also a magic fairy or a silver bullet which can be used to achieve rural development, in all cases. The logical question left is "do we have another option"? The answer of institutional economists is: yes indeed!

---

[7]Given imperfection in labor market this may not be always true but it is true in most cases.

[8]This is commonly observed in China public sector companies (Hayami, 1997).

[9]This is good example how imperfect information can result on Pareto suboptimal resource allocation, when everybody is promoting his/her own interest. The best outcome would be for workers to work hard and state to pay them more. But the incentive structure will not encourage such action.

6.5 MARKET AS DEVELOPMENT INSTITUTION

It has already been discussed before that free market is Pareto optimal. Or in other words market allocation will result in the best possible allocation of resources. The central assumptions are as follows:

There are a large number of buyers and sellers. Everyone will take the market price as given in the market. Nobody will have the power to fix price, which is determined by market demand and supply (collective action of all participants).

Secondly, in the economy, technology is given and anyone can use that technology without any restriction.

Thirdly, there is perfect mobility of factors. Factors of production, like capital, labour, land and raw material, can freely move from one location to another without any need for additional cost.

Next, there is perfect information about price, output, market demand, and supply level and so on. Thus, there is no risk and decision is done under perfect information.

And since there is free entry and exit, nobody can earn any abnormal profit and only the fittest, the one with best quality products and least cost of production and marketing will survive.

All benefits and costs are accruing to those who are responsible either for the consumption or production of the goods and services.

Lastly, human beings are making the best possible decision on time use, production, consumption and saving, after considering all important information.

Thus, under these assumptions market will result in the best possible resource allocation or Pareto optimal resource allocation. Means there is nothing that can be done to improve market efficiency. The market is Pareto optimal under the following circumstances:

First of all most important is efficiency in consumption. It is not possible to increase utility of customer by changing the composition and quantity of goods consumed by the customer. Means customers are generating the best possible utility that can be generated from the limited resource that society has.

Next important factor is efficiency in production. It is not possible to increase level of production by improving technology, input composition and efficiency of input use. Means what can be produced from the limited resources is already produced and there is nothing that can be done to improve it farther.

Lastly goods and services produced from the limited resources are produced and distributed optimally.

If these assumptions are right, resource allocation which is the cornerstone of any development effort can be coordinated by market forces only. In other words, the institution needed to achieve rural development is market only. Free market will provide optimal inputs to the rural residents and will create optimal market for their output demanded by the people. If these assumptions are right, rural and national development could be as simple as letting the market free or getting the price right.

"The model virtually made economics a branch of engineering (with no aspersions to that noble profession), and the participants in the economy better or worse engineers. Each was solving a maximization problem, with full information: households maximizing utility subject to budget constraints, firms maximizing profits (market value), and the two interacting in competitive product, labour, and capital markets" (Stiglitz, 2001, 11-12). The problem is that in order to reach such mathematically precise conclusion, they have to assume many things which are unrealistic. The shortcomings of the perfect market approach can be classified into traditional market failures and none traditional market failures.

Traditional Market Failures

Omission of the existence of externality. Given negative and positive externalities are widely observed in any economy; market allocation will not result in the best possible resource allocation or Pareto optimal resource allocation, by itself. To understand this fact, a market demand and market supply curve has been developed (Fig. 6.1).

Market allocation, based on market demand and supply, will generate optimal output of Q^* and optimal market clearing price of P^*. If either price or output is changed, it will result in suboptimal allocation of resource. If more output is produced, the social marginal cost of production (supply curve) will be greater than the monetary value of the marginal social benefit of the good (demand curve). As result the additional output will generate negative social gain to the society. If less output is produced, the marginal social benefit (demand curve) of additional output in monetary terms will be greater than the marginal social cost (supply curve) of additional output. Means more utility could be generated, if more output was produced and consumed. In general, the social optimal output is Q^*, which is related to point where demand is equal to supply.

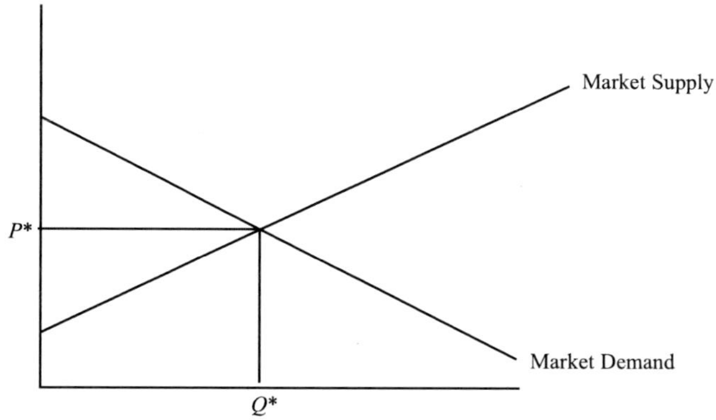

Fig. 6.1 Market demand and market supply curve

If price is greater than P^*, there will be excess supply of output compared to demand. This will result in waste of scare resource; given the excess output produced will not find a buyer. If price is less than P^*, the economy will face shortage of goods and services. Means, people who are willing to buy the goods or services at market price will not be able to do so. In general, under perfect market, social welfare will be maximized, if and only if the market clearing price and output are not altered. This is why, neoclassical economists assume market will result in Pareto optimal resource allocation or in the best possible resource allocation. However in reality, than in assumed economies, there is difference between market demand and supply curve, and social demand and social supply curve; due to positive and negative externalities.

(a) Influence of negative externality. The market supply curve is based on private marginal cost for producing each additional output. However, if there are negative externalities exerted on other economic agents and the environment, it will not be equal to the social marginal cost of each additional output. The private sector will pay for cost of labour, land, capital and other private costs, but it may fail to cover the cost related to river pollution, air pollution and other negative externality exerted on people and the environment.

The cost of negative externality extended on the environment can be achieved by shifting the social marginal cost or social supply curve upward. Based on the private demand and supply curve, the market will supply Q_m level of output at P_m price level. (Fig. 6.2) This is the point where profit of producers and surplus of customers can be maximized. It is optimal resource allocation from private gain point of view. However, at Q_m level of output the social marginal cost is higher than the private marginal cost. Means maximum social welfare is not attained at Q_m level of output. The socially optimal level of output is at Q^* with socially optimal price of P^*. Any production behind Q^* will cost more than the benefit it can generate to the society.

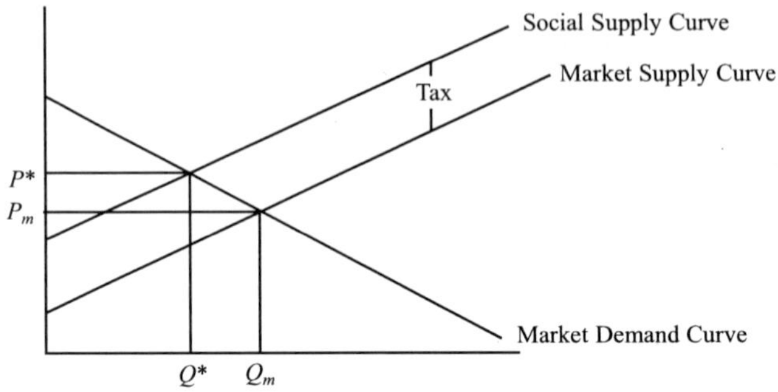

Fig. 6.2 Negative externality

The above graph clearly shows the fact that when there are negative externalities; market allocation will not result in Pareto optimal or the best possible resource allocation. By introducing taxes equal to $P^* - P_m$ better resource allocation can be attained. Means there is possibility to improve market allocation. When taxes are laid on the private sector, the private marginal cost curve will be equal to the social marginal cost curve. Producers in order to maximize profit and customers in order to maximize utility will produce and consume, respectively, socially optimal output of Q^* at socially optimal price of P^*.

(b) Influence of positive externality. Education, healthcare, skill development, research and development will not only benefit the person who is paying for them, but also the wider society. Healthy people for example, can have better and enjoyable life, which will lead them to pay for healthcare. However, the benefit to society is much higher than that. For example, a healthy person will not transmit contingent diseases. Thus, when one person is healthy other people have more chances to be healthy too. These are social benefits, which are not directly accruing to the individual. Based on private benefit, the market demand for healthcare will be presented by market demand curve. However, considering the social benefit, the social demand for health care will be higher than the market demand curve. (Fig. 6.3)

Based on market allocation, private consumer and producer surplus are maximized, when Q_m level of output is supplied at P_m level of price.

However, at Q_m level of output social marginal benefit is much higher than the private marginal cost of production. As a result, social welfare can be increased by producing and consuming more output. Socially optimal level of output of Q^* at price of P^* can be supplied, if a subsidy equal to $P^* - P_m$ is given to customers of healthcare service.

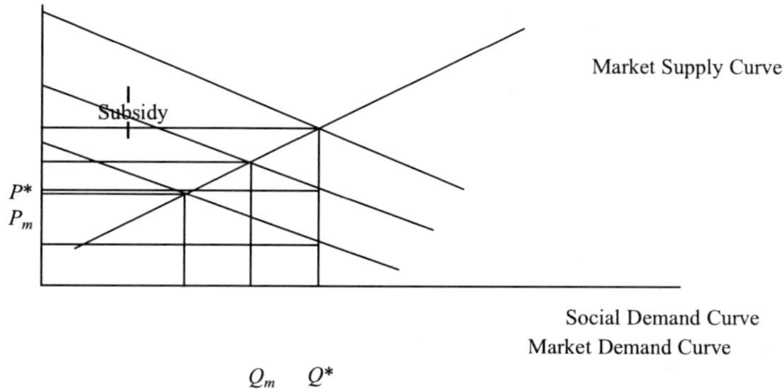

Fig. 6.3 Positive externality

This is a clear indication of the fact that when private benefit and social benefit are different, due to positive externality, market allocations will not result in Pareto optimal or the best possible resource allocation. So, state or other third parity can use tax and subsidy, to improve market allocation. **Omission of the existence of public goods and services.** Private goods and services which can be supplied efficiently by market are rival and excludable in character. If bread is consumed by you, nobody else can consume it. So, it is rival. Moreover, you can easily exclude others from consuming your bread. That is why bread is a private good. However, a road, a bridge, a railway station is not a rival since, once built it will be of use to everyone and not just for the person who built it, without increasing cost. And once built, it is not possible to exclude others from its use. In other words the above said are none excludable services. And so called, public service.

Public goods and services are goods and services which are none rival and none excludable in character. Public goods and services include policing, public administration, defense, infrastructure and so on. For these goods and services private allocation will result on suboptimal resource allocation and the states have to supply them by imposing mandatory taxes. How the market can undersupply such public goods has been shown in Fig. 6.4.

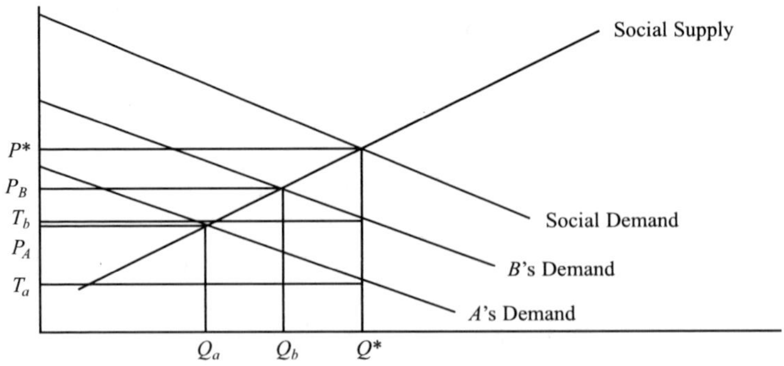

Fig. 6.4 Public goods and services

If only A is in the market, it will demand Q_a level of output at P_A level of price. If only B is in the market, it will demand Q_b level of output at P_B level of price. However, when both are in the market and the good (service) is none rival, consumption by one will not reduce consumption by other. As a result social demand will be vertical than horizontal summation of each individual's demand. Q_a level of output can be consumed by both A and B at the same time, so the market price for Q_a level of output is the sum of the price that can be paid by each. In Fig. 6.4, the social demand is derived by using vertical sum of A's and B's demand curve.

The social optimal level of the public good (service) is Q^* and the social optimal price is P^*. However, market forces will not give optimal incentive for each person to pay for optimal level of public goods and services. Suppose the public good is a road, and the optimal level is 10 km, 7 km is demanded by B and 3 km by A. Now let's assume B builds 7 km road. What does A have to do to maximize profit? He/she can use the 7 km built by B, which is more than what is demanded by him/her or can pay for additional 3 km, which has no value for him/her. Logically, without paying for additional road construction, she/he has to move her/his business toward the road. As result, the market will only supply 7 km road. This can be observed in actual behaviour of people. People normally reject to pay more tax for road construction, but if road is built they will open their business around the road. This is because road is neither rival nor excludable. Thus, from Fig 6.4 it is clear that even though A was willing to pay for 3 km (Q_a), it will try to be a free rider once the 7 km (Q_b) is built by B.

Now if A builds the first 3 km (Q_a). This will not be enough for B, who is looking for 7 km (Q_b). B has to invest more, but the question is how much. One option is to invest in the additional 4 km (Q_b – Q_a), so he/she can have the needed 7 km. Another option is to invest on new 7 km (Q_b). To maximize profit the rational action is the first option. A will build 3 km (Q_a) and *B* will build 4 km ($Q_b - Q_a$), and the economy will have 7 km (Q_b) road instead of 10 km. Means B will use road built by *A*, as free rider, and is only adding the road needed from *A*'s road to his business.

One way or another, market forces will supply less than optimal public goods and services unless state (or any third party) is able to impose mandatory tax, on both *A* and *B*, to supply optimal level of public good and service. The state will charge T_a level of tax on *A* and T_b level of tax on *B*, to supply optimal public good of Q^*. This will not only maximize private benefit since the marginal cost and marginal benefit are equal for each person, it will also lead to socially optimal supply of public goods and services. This is why market allocation of public goods and services is not Pareto optimal or the best possible resource allocation.

The above market failures are traditional, in the sense they have been known for decades. Moreover, there is nothing special about these market failures to rural area. These are market failures which have been widely discussed in economics. However, "these market failures were highly circumscribed" (Stiglitz, 2001) and did not represent all important market failures, that can be faced in development process.

Non-Traditional Market Failures

High transaction, overhead and administrative cost. Rural areas are known for their sparsely populated areas. Give their low population density, the transaction and administrative costs of supplying goods and services will be very high. Facing such high administrative and overhead cost, the state will often undersupply public goods and services to rural areas. A 10 km road can serve 10, 000 people in urban areas, but to serve 10,000 people in rural areas, the state has to build much longer roads, say 50,000 km. This means to provide the same level of road service in both rural and rural areas, for each ₹1 spent in urban areas the state has to spend ₹5 in rural area. This will result on low availability of public infrastructure. Similarly, high administrative cost, that can be expected with low population density, will result on undersupply of stale administrative services like police, judiciary, local administration and so on. This is, partially why rural areas are having less public goods and services compared to urban areas, all over the world. The private sector, facing hardly adequate supply of public goods and services and high transaction costs, will under-supply private goods and services, too. As a result, most of the private market is observed to be missing or malfunctioning. The missing markets include banking, insurance, information, recreation, and so on. In other words, the private sector does not have economic incentives to supply Pareto optimal goods and services to rural areas. Even though rural areas can be in equilibrium, it is low level equilibrium and they will remain trapped in poverty. If there are ways to reduce these transaction costs, it is possible to improve rural life by non-market forces. Thus, market does not result in the best possible allocation of resource and still there is scope for further improvement.

Imperfect information or asymmetric information. Imperfect information is observed, when people do not have perfect information about course of events. Asymmetric information is observed, when all concerned bodies are not having balanced share of information.

Imperfect information is the norm than exception of life. Farmers can make rational decision on their grain choice and input use, if they perfectly know the state of nature and market in the future. They will produce products which are highly demanded by customer, which can fetch higher price, at least possible cost in order to maximize profit. The problem is that let alone farmers, even a professional meteorologist cannot have perfect information about the state of nature, even with the most sophisticated instruments they use. It is possible if price of *A* is higher than *B* now, it can be *vise versa* next time. So what seems optimal now may not be optimal for the future. So if one introduces mechanism to reduce the uncertainty or to improve the risk management capacity of rural population, one can do much better than market allocation. If state can stabilize prices around their long run equilibrium; it will improve market allocation by eliminating the risk faced by rural population.

According to proponents of free market economy, given that people have to use some of their resource for information collection than for production, the level of output under risk will be lower than what can be under perfect market. But still market is constrained optimal. If state can collect information about the long run behaviour of prices, the market can do it better. Stiglitz (2001) states that if we include the cost of information market economies are constrained optimal. Thus, the cost of providing welfare will increase by cost of information; but still market economy will provide the most possible higher welfare that can be generated from the given resources. As such imperfect market will not generate the best possible allocation of resources, but it will result in the next best allocation of resource. Even then the following two points are of major significance.

First, information is a public good. If I have information that I able to collect at given cost, 1 can freely share it with all people without any significant addition to cost. In other words, information is not rival. If I freely share it with any one, others will have incentive to be a free rider, since I am not excluding them. Means information has pure public good character; as a result will be undersupplied by market forces. Another option that I have is to hide the information and this will reduce the level of information available among the public. Again this will result in suboptimal supply of information. One way or another imperfect market can't supply optimal level of information, so it will not result on the next best resource allocation.

Second, information is conveyed not only by actual communication, but also by agents' action. When a big trader, who is known to invest on information, start buying grain, all small traders will follow his lead to benefit from his investment, by being a free rider. So if he/she wants to make more profit, not only it has to hide the information that he/she has but also he/she has to manipulate his/her behaviour to give distorted signal to the competitors and free riders. So market economy is not only facing imperfect information, but is also creating additional imperfection of information. This is why information economists like Stiglitz stress the fact that "perfect competition — model was not robust — even slight departures from the underlying assumption of perfect information had large consequences.... In the standard paradigm, the competitive general equilibrium model, there were no shocks, no unanticipated events: at the beginning of time, the full equilibrium was solved, and everything from then on was an unfolding over time of what had been planned in each of the contingencies." (Stiglitz, 2001)

"Under the imperfect information paradigm, markets are almost never Pareto efficient." (Stiglitz, 2001) Means there are many ways to improve market allocation. Unless we assume there are complete and efficient credit, information, insurance and future markets, market allocation will not result on the best possible resource allocation, under risk (Stiglitz, 1981).

Farmers have the choice of which input to use and which output to produce, without knowing how much output they can get from each effort. Different inputs have different productivity under different weather conditions, which are behind the control of the farmer. For example, fertilizer can give different levels of output based on moisture content of the soil, which depends on natural weather conditions. At the same time different grains have different resistance to different shocks.

That is why there is high output uncertainty in farming. Unfortunately, given the nature of most agricultural products, random change in output will generate more than proportional change in price. Means production decisions have to be made in the face of high output and price risk. If market forces can supply optimal information to economic agents, market based allocation of resources will be, still, constrained optimal decision*. But given the fact that information is public good, market forces has tendency to undersupply it. As a result, farmers have to make production decision with less than optimal information.

One important thing to remember is that: even if there is enough information in the market, market allocation needs additional institutions to be constrained Pareto optimal. First the information has to be squeezed into simple values that can be easily understood by economic agents.

But market will never have perfect information. Some information is not perfectly available like weather condition and other information is too costly to collect compared to the benefit it can generate. What we are expecting is to make sure that the best and cost effective prediction is available to economic agents. And to make sure that economic agents are making decision based on such efficient prediction. As a result economic agents are still exposed to some risk. That is why insurance markets must be functional to allocate risk from risk averse individuals toward risk takers, for price. If a farmer can produce wheat valued at Rs 10, 000 from input cost of ₹ 8000, there will be a profit of ₹ 2000. However, if the farmer is risk averse and needs a risk premium of ₹ 3000 to take the risk on his/her ₹ 8000, he/she will not engage in the production activity. As result value of output will decline by ₹ 10, 000. And what if someone can give the farmer full insurance of ₹ 10, 000 for premium of ₹ 1000? So to achieve the best possible allocation of resource, the farmer needs to buy insurance for ₹ 1000 to produce and earn net profit of ₹ 1000. That is why for market allocation to be constrained Pareto optimal under risk; there must be functional insurance market or similar institution.

Finally, there must be functional financial intermediaries or banks, too, for people to stabilize their investment and consumption in face of random income by lending, borrowing and saving without limit. In general, even if there is risk in a market, there are—

- enough information in the market,
- functional future market,

---

*Constrained Pareto optimal implies considering the cost information, market allocation is still the best possible allocation. Some resource that can be used for production will be used for information collection but still market allocation is the best possible allocation. Means there is nothing that one can improve on it.

- functional insurance market or related institutions, and
- functional financial intermediaries (banks).

Market allocation will be the next best possible (constrained Pareto optimal) resource allocation and there is nothing that can be done to improve it further. Under such reality, decisions will be based on the best possible information and all risks will be efficiently managed by financial markets (insurance and banks). Under such reality there is nothing that the state or other institutions can do to improve farmer's decision than to respect market allocation.

It is an established fact that in any economy market will undersupply the needed information. Rural farmers, who do not have neither the means nor the large-scale production to invest on information, will have less than fair share of whatever inadequate information there is in the economy. Future and insurance markets are virtually absent in rural areas and financial intermediaries are highly imperfect, if not absent. Under such reality changes in market outcome, which can either reduce risk or improve risk management capability of agents, can have positive impact on market allocation. In other words, market allocation under imperfect information is not constrained optimal.

In perfect competition we assume perfect information, among other things, so invisible hand can efficiently coordinate the egocentric action of each agent to ward social welfare maximization. Unfortunately, under imperfect information, which is the norm in real life, efficient coordination of resource allocation by market forces is not granted. Lack of information and risk in rural areas is observed not only in output and price side, but also in lack of clearly defined grade and standards, lack of information about hired labour efficiency, lack of information on the best technology and farm management technique that can be used.

Manipulative middleman: Perfect competition assumes the existence of large number of buyers and sellers, in which everyone is a price taker. However, in rural areas large and unorganized rural agents are trading with small number of middlemen. First rural agents will have neither the production capacity, nor the resource to invest on information.* On the other side, traders can afford to invest on information and this will create asymmetric information, to the disadvantage of rural residents. Again farmers lacking adequate storage and financial resource will be under stress to exchange their output at whatever price. This will create asymmetric

*Since information is non-rival large-scale producers can benefit from economic scale of information, which is not available to small farmers.

bargaining power in hand to manipulate middleman. Moreover, farmers will come to market with their grain, which needs more transaction (mainly transportation) cost, and middleman with their money, which needs less transaction cost. Rural agents are thus under more stress to sell at whatever price compared to traders. These facts will concentrate marketing power in hand of manipulative middle man, to result on Pareto suboptimal resource allocation. In such a situation farmers will lack the incentive to be innovative, to be productive and to take risks. That is why, any change which can improve this structure directly or indirectly can improve market allocation.

Factor immobility under imperfect information. If factors of production are mobile and if investment decisions are done under perfect information then market allocation could be Pareto optimal for private goods and services. Mobility implies that inputs can take any form in the process of production. If capital is invested in a juice maker and the juice business is not profitable, the juice machine can be changed into a tea-coffee machine to open cafe. If not, any intervention which can improve resource allocation under imperfect information means which can help you to start cafe than juice service at the start, will improve market allocation. Since most activities in developing rural areas are less capital intensive, this shortcoming is not a serious challenge into market allocation in rural areas.

This is why market, as an institution, is important, yet not a perfect institution for every developmental problem. There is no doubt that market is the most effective institution in allocation of resource, compared to any alternative institution. But it is always better to let the market to take the leading role and use other institutions to make it more effective by solving market failures directly and indirectly. If you use other non-market institutions, there is no guarantee that the outcome will be Pareto optimal. But if market failures are somehow mitigated by other institutions, there is theoretical (neoclassical) knowledge and empirical evidence (from former Communist economy, newly industrialized nations and western economies) that market is not perfect, but it is the most effective institution in the process of economic development.

6.6 EVOLUTION OF ALTERNATIVE INSTITUTIONS

The two most important institutions for development are market and state. If market is perfect on coordinating diverse and self-promoting act of rational agents on production, distribution and consumption of private goods and services, and the state is perfect on internalizing externalities and on supplying public goods and services; all that is needed for efficient attainment of development is a perfect mix of market and state institutions.

But in real world imperfect market and state, will face high cost of doing things, which will hinder their efficiency. Thus, complementary institutions are needed, to give complementary signal in order to improve the efficiency of the invisible hand of the market and the visible hand of the state.

If market is perfect, as assumed in neoclassical economics, the only institution that we need to coordinate the self motivated action of economic agents, toward social welfare maximization, is market and its matrix of institutions. However, when market is imperfect, we have to look for alternative and complementary institutions which can handle, diverse market failure problems. Since perfect market can result on Pareto optimal or the best possible resource allocation, any alternative or complementary institution can't do better than perfect market. No one can do more than what is best possible! However, when market is imperfect, alternative institutions can improve market allocation to take market allocation closer to the outcome of perfect market. The general pattern of economic development can be explained by institutional development not because institutions are sufficient condition for economic development, but because appropriate institutions are necessary conditions for any economic development. This is because the same level of resource will have different levels of productivity, when different institutions are at work, as was the case in the above example. Institutions will not produce optimal output by themselves, but fast and sustainable development is unthinkable without evolution of efficient institutions. Efficient institutions will create appropriate incentive for economic agents to be efficient, innovative, productive and risk taker.

What determines the evolution of such efficient institutions. Demand for institutional changes is the result of demographic changes, which create demand for factor accumulation, human development and technological innovation. For this change to happen right institution must be established to give appropriate incentive for individuals to engage in such productive activity.

This can be seen from the fact that when regions was sparsely populated, the mode of production was based on simple tools (capital) like stone and wood, which facilitate hunting and gathering. Such technology and capital did not need any form of advanced institutions to guide the behaviour of economic agents toward social welfare maximization objective of the society. In such society the rule of the game was that forest and everything in it are common property of all community members, in which everybody has right but not exclusive ownership right (private property). If private property is enforced, the enforcement cost will simply overweigh its benefit. If there is more than enough fruit to collect and game to hunt, there is no need for enforcement of costly private property. But when population growth resulted in scarcity of food items, they need to develop advanced institutions to generate more food items.

Agricultural production, in the form of plant cropping and animal husbandry, will become option less way of life, in order to provide food items and means of survival for ever increasing population. This, in turn, will need investment in technology and capital to make farming possible. Hunter and gatherers need to develop all necessary know-how of farming methods and need to invest in farm tools. Unfortunately, the older institutions, which make all resources and products a common property, will not encourage such optimal reaction to change in factor endowment. Means the existing institutions, which provide optimal rules for earlier factor endowment, will become fetter of development with changing conditions. So in order to create conducive conditions and incentives needed for technological progress and capital accumulation, new institutions will be developed. The change in factor endowment is increasing the benefit of the new institution to make it useful for the society. Notice that enforcing such private property will demand higher enforcement cost compared to common property.

With time, population growth will create further shortage of food items. First, large population will reduce the fallow period of land, which will reduce the fertility of land. Second, there is large number of mouths to feed now. To solve the food problem, productivity of land has to increase. The challenge is that free use of land, which used to work under slash and bum method, will not encourage people to make investment on their land. Now the benefit of private property on land will overweigh its enforcement cost, so private property will be also extended to land, too.

In modern ages, based on our period, advent of medical technology did result on population explosion all over the world. Under such reality, nature based technological progress and land improvement will not generate enough food items to feed every one. Science based agriculture is needed to solve the problem. The challenge of science base agriculture is

1. It will demand huge cost on research and development (R&D)
2. It is very risky, since each research effort will not generate a new technology
3. It has public good character, so the market will undersupply it.

That is why public provision of education, public spending on R & D, enforcement of copyright and patient rights becomes beneficial to society, despite its huge cost. Means private property has to be extended to intangible intellectual property rights.

In general, when a given technology, capital accumulation and factor endowment prevail optimal institutions will emerge; assuming supply rigidity does not exist. But when factor endowment is changed to demand change on capital accumulation and technology, the old institutions will become fetters of development. As a result demand for new and more efficient institutions will increase. Assuming supply side rigidity does not exist, new and more efficient institutions will be enforced. This will make all existing resource more productive. Institutions are organizational technologies and the use of new and more efficient organizational technology will make all resources more productive. However more advanced technology is also more costly. So cost and benefit analysis need to be done, before use of any new technology.

Now what determines the supply of institutions. Like any thing in economics the supply of institution is determined by cost of production, which is enforcement cost. If institutions can be easily enforced with low cost, they will be easily supplied; given they are beneficial. Factors which can reduce the enforcement cost of any institution are explained below.

1. Informal institutions in society

If the informal values, norms and religious beliefs of the society support the enforcement of such institutions, they can be easily enforced. The appeal is not to third party enforcer, but to superego (cultural value) and ego (personal moral belief) of economic agents. If people feel breaking the formal institutions will create either mental dissatisfaction or social sanction, it is cheaper to enforce formal institutions. As was stated above, any formal institution which contradicts the moral of the people can't be easily enforced.

2. Distribution of benefit

If benefit from new institution is widely dispersed and majority are benefiting from it, it will be easy to enforce new institutions. Moreover, if the powerful elite in society can benefit from the new institution, cost of enforcement will be very low. The ideal condition is for majority including the elite to benefit from institutional change.

3. *The importance of the institution in wider institutional matrix of society*

Institutions are evolved through long term trail and error process. As a result, there will be huge interdependence among institutions of society. Institutions will have direct and indirect impact on the welfare of society. Think tenancy for example, the landowner is not only supplying land, but also protection, credit, input and other social goods to the tenants. The tenant will not only use land, but will also help in social activity of the landowner, will stand beside him in any social function and possibly will be part of his army. When tenancy is abolished, it is clear the tenant will benefit from his land, ownership. But it is not clear, what the impact of lack of credit, protection and inputs will be. Means any institutional change, which alters the *status quo*, will have uncertain outcome, if the institution is highly interlinked with other social institutions. In general, the less interdependence there is between the institution to be changed and wider matrix of social institutions, the less risky will be the proposed institutional change and it will be easy to enforce.

Unfortunately, there are structural reasons why dysfunctional institutions could be preserved in society. First, any institutional change which does not benefit the powerful elite will not be adopted. Second old institutions which are stamped in psychic of the population is not easy to alter. Third, given institutions are highly interdependent on each other, any institutional change will have uncertain outcome. As a result the proponents for change will be less organized than the opponents of change. In such reality the supply of institutional change will normally lag behind the change in factor endowment.

In simple words institutions will not only work under existing power structure, but also they will work to preserve existing power structure. So there is no gurantee that existing institutions are the best institutions for the society. If they exist, it means they are functional but it does not mean they are Pareto optimal. The problem is that there are many important steps that have to be followed before a new institution can be adopted. First people have to recognize the importance for change (cognition must be developed), second enough number of people must accept the need for change to generate social demand for institutional change (group mentality must be developed) and finally the powerful elite must support the change. Institutional change can be hindered, if one of the above steps is not completed.

The first problem is that people may not know the existence of better alternative. How do communities know that private property on land is the right institution for settled agriculturalist and communal ownership of land is the right institution for pastoral communities? In early times communities do not actually know. But the social evolutionary process has tendency to pick communities with functional institutions. Based on their historical path, some communities did adopt the right institutions and others did not. Over long run when natural shocks, wars and other calamities are injected into social game of institutional development, only societies with best functional institutions will survive over long run. Second, even if there is private acceptance for change, institutional change needs an organized effort. If the society is not open for change, it may not be easy to organize people to create group mentality to generate change. However, the evolutionary process will eliminate all societies, which are highly rigid compared to others. Third, if there is unbalanced distribution of power in society, the powerful elite may create huge enforcement cost for any new institution. Again any rigidity created by the elite will end up either in the elimination of the elite (or their replacement by other elite), if not the evolutionary process will eliminate the community. In short, the social evolutionary process will select communities with functional institutions by eliminating others. The existing institutions are functional, but there is no guarantee they will be Pareto optimal (the best possible institutions).

In contemporary times with expansion of information technology and globalization, the cognition problem is not as restricting as it used to be. So cognition is still relevant. Moreover, rigidity that can be generated from lack of cognition, lack of group mentality and existence of powerful elite can be easy to manage, if there is charismatic leader who can mobilize the public. The importance of charismatic leader to introduce institutional change is widely documented in religious documents and modern community development efforts. Putting the above facts in line, it is time to focus on some alternative institutions that can be used for rural development.

6.7 SERVICE COOPERATIVES

If the transportation, storage and information costs are a determinant factor for efficiency of a marketing system, small-scale farmers, which are failing to benefit from storage, transportation and information economies, will be affected the most. Moreover, given financial stress related to obligations to pay debit and tax or to cover expenditure needs, small-scale farmers will be forced to sell their output at whatever terms. Additional stress will also be created from lack of proper storage facility. As a result, having low transaction cost and better information, manipulative middleman can develop unfair trading relationship with small scale farmers. The negative effect of these market failures on farmers' incentive to be productive, efficient and innovative is inversely related to their size. Means the intensity of the problem is directly related with smallness of the farmer production system. The natural solution for market failure related to smallness is cooperation.

One possible way that can be used to improve the bargaining capacity of small-scale farmers is to organize them into service cooperatives. Collective action under service cooperatives is a natural reaction for problems related to smallness. This will enable them to have more market power that can balance the power of manipulative middleman. Moreover, by consolidating their sale and purchase, they can benefit from economies of scale on transportation, storage, information collection and so on. This will reduce the transaction cost they face in exchange.

If the marketing function of cooperatives is beneficial to its members, the supply of credit can be easily facilitated by cooperatives, too. This can be done by linking the marketing role of cooperatives with their credit service. The flow of cash through cooperatives can be used to collect information about the creditworthiness of each potential borrower. Means there is no need for additional screening cost, since the information is available in the cooperative financial books. Moreover, debit can be recovered from income of the borrower that is flowing through the cooperative. If a tea farmer is having much higher benefit from the cooperative marketing service, he/she will think twice before taking higher risk with cooperative money. This will reduce moral hazard and adverse selection problems. These problems can be easily reduced further by observing the cash flow of the farmer. Additionally, there is no need for army of bankers to collect repayment of debit from the borrower, since debit can be easily recovered from the cash flow of the borrower. Means efficient service cooperatives can easily extend credit at low transaction cost to its members.

The supply of local public goods, like irrigation facility, adopted technology, land improvement forestation, extension and other local public goods, can be easily organized by local (service) cooperatives. A single small-scale farmer can't invest in adoption of new technology to local condition. However, 10,000 small scale farmers paying ₹100 each can accumulate ₹1 million to fund such research and development project. In general, if the market failure is inversely related to size, the natural solution to such market failure is cooperation. Conditions necessary for service cooperative's success are:

1. The difference are between transaction cost of normal trading and transaction cost under cooperative marketing needs to be greater than the administrative cost of running the cooperative. It means that the transaction cost saved by cooperative needs to be larger than the administrative cost of running the cooperative.
2. To provide credit not only the transaction cost saved need to be more than the administrative cost, but also the lifetime saving in transaction cost for the borrower need to be much greater than the short-run benefit of default for the borrower. This is a necessary condition to discourage default and unacceptable risk taking by a borrower.
3. Membership needs to be a privilege than a duty. People must join a cooperative, if and only if, they think it is beneficial to them.
4. The cooperative needs to face strong competition from the private sector.

The last two conditions are needed in order to make the cooperative management efficient enough to compete with the private sector. If the cooperative management is competing with traders for farmers' supply and consumer demand, the only way it can win the battle is by becoming more efficient than traders.

6.8 VALUE CHAIN AND CONTRACT FARMING

In buyer driven market economy an exporter, a wholesaler and a manufacturer needs a sufficient and reliable supply of agricultural products from a large number of small-scale farmers. The problem is farmers are constrained by lack of credit, lack of appropriate technology, lack of extension service, lack of irrigation facility and high level of market uncertainty. These are related to finance, information, technology, capital and output market failures. Under such reality, small-scale farmers may not be able to supply reliable quantity of agricultural products to other economic agents. As a result, both farmers and other economic agents may not able to achieve what is best for both of them and the society. The problem is related to existence of anonymous exchange between buyer and seller. If buyer and seller are anonymous and operating under imperfect market, economic agents will not have adequate incentive to avoid moral hazard and adverse selection problems.

By changing the institutional setup from anonymous exchange into contract farming, much better outcome can be generated under imperfect market setting. In contract farming a buyer, could it be a manufacturer, wholesaler or exporter, will supply credit, new input (technology), extension, irrigation facility and other inputs to the small-scale farmers. For doing that he/she will have exclusive right to purchase their output, at predetermined price. In such an arrangement farmers will not only have cheap access to agricultural inputs, but also assured market for their output. The buyer will also have assured access to reliable quantity and quality of agricultural products.

In contract farming, market failures are managed by interlinking input and output markets. Any input cost or unpaid credit can be easily recovered from the income of the farmer. Adverse selection and moral hazard problems will be avoided, first by using the information in cash flow of the farmer and second by beneficial transaction cost advantage of contract farming. Starting from the second point, the farmer will think twice before he/she takes any action that can jeopardize such beneficial arrangement. Additionally, any one who is credit unworthy can be easily screened out by using the cash flow information found in the hands of the contract buyer. Even if the contract buyer is providing any unpaid input or extension service for the farmers, he/she will be compensated by low price that he/she has to pay for the farmers. So the contract farmer and buyer will have lower transaction cost and higher incentive to be efficient, under the new arrangement. This is why in contract farming beneficial exchange can be made possible, even when most markets are dysfunctional or missing.

Moreover, such arrangement will enable the buyer to trace his/her final output up to the farm. Under buyer driven market filled by environmental sensitive customers, traceability of output is a necessary condition for market penetration: A tea exporter in order to supply tea to international market needs to show buyers that the tea is produced and processed according to their specifications. Their specifications can be about chemicals usage, processing method and use of labour, for example. This can be done only under such arrangement. This is not a problem in perfect market since there is perfect information about everything.

At society level the main advantage of contract farming is related to the optimal inputs that are supplied by the contract buyer. If the buyer supplies less than optimal inputs, he/she may not get reliable quantity and quality of output to maximize profit. If he/she is oversupplying inputs, the cost will be greater than the benefit. One way or another the contract buyer will maximize profit, if she/he is supplying optimal amount of fertilizer, credit, improved seed, irrigation and other inputs to the farmers.

Contract farming is one example of value chain management and governance. Value chain, in agricultural products, involves the value added, generated and the interlinked activity preformed from the time an agricultural product is produced, on farm, and until it reaches the mouth. If markets are perfect, the invisible hand of competition will efficiently coordinate every activity horizontally and vertically. So there will be no need for any additional management. Unfortunately, what we have is a highly imperfect market. Under such reality, value chain management is developed in order to generate optimal resource allocation on vertically integrated activities. When the invisible hand of competition is failing to do its job, visible coordination will be introduced by one or few economic agents found in the vertically integrated activities. In value chain the role of the value chain governor is not to micro manage the entire chain. Governance in value chain is about fixing optimal norms that have to be followed by each firm in the value chain. These norms are enforced by the multifaceted relationship that exists among value chain members. If a farmer fails to supply good quality tea or to pay fertilizer credit, he/she will be excommunicated from the value chain. Means he/she will not share the future benefit of value chain. If the expected value of all future benefits of the value chain is large, it is at the best interest of the tea farmer to follow the value chain norms. Value chain members will normally solve credit, information, market, technology, extension and other factors related to problems of other members.

A good example for successful implementation of value chain management is operation flood implemented by Dairy Cooperatives of India. Dairy products, which use to be wasted in small-scale farmers house due to lack of market, was efficiently distributed to the whole country by the dairy cooperatives. The cooperatives were not only intervening to improve productivity of farmers, but also it was managing the entire chain from farm to mouth. Management here is not about selling milk to the customer, but making sure that other agents in the chain are efficiently operating to make the vertically integrated milk market functional.

Value chain management can be effective, if and only if the comparative advantage it has over the next best alternative is high to discourage members from breaking the agreed codes of conduct. Traders may force farmers to sell their product at lower price, claiming they are supplying poor quality grain, when the contrary is true. Farmers can fail to repay credit or can supply poor quality grain. To avoid these problems the present value of total expected life time benefit should be greater than the benefit of any moral hazard. This fact implies: value chain, in particular, and contract farming, in general, can be functional, if the area is having adequate flow of products, in the face of market failures.

6.9 MICRO FINANCE INSTITUTIONS

People facing asymmetric information, that can generate adverse selection and moral hazard problems, will reject to lend to someone, who is willing to pay them acceptable level of interest rate. This is because they are not sure about the actual risk of the exchange. Actually, asymmetric information has a tendency to increase the risk faced by the lender. At the same time the search cost for potential borrower or lender, the cost of signing a contract and enforcement cost of a contract will be high. Enforcement cost is very high, because the legal system is less efficient, less predictable and more sluggish in developing economies. Given these facts, direct financial market, in face of high transaction cost, will exist in the form of informal money lenders, only.

The informal moneylender will use his multifaceted relationship based social capital and local knowledge to reduce transaction cost, moral hazards and adverse selection problems. First, by living and working in the area, the moneylender will have better local knowledge compared to bankers. This knowledge will be used to screen borrowers at low cost. Second, moral hazards can be easily managed, given the moneylender is important trader, civil servant or landlord in the area. Means borrowers are dependent on him/her not only for loan, but also for land, merchandise and other services. Under such reality, in order to preserve their multifaceted relationship, borrowers have less incentive to develop moral hazard problem. Unfortunately, this informal market is not Pareto efficient. First, since the moneylender can't raise saving, he/she is dependent on his limited wealth. Means the amount of loan he/she can make is very limited. Second, given the existence of high risk in developing rural economies, he/she will demand high risk premium. Third, given he/she is operating in a highly imperfect market, which can generate him/her high level of abnormal profit, the opportunity cost of lending is very high for him/her. These facts will restrict the amount of finance that can be accessed from the moneylender and he/she will demand extremely high interest. In other words, in rural areas the only functional direct financial market is the inefficient informal moneylender.

However, financial intermediaries or banks, by introducing different institutional mechanisms, can reduce the transaction cost of direct financial market. Search cost will be reduced by supply safety, interest income and liquidity to depositors. Borrowers and lenders do not need to search each other, they just have to come to the bank. By benefiting from economies scale of contract, the bank can reduce the contract cost of lending. If a standardized contract is developed, it will become non-rival and as a result it can be used unlimited number of times, without significant addition to cost. Asymmetric information and associated risk can be reduced by diversifying portfolio, by checking cash flow of customer, by demanding collateral, through screening and monitoring. These activities will be cost effective, because the bank normally uses professional loan officers, it will lend in large sum and some information is freely available to the bank, like cash flow data. Moreover, special state laws, which allow repo (repossession), will make contract enforcement extremely effective to the bank. That is why an institutional change which links lenders and borrowers through the bank, than directly to each other, will result on functional financial intermediaries (banks) found in urban areas.

However, rural areas will create their own special problems to result on missing financial intermediaries. First, rural areas are dependent on risky agriculture. This is because of high dependence of agriculture on erratic nature and high quantity elasticity of demand faced by agricultural products. Second, rural population will have less marketable asset to serve as collateral. This will increase both moral hazard and adverse selection problems. Third, banks will face high level of diseconomies of scale on transaction cost. This is because the amount of money that can be borrowed by small-scale farmer is smaller than the money that can be borrowed by an urban investor. Finally, given low population density, the bank needs to open large number of branches in rural areas to give the same kind of service the given urban areas. In simple words, the bank will face huge transaction cost, if it wants to serve the rural population. Given this cost will be higher than the interest rate it can possibly charge, the bank will normally ignore the rural population, resulting in missing financial intermediaries.

Unfortunately, achievement of rural development, in the face of vicious cycle of poverty which is very common in rural areas, is unthinkable without access to finance. For farmers to adopt technology, to invest on their own human capital, to specialize and commercialize, they need cheap access to finance. But the formal financial market, which does not exist in rural areas, is not in position to supply the necessary finance to rural population.

To deal with the challenge innovate institution is proposed in the form of Micro Finance Institution (MFI). This institution is created by taking the strong sides of both the formal bank and the informal moneylender. The strength of formal bank is related to its capacity to rise saving. The strong side of the moneylender is related to its capacity to reduce transaction cost by depending on social capital and local knowledge of the community.

MFIs lend not to individuals but to group of individuals. The idea is to use social capital, local knowledge and peer-pressure for productive purpose. People living in the same community will have better understanding of each other's behavior than outsider. Since under group lending, default by any member is recovered from income and asset of other group members, they will use their local knowledge to screen potential group members. People will form group with trustworthy community members only. This will reduce adverse selection problem. Moral hazard problem, too, will be reduced due to two factors. On one side, community members have better capacity to monitor each other than an outsider. On the other side, given the multifaceted nature of their relationship, economic agents under imperfect market will care more for social than legal sanction. So fear of social sanction and peer pressure will further reduce the level of moral hazard. By depending on social incentive and local knowledge of a community, MFI can reduce the transaction cost of lending to make the rural poor bankable.

MFI can also give additional banking service to the rural poor by using locally available cheap, but somehow educated labour force with minimum office facilities. It could be costly to open 10 modern bank branches in rural areas, but it is not costly to open 10 rural MFI offices staffed with cheap local labour. This will enable the MFI to raise saving and implement its frequent repayment requirement without having high transaction cost. Some MFIs also demand mandatory saving from its customers to raise saving and introduce culture of saving.

However, MFI cannot solve the financial problem of each and every rural poor, everywhere. First, the poorest of the poor have less probability to be selected as group members. Means the benefit of MFI will occur to the average poor, but not for the poorest of the poor. Second, in areas with low social capital, group lending will not be effective. Third, if risks are unavoidable and systematic in nature, group lending will not reduce the risk of lending. Systematic risk is a risk which affects all economic agents at the same time. This includes drought, floods, war, political instability and so on.

6.10 WAREHOUSES

Due to lack of proper storage facility, small scale farmers will lose significant portion of their output due to spoilage, rodents and insects. To avoid this problem, the only option available for small-scale farmers is to sell their output just after harvest. It is very urgent to sell to pay for tax, debit and other monetary expenditures, under dysfunctional or missing financial markets. When large number of small-scale farmers sell their grain just after the harvest, market price will collapse. Even when prices are getting lower, the only option for small-scale farmers is to supply more in order to satisfy their financial constraint. This will create vicious cycle of poverty.

To solve this warehouse problem, a warehouse provider can charge very low fee to provide storage facility to small-scale farmers. Given the existence of dimensional economic of scale in storage, large storage facility is more cost effective than small-scale storage facility.

After storing grain in certified warehouse, farmers will be given a warehouse receipt. The receipt is certificate of deposit and it will show the type of grain stored and its quantity and quality. This receipt can be used as collateral in accessing bank loans at discount base. Grain depositors can borrow some percentage of their grain value from banks. This is known as discounting. This will also solve the credit constraint of small-scale farmers. If the market is well developed, the warehouse receipt can also be used in market. Not only people can borrow by using their deposit of grain as collateral, but can also trade on the deposited grain. So warehouse receipt system is an integrated solution for storage and liquidity problem of small-scale farmers. But again it cannot solve all credit and storage problems of small scale farmers.

For warehouse receipt system to be cost effective there is need for proper grades and standards to be enforced. If proper grades and standards are not used, economic agents will have incentive to supply the lowest quality grain. When all of them supply third quality grain, the stored grain will be of poor quality and nobody will be willing to buy it. That is why, for successful use of warehouse receipt system, properly defined grades and standards are mandatory. So in locations without clearly defined grade and standard, warehouse receipt system is impractical. Moreover, for warehouse receipt system to be cost effective, it needs large demand for storage. So it can only be effective in high potential areas of a country, not in all locations.

6.11 COMMODITY EXCHANGE

Market failures related to imperfect and asymmetric information, ineffective contract enforcement, lack of proper storage, risk, lack of proper grade and standard and lack of finance are norms, than exception in developing economies. Under such reality failure will breed failure, in which failure on side of the market will increase the probability of failure in other side of the market. To be effective long-term solution needs to be an integrated solution to the market failures observed in output, credit, insurance and information markets. Well financed traders will have a higher capacity to manage risk, even under missing or dysfunctional insurance markets. But a trader operating with high level of financial constraint will have low capacity to manage risk. The lack of insurance, in turn, will increase the level of risk banks are exposing themselves, which can easily bankrupt them. That is why an effective solution needs to be an integrated solution.

A market with high level of potential trading gain has a tendency to generate spontaneous local institutions to fill the gap created by market failures. Traders by developing network, based on long-term personal relationship, can easily deal with most of the problems. Networking is integrated but informal institution used by traders operate under imperfect market. To understand the importance of networks, we need to understand the importance of trust or as commonly called social capital in economic development.

Under imperfect and asymmetric information, missing and dysfunctional markets, only one agent can depend on for credit, risk sharing, information, training, exchange and other services is another agent. However, such dependency will generate high risk and cost due to asymmetric information and poor enforcement of contracts. You can lend your capital to someone, but what guarantee do you have? That can assure you, the fact that you are going to be repaid? The only way this exchange can be made possible is if you are willing to take the high risk it may generate. Think about information. It is true you can get some information from another agent, but what is the guarantee that it will be reliable information?

That is why under reality with imperfect information, where the cost of information is very high, trust is a very productive capital. Through long term multifaceted relationship and built in local knowledge, economic agents know who is trustworthy and who is not. Once people are known to be trustworthy, you can lend them, exchange information or exchange goods and services without having adequate information, based on trust. If market is perfect, there will be zero transaction cost by assumption. But under imperfect market, this is not necessarily true. Fortunately, if people are trustworthy, they can exchange things with full faith under imperfect information. This will reduce transaction cost. Now transaction cost is close to zero by social virtue not by assumption.

That is why traders need to develop network of trusted traders to share information, finance, risk management capacity and other factors of production. In addition to that, high screening cost, expected in exchange under missing grade and standards, can be avoided, if traders can trust each other. If you trust another trader in the exchange, you don't need to screen the quality of each grain you are purchasing. This will avoid the screening cost needed under imperfect information. In other words, traders will develop micro level social capital to reduce transaction cost.

The problem is that if the net present value of all expected future benefits from one relationship is very low, agents has incentive to develop moral hazard and can breach a contract. That is why meso level social capital is very important to enforce contracts, effectively. If all traders as community can sanction unacceptable behaviour, the net present value of all future benefits will be much higher than the benefit that can be generated by breaching any contract. Under such reality it will be easy to enforce community norms and enforce contracts. Means by excommunicating or by using collective sanction on misbehaving members, they will discourage moral hazard problem among members. Under such network arrangement, traders can lend and borrow without any formal papers, can buy and sell without detailed inspection of quality and can honestly inform each other. Means they will solve the market failure problem related to high transaction cost, imperfect information and missing markets, by using an alternative institution of networks than anonymous market.

The problem is that this institutional response is functional, but not Pareto optimal. Means this arrangement can work, but will not generate the best possible welfare to society. To understand this we need to understand micro, meso and macro level trust. Perfect market or functional mix of state and market, will create macro level trust or trust on the system. If there is macro level trust, people will exchange, produce, invest, invent and save believing the system is reliable. Under such reality there is no exclusion of economic agents. If macro level trust is weak, either due to malfunctioning state or malfunctioning market, economic agents will depend on either meso or micro level trust. If a group of firms in one industry, group agents (traders) in one community (market) or group of community in one socioeconomic group (say race or religious domination) trust each other more than others, they can exchange private property under imperfect information based on trust of the meso group.

Meso level trust is the trust observed between members of one socioeconomic group. The socioeconomic group can be defined in terms of ethnicity, religion, spatial location and so on. But both meso and micro level trust are highly inefficient, though functional, compared to a functional mix of market and state, or macro level trust. The inefficiency of such trust is related to exclusion of economic agents, which does not belong to the specific group. To use the economic term, there is lack of free entry. As a result, resource, knowhow and technology, which is not possessed by the specific social group, will not be utilized. Under such reality meso trust may improve the functionality of imperfect market, but is not Pareto optimal.

Trust can be also found at micro level. A trader will have more trust on people he often transacts with and know for years than others. If there is lack of macro and meso level trust, agents have to depend on micro trust for exchange. As a result, they will have lower transaction cost, if they restrict their trade with limited number of network members, only. But lack of free entry will restrict the efficiency of the market. If they wish to transact with others, they will face full transaction cost of imperfect market. One way or another both meso and micro level trust can be functional, but will not be Pareto optimal.

Lack of optimality is also caused by concentration of market power. If trust is used as means of exchange, trusted network (social group) members will have more market power than others. These will distort price discovery process, to result on suboptimal resource allocation.

Commodity exchange is an integrated solution, which builds on the strong side of both meso and micro trust, under imperfect market, with objective of building macro trust. In other words, commodity exchange will do what networks or socioeconomic groups are supposed to do and at the same time will solve the problem created by them. Moreover, storage problem, grade and standard related challenges and other problems not fully addressed, either by networks or socio-economic groups will be also effectively addressed by commodity exchange. That is why, it is an integrated solution for market failures, widely observed in developing economies.

Commodity exchange will develop appropriate grade and standards. Since grade and standards are public goods in character, it is cost effective to supply them by central body, like commodity exchange. Once appropriate grade and standards are introduced, warehouse receipt system will address both storage and financial problems of both traders and farmers. Using warehouse receipts and clearly defined grade and standards, exchange will be facilitated by using auction system. The auction system will result in efficient price discovery and exchange at least cost possible. Rather than wasting significant amount of resource and time to search contracting bodies, brokers and traders will simply come to commodity exchange to participate on auction. This will reduce the search cost. By using standardized contracts, the term that has to be discovered in auction is only price. Grade and standards are developed and how much quantity can be traded is fixed by standard contract, so less time and resource will be wasted in the process of exchange (auction). Thus, commodity exchange will reduce problems related to high search cost, high contract cost, high storage cost, lack of finance and high screening cost. Moreover, it will also reduce the information cost, by collecting and disseminating market and industry level information to the general public, at much lower fee. Since information is public good, commodity exchange has natural advantage on information market. But still there is problem of contract enforcement. This is addressed by taking a strong side of meso and micro level social capital.

Since the legal system in developing economies is highly inefficient to enforce contracts and it is not possible to contemplate all possible contingencies in any contract, there is high contract risk that can be expected in any contract. Fortunately, commodity exchange can exclude only untrustworthy economic agents and will create free entry for all productive economic agents. As a result, society will benefit from all productive resources, skills and technology available. In social capital you are guilty until proven innocent, but in commodity exchange you are innocent until proven guilty. This will create macro level social capital without avoiding sanction targeted at rent seeking agents.

There are some basic conditions that have to be satisfied, before commodity exchange can be successful. These conditions are:

1. There is need for large flow of trade to break even with huge overhead or fixed cost. The most important cost in commodity exchange is overhead cost. Means like any fixed cost, the average cost will decline with increase in use or production. In order to break even with such huge average fixed cost and ensure the sustainability of such an exchange, there is a minimum trade volume that has to be attained. The implication is that in areas with less than optimal grain flow, commodity exchange is not a valuable option.

2. Variable cost is related not to size of transaction, but to number of transactions. As a result, only economic agents which can trade in bulk, within the commodity exchange, can have low transaction cost. Unless small-scale farmers and small-scale traders are able to trade

in some form of collective, for them commodity exchange may not have transaction cost advantage over normal way of trading.

3. Large-scale traders, which already have efficient trading networks, may not have the necessary incentive to join commodity exchange. First, for them the transaction cost of normal trading will be much lower than the market average. Second, such institutional change will reduce their market power. Under such a reality, commodity exchange may not be a viable option for them.
4. The success of any commodity exchange depends on the availability of vibrant and dynamic management, which can find dynamic solutions for ever evolving challenges. One thing common among all successful commodity exchanges is that all are endowed with efficient and flexible management.

In simple words, commodity exchange cannot solve every market failure problem everywhere. Like any institution, there are conditions that have to be satisfied, before its potential benefits can be realized. The condition is that both direct and indirect costs of commodity exchange have to be less than the cost expected in normal way doing business.

6.12 SOCIAL CAPITAL

It has already been seen that in an otherwise perfect market, if we avoid the perfect information assumption there will be moral hazard problem. This is reflected in breach of agreed terms of contract, labour inefficiency, unless intensively supervised, lack of incentive to minimize risk by insured agent and so on. Ideally, these problems could be dealt with, by the judicial system, but given the low efficiency of developing economies judicial system, the cost will be more than the expected benefit from such a process.

Viewed from socio-cultural dimension of life, however, ideologies like religious codes, norms and values can easily suppress moral hazard problems. The incidence of moral hazard problem should be lower among people; whose personal interaction is so intense, in which one can easily predict the action of the other even without having complete information. This will result on mutual trust among community members.

Mutual trust, nurtured through close personal interaction, should work as a brake on committing moral hazard Community is a group of people tied by mutual trust, based on intense personal interactions and fear of losing multifaceted relationship. This will result in development of micro level trust. Moreover, meso level trust can be developed, through statistical discrimination. When people know on that some socioeconomic group is more reliable and trustworthy than others, any anonymous member of the socioeconomic group will be accepted as trustworthy, without having adequate information about his behaviour. When economic agents have to make decision without adequate information, they will make decision based on average behaviour of the socioeconomic group that the agent belongs to. Under such reality, social capital of trust will be defined in socioeconomic dimensions. If individual or collective sanctions are used, if community members share information among each other and there is mechanism in society to refine gossip from facts, economic agents will have incentive to be trustworthy as they are expected to be beforehand. Even though macro level trust is more productive and inclusive than both micro and meso level trust, when there is no way to develop macro level trust or development of macro level trust demand more time, one needs to make best use of micro and meso level trust by minimizing their failures.

Mutual trust and multifaceted relationship or, in short, community social capital can promote collaborative relationships within the wider community. Benefiting members will reject to collaborate with any one with bad past record of breaching agreements. The stronger the fear of social sanction by the community, the more firmly would the convention of honouring contracts with members of the same community be established. Seen from this point of view trust will increase efficiency and reduce costs associated with division of labour. In this regard trust is a kind of social capital similar to social over head capital.

Community principle in rural village of developing countries has its potential to be an important part of modern organization to facilitate the process of rural development. However, traditional norms and conventions are not by themselves efficient in organizing modern rural development. This is because of community failures which include:

(1) Due to supply lag and historical dependence on cognition, community norms could be functional but are not necessary optimal. First, community could not possibly know all possible ways to organize society. What a community knows at given time period is dependent on historical incidents of that community. Since history is always partial, what is known by one community will be always partial. Second, even if there is cognition and demand for new institution, supply may lag due to aforementioned reasons.

(2) Mutual trust and cooperation among community members are often supported by rivalry, fear and hostility towards others. This will result in lack of cooperation and war among different communities. The exclusion of resource, technology and skill belonging to none community members will reduce the efficiency of community social capital.

(3) The possibility should not be overlooked that mutual help and cooperation, based on community relationships, works in the same way to promote mutual shrinking and back scratching. Life time employment in any management will be really effective, if and only if the company is profitable in the face of intense competition. But there is a possibility that the employees' work moral is low and their cooperative efforts are directed towards maintaining the *status quo* of living and working condition, rather than improving productivity. This shows the fact that community relationships without appropriate mechanism to create incentive for community level efficiency will tend to work as a social mechanism for penalizing and ostracizing innovators, who deviate from established norms and conventions there by preserving absolute and dysfunctional institutions. Community social capital without state and market institutions to complement it will work to preserve dysfunctional system than promote efficiency.

(4) Community social capital is not only Pareto suboptimal, but will also kill the capacity of market and state to develop much better institutions. And, development of traders' network is expected to reduce the level of demand for commodity exchange. This is so, despite the fact that commodity exchange is much efficient than trade networks. It has been seen that the social networks, which supply some form of insurance to individuals under missing insurance market, will not only supply less than optimal insurance, but will also kill the capacity of market to develop better and efficient formal insurance markets.

As other institutions of development, community social capital too cannot solve all market failure problems. It has its own advantages and disadvantages. So it has to be used in a way that can maximize its benefits and restrict its failures.

6.13 CIVIC SOCIETIES AND NGOs

The public sector is found to be highly inefficient to deal with market failure problems. Public sector within the labour market does face adverse selection and moral hazard problems, which can reduce civil servants efficiency. The above fact, coupled with the use of social capital to preserve the inefficient *status quo*, will result in self-sustaining trap of inefficiency. The bureaucratic system, which is used in public sector, will complicate the problem by reducing the flexibility of the public sector. Armed with inflexible system and less efficient civil servants, the state may not be in a good position to correct all market failures, everywhere.

A good alternative to state is civic society, in general, and non-governmental organizations (NGO), in particular. Civic societies are established by value oriented individuals with high value for civic duty. A group of teachers may organize themselves to eradicate illiteracy. A community in one location may organize themselves to clean the street. These are example of civic societies. The advantage of such civic societies is that the people involved are value oriented, their system is flexible and their social capital will be used for efficiency than shirking. Civil servants are working to have salary, but civic society members are working to achieve their value. Under imperfect information, a rational civil servant has to develop moral hazard, since his salary is not related to his efficiency. Fortunately, civic society members will not develop moral hazard problem, because their satisfaction comes from achievement of their value, not salary. The harder they can work and the more of their value is achieved, the more satisfied and happy they will be.

Moreover, their value orientation will reduce the importance of hierarchy in decision making. Since a leader can't benefit anything by blaming the failure on others, he will collaborate with others like close community for achievement of their common value.

Many a times a person at top may reject good ideas coming from the bottom, only to preserve his prestige. However, value oriented boss will be flexible to all ideas coming from all people with similar value orientation. This will not only improve efficiency, but also will create community kind relationship, where everyone is cooperating and supervising each other for a common goal. By avoiding hierarchy, civic society can supply the needed high level of flexibility in solving market failure problems. Thus, a civic society established by value oriented individuals has structural advantage at micro development.

NGOs could be established by value oriented individuals, but are not necessarily filled by value oriented workers. However, their capacity to pay higher salary, compared to public sector, will reduce the occurrence of moral hazard and adverse selection problem. Since they can pay more than the average salary, they have capacity to attract efficient workers. The higher salary that they pay will reduce moral hazard problem from two directions, too. First, the feeling of being fairly treated will create incentive to be a hard worker. Second, the increase in lifetime income, once people join NGO, will increase the opportunity cost of losing the current job. This will reduce moral hazard problem. If you are paid market average or below market average, you will not lose much by losing your current job. But if a worker is paid more than the average, the lifetime opportunity cost of being fired will be very high. Under such reality, even if the probability of being discovered is low, still workers will try to avoid development of moral hazard. The negative effect of salary on moral hazard will be stronger, if there is high level of unemployment, which is the case in developing economies. In general, NGOs can reduce moral hazard and adverse selection problems by paying efficiency wage than market wage rate.

Small NGOs specializing in micro development can also have more flexibility than state bureaucracy. Small NGOs do not need to build a complicated hierarchy and this will make them flexible and efficient for micro development. This is why many international organizations, like World Bank (WB), insist for leading role of NGOs and civic society on rural development.

Unfortunately, in reality any institution is not a perfect solution to all problems everywhere. Practically, it is safe to assume anything extreme is always wrong. Many problems do crop up by the expansion NGOs and civic societies

A. NGOs and civic societies are not always established by value oriented individuals. This is the reality we face, where NGOs and Civic Society are established by agents looking for easy way to riches. Given irrational and unfounded insistence by international organizations to call all NGOs or civic societies a perfect solution for all rural development problems, the other side presents an extremely negative picture of such organizations. The practical truth lies in the middle, in which some NGOs and civic societies are extremely productive, but majority of them are nothing but a corruption machine.

B. Improper use of social capital. NGO or civic society workers can use their social capital for productive or mutual shirking and back scratching. Unfortunately, use of social capital is observed to be the most dominant use of social capital in NGOs and civic societies.

C. Lack of integrated strategy at both sectoral and spatial levels. Since civic society and NGOs are efficient under micro development only. If civic societies and NGOs increase in size, they will develop bureaucratic system of management losing their advantage in terms of flexibility. In a way they will lose their advantage at micro development. As a result rural development can't be managed by either civic societies, in general, or NGOs, in particular, only. State is needed to integrate the effort civic society, NGOs and other institutions of rural development.

D. NGOs and civic societies are funded by international donors and the donors mostly have their own agenda. That is why when the international agenda or agenda of the donors' is changes, everything in the process is abandoned. In spite of the donor having a keen interest of developing economics welfare, rarely NGOs or civic society everywhere are promoting social welfare of recipient community.

E. High wages which are fixed very high, by taking international wages into account, although attract international and domestic best expertise, NGOs will not have enough finance left for their development efforts. But NGOs have a tendency to spend significant portion of the budget on wages and salary of their workers.

NGOs and civic societies are important institutions, but cannot solve every state failure problem everywhere. They have to be evaluated one by one. Moreover, the integrating role of the state in rural development process can't be ignored. There are many schools of thought pertaining to development economics. In 1950s and 1960s state was taken to be the solution to the growth problem. In 1970s agricultural fundamentalism did take a root. In 1980s the market is ignored and welfare oriented redistribution policy became dominant. In middle 1980s and early 1990s the state was ignored and market become dominant. In late 1990s poverty reduction within market became dominant. Around 2000 the focus was on globalization and marginalization. And now every thing is about environment.

Sustainable improvement in quality of rural life has to be achieved in spite of malfunctioning market and highly inefficient state. To make things worse there is lack of Pareto optimal alternative institutions, which can efficiently coordinate rural development process in all locations. The problem for rural development is that what we have is only large collection of incomplete theory and limited historical data. The theories are reliable under their restricted assumptions only and the restriction imposed by those assumptions can't be evaluated by large quantity of empirical data. The right and logical step is to start the development effort from what you know and perfect your knowledge through try and error.

Institution with low level of failure should have a leading role and other institutions have to take complementary role, to fill the gap of the leading institution. But one can't fix what state, market or any other institution has to do everywhere. Pragmatically, it is advisable if the market is given the leading role in the long run, though. If market is perfect, it will give Pareto optimal rural development. Since the market is imperfect, it is possible that other institution can do better. The problem is any alternative path is not clear where it leads to. What we know is that in some cases, some institutions can perform better than market. Unfortunately, there is lack of clear knowledge about how non-market institutions can achieve sustainable development in the long run and all sectors. If market failures are deep and not easy to correct, and if there are functional alternative institutions, it is pragmatic to depend on non-market institutions. However, if market failures are not that serious or alternative institutions are not that better, it may be better to concentrate on market.

One way or another, over long term, it is rational not to defy the market as the best institution given the limited contemporary knowledge that we posses.

Market outcome even if it is efficient, will not be necessarily egalitarian or fair. Thus, one needs to address inequality in a way that does not compromise the efficiency of the system.

CHAPTER 7

Role of Institutions and Organisations in Rural Development

CHAPTER OUTLINE

- Role of Institutions and Organisations in Agriculture Sector
  - Fertiliser supply
  - Seed supply
  - Agricultural Research
  - Agricultural Extension Systems
  - Livestock and Veterinary Services
  - Rural Credit
  - Marketing agricultural output
- New Approaches to Agricultural Development
  - Participatory and Client Oriented Approaches
  - Participatory Watershed Development
  - Farmer Participatory Research and Extension
- Neo-Institutionalism and the Role of Organisations
  - New Institutional Economics
  - Managing Common Property Resources
  - Institutional Arrangements
  - Institutions, Poverty and Community Based Property Resources

7.1 ROLE OF INSTITUTIONS AND ORGANISATIONS IN AGRICULTURE SECTOR

What are public goods? Broadly, they are goods or services which are jointly consumable, and from which people cannot normally be excluded from consuming once the good is produced. Kherallah (et al.) refer to public goods as:

> *"...goods and services whose benefits cannot be captured privately owing to significant fixed costs and prohibitively high exclusion costs."*

Whereas according to Dasgupta (1993), the key point about public goods is that, because benefits cannot (easily) be captured privately, it is generally assumed that the private sector will not supply these valuable goods and services, and that therefore the public sector should do so. A good example is the research into new crop varieties conducted by the agricultural research institutions. These new varieties are made available to all farmers (or at least to national agricultural research systems) at no direct cost.

One problem that has arisen where the state has withdrawn from activities previously associated with it has been the undersupply of important functions such as provision of information, law enforcement, product standardisation, grading and inspection, buffer stock schemes, and infrastructure investments. Kherallah (et al.) recognise that it is important to re-evaluate the respective roles of State, market, and civil society, in order to develop institutional arrangements which are best suited to broad-based development.

The major reasons for reform are as follows. The State's direct involvement in agriculture through, for example, parastatal market boards,' monopoly provision of inputs and finance, control of prices and the exchange rate, and politicisation of farmers organisations, resulted in major inefficiencies, were a major cause of low rates of growth in agricultural output, and were ultimately unsustainable from a budgetary viewpoint. Structural reform has resulted in abolition of many parastatal marketing boards, price liberalisation, reduction or abolition of input subsidies, withdrawal of state-provided credit (which was often not repaid by farmers), and the dissolution of politicised farmer co-operatives.

Market optimists expected that withdrawal of the State would result in a vibrant private sector rapidly responding to market incentives and filling the gap, this has not happened to the extent anticipated. For example, detailed analyses of the role of parastatal marketing boards (e.g., Dorward et al., 1998; Reardon et al., 1999) noted that, in the absence of competitive input, credit and output markets, these marketing boards were institutional mechanisms which, by interlinking input and output markets, enabled credit to be delivered on a scale greater than the private sector could have achieved. The abolition of such boards, although justified in many respects, has in particular resulted in a decline in the availability of seasonal credit for many farmers, and, particularly in more remote areas, has resulted in farmers either being unable to market produce, or being able to do so only to a limited number of monopolistic traders on unfavourable terms.

Therefore, recently there has been some reassessment of the role of the public and private sectors, with a degree of greater acceptance — although there is no consensus on this — that there are many areas of agricultural system where the State needs to continue to play a role, and where the withdrawal of the State may, in fact, has gone too far.

In addition, there is a wider appreciation of the benefits of a plurality of actors – including NGOs and farmer-based organisations – as players in the areas of food security, agricultural support services and associated natural resource management issues. The role of NGOs and farmer-based organisations has been particularly important in the development of more participatory processes in agricultural development and natural resource management.

Carney's (1998) overview of the changing roles of the public and private sectors summarises some of the key shifts in thinking on agricultural service provision, although it does not do full justice to the diversity of approaches now in operation. Some of the key points of Carney's analysis have been summarised below. The primary economic justifications for continued public sector involvement in the agricultural sector – which as is often pointed out, is dominated by private producers, unlike other more obvious areas of public action such as education and health – lie in:

(a) the identification of the public goods nature of certain agricultural services;
(b) the need to correct a variety of *market failures;* and,
(c) going beyond a purely economic perspective, the need to provide specific support to poor and marginalised groups.

If a particular product or service has public goods properties, private markets in such goods or services are less likely to develop. Carney differentiates between public and private sector roles, and the specific requirements of the rural poor, with respect to the main agricultural service functions of:

- Fertiliser supply
- Seed supply
- Agricultural research systems
- Agricultural extension systems
- Veterinary services
- Rural credit
- Agricultural produce marketing.

Although there is an increased awareness of the need for holistic approaches and that sources of non-farm income are important for rural households, there is still a need for detailed analyses of sub-sectors to develop effective, efficient and transparent institutional arrangements to best serve the goal of a broad-based and sustainable expansion of agricultural output.

7.1.1 Fertiliser Supply

In principle, fertiliser can be regarded as a private good. However, in practice trends towards privatisation of fertiliser supply, accompanied by abolition of fertiliser subsidies, have in some countries resulted in declining use of fertilisers. Governments have long justified the use of fertiliser subsidies as a means of mitigating the risk which individual farmers face in purchasing fertiliser when outcomes are uncertain. In addition parastatals which previously supplied fertiliser as credit in-kind were in a better position to recover input costs due to their control over farm output.

Poorer farm households are unlikely to have benefited significantly from liberalisation and abolition of subsidies. This is in part because such households do not use significant quantities of inorganic fertiliser. Since fertiliser use especially by small farmers is highly price-elastic, i.e., a small increase in price can result in a relatively large decline in demand – then the abolition of fertiliser subsidies is likely to reduce even further small holders' fertiliser use. Furthermore, given their low levels of demand, private traders may find it uneconomical to supply to them, more so if they are in remote locations where high transport costs would be incurred.

In order for a more comprehensive reform to take place while at the same time ensuring that poorer households have access to fertiliser, some combination of support to private traders and some level of targeted subsidies to poorer users could be possible policy measures.

There are also environmental externalities in regard to fertiliser use that might influence the extent and direction of any public intervention. There are different opinions about the environmental effects of low fertiliser use. While some analysts conclude that low fertiliser consumption will be environmentally beneficial, there may be opposite effects, as described by Reardon et al. (1999).

Various national and international scientists have put together evidence of how counter-productive fertilizers have become and the havoc they are playing with Indian soils. On the basis of various scientific studies and solid data, it has been found that while fertilisers did raise productivity in the early years of the Green Revolution, they are no longer doing so. In fact they are reducing productivity in many areas due to several factors such as soil degradation caused by destruction of organic matter, nutrient imbalances, and micro-nutrient deficiencies. The human health impacts of fertiliser pollution are also very serious. In Punjab, it has been found that most wells were contaminated with nitrates—20 per cent of all sampled wells had nitrate levels above the safety limit of 50 mg per litre as established by the World Health Organisation. Such high levels can cause diseases such as cancers (of the digestive tract, bladder and ovaries) and blue baby syndrome in infancts. Air pollution too occurs due to the release of heavy metals by fertilisers.

7.1.2 Seed Supply

Seed technology – excluding recent developments in biotechnology – can be divided into open pollinated varieties, which farmers are able to reproduce themselves, and hybrids, for which new seed is required each year. Liberalisation of the seed supply sub-sector has tended to result in some private companies entering the market to supply hybrids, which have private goods properties, whereas open pollinated varieties are common pool goods which are generally informally exchanged between farmers. This characteristic makes it unlikely that seed supply could be fully privatised, and at the same time there is a view that if farmers had sole responsibility to organise the production of open pollinated varieties, there might be undersupply, particularly in risky environments where seed availability might suddenly be reduced. This suggests a continued role for the public sector in ensuring that there are adequate supplies of seed available. This might involve co-operation between farmers and the public sector in seed multiplication, seed storage, etc.

The public sector will still be likely to have a role in terms of research into new or improved varieties, or adapting varieties produced International Agricultural Research Centres (IARCs). As in the case of fertilisers, there is evidence that liberalisation is more likely to meet the needs of better-off than poor farmers, but there are general gains in terms of improving the variety and quantity of seeds available from different sources of supply.

7.1.3 Agricultural Research

The area of agricultural research covers a variety of activities such as scale, commodity mix, and whether the research is basic, strategic, applied or adaptive. The people involved in agricultural research vary from the international (the IARCs, and increasingly the biotechnology companies), to the national (National Agricultural Research systems or NARs), sub-national (for example commodity-focussed organisations or NGOs), and last of all, farmers themselves (Fig. 7.1).

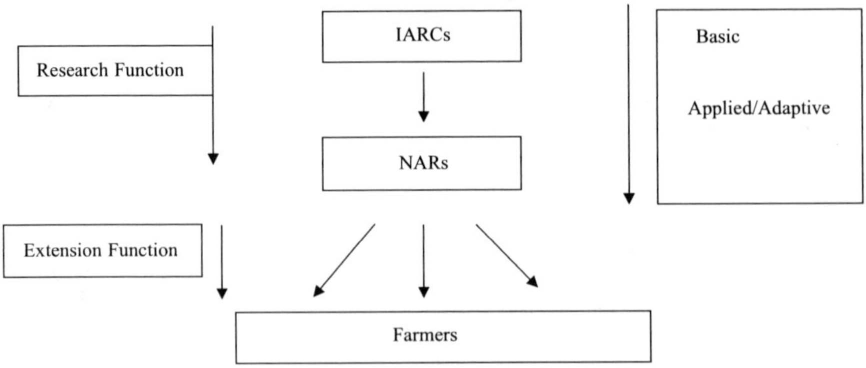

Fig. 7.1 Traditional agricultural research and dissemination model

Here new varieties, vaccines, etc., were developed through basic research in IARCs, developed through further applied or adaptive research in NARs, and then *extended* to farmers as a technological package (most notably the Green Revolution seed-fertiliser-pesticide-water prescription). Farmers were to some extent seen as passive *adopters* of these packages, although it was later recognised that farmer adaptation played a role in modifying IARC products to make them suitable to specific agro-ecological environments. National agricultural extension services based, for example, on the T and V (Training and Visit) system was tasked with encouraging widespread adoption of these packages.

This model still exists, in many countries, but its limitations are increasingly recognised. The limitations of this approach are as follows:

- the top-down, prescriptive nature of the approach;
- the development of packages which may have little relation to the aero-ecological conditions found in farmers' fields;
- the implicit economics of packages which might make them unaffordable particularly to poor farmers;
- the lack of capacity in NARs to effectively conduct applied or adaptive research; and
- the denial of the local knowledge and adaptive capacity of farmers themselves.

Essentially, the fact that this model has not transformed food production and food insecurity problems outside of the Green Revolution *heartlands*, and that even there yields now appear to be declining, has contributed to a reappraisal of the conventional model. There is now much more focus on developing agricultural research systems in collaboration with farmers and taking their identified needs into account. The development of biotechnology and the potential (and threats) of genetically modified crops have brought new issues into the research scene.

Carney distinguishes among mechanical, chemical, biological and agronomic research, noting that these are of "*descending order of attractiveness to the private sector, according to their economic characteristics.*" Under a private system, thereby justifying public sector investment. This indeed is the justification given for the existence of the IARCs in terms of their supply of *international public goods.* However, the development of biotechnology led by the private sector may change this equation.

Evenson suggests that there are three stages in technology development:

- pre-technology
- prototype technology, and
- usable technology.

Evenson regards pre-technology as a pure public good which requires full government support, whereas the other stages require lesser degrees of Government involvement. The existence of significant scale of economies in research also justifies a continued public sector role, although again the advent of biotechnology has indicated that enormous research budgets can be mobilised in the private sector if the expected profit level is high. Where profit levels may not be high, however, this provides one of the strongest justifications for continued public sector involvement in research, in support of other goals such as food security, compatibility of cropping patterns with sustainable soil fertility management, etc., where the financial returns from such research cannot be readily appropriated.

Former President of India, Dr. A.P.J. Abdul Kalam, suggested research missions for ICAR (Indian Council of Agricultural Research) during the period 2012–2030, for accelerating the growth and increase the productivity to achieve 10 per cent growth in agriculture. He has suggested research missions which include development of farm practices for small and marginal farmers, analyzing the mapping of natural resources and documentation of all the agricultural technologies. He also noted that ICAR can develop a self-coordinating mechanism for achieving this goal as an organizational development mission. He had said the above on the 84th Foundation Day of ICAR on 16th July, 2012 in New Delhi.

There is clearly a need for continued agricultural research. Many public sector research institutions have not performed well; hence there is a tendency towards increased experimentation and innovation in research systems and accountability. Innovations include the methodologies of farmer participatory research/technology development; the establishment of competitive research/technology development funds; and attempts to put clients (farmers) in control of research funds to encourage more client-oriented research. It is also important to note that the division between research and extension is increasingly disputed, at least in regard to adaptive research, and there is a greater tendency to attempt to design effective systems which link research, extension and farmers together.

7.1.4 Agricultural Extension Systems

Agricultural extension was once known as the application of scientific research and new knowledge to agricultural practices through farmer education. But now the field of extension includes a wider range of communication and learning activities organised for rural people by professionals from different disciplines, including agriculture, agricultural marketing, health and business studies.

The four paradigms of agricultural extension services are Technology Transfer (top to down approach), Advisory Work (Governmental organisations and private consulting companies respond to farmers enquiries with technical solutions), Human Resource Development (universities giving training to rural people) and Facilitation for Empowerment (experimental learning and farmer to farmer exchanges).

In areas characterised by poor farmers and weak government services, NGOs are in some areas the main providers of extension services. Some of these NGOs have at the same time developed participatory research and extension methodologies, which have to some extent been adopted by the public sector.

The question of whether extension services are a public or a private good depends both on the nature of the extension and on the stage of development of the country. These issues are interrelated. Information in general is more or less a public good (Dasgupta, 1993), but more specialised information needs, which tend to be demanded by more commercially oriented farmers can be privately provided on a fee-paying basis. However, in food deficit countries or areas where there is a general need to raise aggregate output and household incomes, it can be argued that all types of information should be made available to improve general welfare. This requires the public sector or non-profit NGOs to do so.

Institutional pluralism (Antholt 1994) is in favour of the extension sub-sector, but the role of the public sector needs to be strong, and to be developed within the context of national agricultural development strategies (for example, through sector programmes). The role of a broad-based extension service is complex, and extension agents may need to take on new and more generalist roles, including providing information on issues such as credit, marketing and storage as well as the more *conventional* technical/agronomic information. Furthermore, such agents need to learn new, more participatory ways of working.

Finally, although pluralism might be the preferred approach, there is a danger of fragmentation of the supply of services, thereby weakening the link between extension and research.

7.1.5 Livestock and Veterinary Services

The importance of livestock in India is obviously the provision of veterinary services which is a key issue for rural development. Whereas these services were formerly provided free of charge, in most countries services provided by the public sector now include an element of cost-recovery. In addition some parts of the service are now provided by the private sector.

There appears to be little consensus on whether veterinary services should be regarded as public or private goods. Curative services are to some extent regarded as private goods, while preventative services are viewed by different analysts as either public or private. The argument that they are public goods rests on the need to ensure that all livestock owners inoculate their animals against infectious diseases. Failure to do so has obvious externalities in terms of the danger of infecting other herds. Therefore, some analysts suggest that preventative services should be provided by a public or other collective body according to a fixed charge. Differential services and perhaps differential fee rates could operate between more commercially-oriented larger farmers, and smaller farmers with small herds which may be communally grazed.

In relation to poor households, NGO services which are often based on the training of community-based *para-vets* can extend services to a group that formerly had no access. Furthermore, poor households, and women within poor households, often rely on small stock which are generally neglected by large-scale public veterinary services. NGOs often provide particular support in this sub-sector. Support can also be given for the development of membership organisations which can share the cost of service provision. Such groups may be more cohesive if they are organised around marketing.

It will remain important to support regional disease control — the private sector will not deal with the externalities of epidemic diseases.

Animal production is important for most farmers, but this is not reflected in the composition of services offered to farmers. Livestock services have been dominated by veterinary science, but there are many other ways to enhance productivity. Issues that need to be raised include:

1. What kind of livestock services do farmers currently receive?
2. To what extent are crop-livestock interactions understood?
3. Are gender roles adequately understood?
4. Through what channels do livestock owners market their produce?

7.1.6 Rural Credit

The post-liberalisation period saw a paradigm shift in the banking sector which coincided with the growth of a silent micro-finance revolution in India. The genesis of this was a National Bank of Agri & Rural Dev. (NABARD) - initiated pilot, the self-help Group (SHG). Bank Linkage project in 1991, which focused on SHG's as a channel for delivery of micro-finance (Satish of Mehrotra, 2009).

Major changes have occurred in the area of rural credit provision. Public sector credit programmes often had high costs, poor recovery rates, and were prone to political interventions to forgive loan arrears, thereby wiping out the credibility of the loan-giving institutions.

Reardon et al. (1999) noted that where public sector credit, often linked to parastatal marketing arrangements, has been eliminated, the access particularly of small holders to credit has diminished; small holders therefore look to income from other sources (cash crops and non-farm income) to meet financing needs.

In place of purely public sector programmes a variety of innovative rural financial institutions have grown up, many supported by donor finance. The most well-known is the Grameen Bank in India which has since been replicated in many countries. There are, however, many other existing savings and credit associations or cooperatives, including a large number in Indian states, sometimes based on *traditional* savings and loan institutions. These tend to be distinguished according to the extent to which they encourage self-financing based on savings, and also according to ownership structures. The creation of the formal credit structure for financial agriculture and other rural activities commenced in India in the early part of this century with the introduction of cooperatives. The ACRC (Agriculture Credit Review Committee) in 1989 examined the existing rural credit system in detail. This committee recommended greater autonomy for commercial banks. The Narasimham Committee on Financial Sector Reforms 1991, recommended redefining of priority sector, gradual phasing out of directed credit programmes to 10 per cent of aggregate bank credit and deregulation of interest rates.

Donors fund a number of rural financial institutions, including some (such as the Grameen Bank) which are specifically targeted at the poor. Donor funding often covers some elements of operating costs, and therefore these institutions are often not fully self-financing, even though they charge market rates of interest.

In terms of the public/private good nature of rural finance institutions, credit can be regarded as a private good, but given risk factors present particularly in poor rural areas in India and elsewhere, it may not be attractive for private lenders. Hence, the continued existence in many areas of moneylenders charging very high rates of interest. In principle Government should be less risk-averse, but Government programmes generally face the problem of lack of loyalty on the part of borrowers thereby leading to high rates of default. The Grameen Bank-type institutions overcome the problems both of lack of collateral on the part of poor borrowers, and of the risk of default, through the mechanism of group guarantees. In general group-based finance (as in the case of credit unions) can in principle address a number of the disadvantages of public sector programmes, but there are questions about both the scale and the long-term sustainability of such group-based schemes. According to Carney (1998) financial services for poorer people should be as follows:

1. interest rates should in general be market-determined;
2. lending agencies should be decentralised;
3. externally-supported schemes should try to build on existing informal methods of accessing credit;
4. credit and savings should be jointly provided as key elements of a broader financial service infrastructure; and
5. rural savings can be mobilised as a viable basis for lending, in the longer if not the short term.

In terms of organisational arrangements for provision of credit particularly to smaller farmers, micro-finance institutions provide one option, but other options could also be explored, including co-operative finance, savings and credit associations, agricultural development banks, etc. In addition, where contract farming develops, the end-users can develop credit arrangements with farmers supplying on contract.

There are many issues in the design of effective 'micro-finance' and broader rural credit programmes, which require in-depth consideration. Key recent issues are as follows:

1. The notion of credit has changed. It is now viewed as one of a range of financial services to which people should have access rather than a way to kick-start rural enterprise.

2. The importance of savings is recognised.
3. There is more appreciation of how rural finance can contribute to poverty reduction, improvements in food security and empowerment.
4. Financial sustainability issues are critical.
5. Issues of whether the provision of financial services should be part of a broader rural development package or stand-alone intervention.
6. How to reduce transaction costs of lending to small borrowers while increasing repayment rates.

It is vital to understand the existing financial systems and the debt-bearing capacity of local people, especially poor households – some questions include:

1. Are people already accessing informal credit, and can these systems be used or should new systems be developed?
2. On the other hand, are informal systems essentially being used to help poor people repay loans taken from the formal institutions? If so, to what extent are poor people actually benefiting from using such services?
3. Is there a need for the parallel development of insurance services to reduce risks for borrowers?

There is also a clear gender element to the provision of rural finance. Many schemes focussed on poor people lend particularly to women, either individually or in groups. There is evidence to suggest that women repay at a higher rate than men. In addition, it is often thought that finance targeted at women helps them to gain some economic independence within the household, perhaps particularly when their roles in agriculture, or access to income resulting from agriculture, are restricted. But for some women who borrow, and there could be a danger of actually weakening their position further if they become caught in a cycle of debt. Therefore, the benefits to be derived from any lending scheme need to be carefully assessed.

Group formation is often an element of setting up rural finance institutions. Groups have a number of advantages – transactions costs for lenders are reduced, transparency is increased; but there are also costs involved in group-based lending. Borrowers themselves are often reluctant to get involved in such groups because they will then be held liable for any defaulting by other members.

With regard to lending to poorer people, there is some more consensus besides the given by Carney:

1. Lenders should not become bogged down in monitoring the exact use to which loans are put: the main issues are to ensure repayment and that there are incentives to encourage borrowers to do so

2. Schemes should not expand too fast but need to learn from experience and adapt.

Financial services may need to be complemented by a range of other community development interventions or other actions. With regard to the establishment of financial services, few rural financial services are fully self-financing. Some kind of external subsidy is usually required for training, administration and start-up costs. Generally, neither government nor bilateral donors should be directly involved in financial service provision, but should work through NGOs or intermediaries in the financial services area. Institutional sustainability is a key consideration.

Expansion problems of micro-credit organizations

Osmani (2000) raises an issue that is of interest in the development of micro-credit organisations. What happens when they expand vertically in terms of increasing loan size?

The Grameen Bank itself has run into difficulties in this respect. As average loan sizes have increased (more than fivefold in some areas compared with original levels) repayment rates have fallen, from the often-quoted 98 per cent to less than 80 per cent in recent years. In addition, many borrowers are becoming dependent on village moneylenders to be able to make the weekly repayments – which defeats the purpose of the loans in the first case – and, on the other hand, the larger size of loans available is inducing non-target group households to become borrowers, thereby undermining the self-targeting nature of the credit programme and potentially threatening the group guarantee mechanism (which to a large extent depends on a relatively homogeneous group of borrowers).

The basic dilemma is that, while loan size should increase over time to have a significant impact on incomes of the poor, too great an expansion can undermine the whole system. The degree to which self-targeting can be maintained is also a critical question; perhaps alternative, more explicit targeting mechanisms are required.

7.1.7 Marketing Agricultural Output

The National Commission on Agriculture defined agricultural marketing as a process which starts with a decision to produce to saleable farm commodity and it involves all aspects of market structure of the system, both functional and institutional, based on technical and economic considerations and includes pre- and post-harvest operations, assembling, grading, storage, transportation and distribution. The ICAR defined involvement of three important function, namely (a) assembling (concentration) (b) preparation for consumption (processing) and (c) distribution. In the older days selling of goods was easy, but now in the modern world it has become more challenging with the latest technologies and involvement of middlemen, commission agents who keep their margins and move the produce further. In the entire process of marketing the producer gets the lowest price and the ultimate consumer pays the highest due to the involvement of more middlemen in the entire distribution process.

The core principle of marketing in India is price, product, place and promotion.

From the above discussion it is clear that the assumption that liberalisation would bring an automatic response from private traders has been shown to be over-optimistic, particularly in regard to small producers in more remote areas. In those areas the limited trading activity has resulted in farmers having few options but to accept the low prices offered by traders.

In terms of its economic characteristics, buying and selling of output is at the core of private sector activity and, given a liberalised environment, it would be expected that private traders would enter the market. However, certain characteristics of the agricultural sector provide potential justification for continued public sector involvement. These characteristics include:

1. agriculture is inherently risky and major price fluctuations might suggest a role for government in price (and income) stabilisation;
2. food security considerations justify government involvement, for example, in building up food security reserves; and
3. government intervention might be needed particularly to support small holders who otherwise might be exploited by private traders.

However, even if these arguments are accepted, it does not mean that direct government intervention in terms of market purchases should continue. The extent and nature of such interventions depends on specific country circumstances.

There are some arguments to support the view that cash crop marketing, because of its greater profit potential, is likely to attract more private trader involvement than the marketing of basic food crops. For example, Dorward et al. (1998) argue in favour of continued liberalisation of cash crop marketing.

In relation to food crop marketing there may be more justification for Government involvement, but again this could be in a variety of ways, for example:

1. Supporting the development of farmers' organisations which might play a greater role in developing marketing channels and/or provide countervailing bargaining power in negotiations with private traders.
2. Supporting the development of financing institutions for small holders.
3. Limited market support arrangements where prices have collapsed.
4. General infrastructure development to improve the prospects and reduce the costs of market exchange.
5. Providing improved market information, etc.

The fragmentation of production and marketing systems suggests a role for groups. Marketing co-operatives have failed in the past but still have potential. Alternatively, less formal farmer enterprises can play a role in bulking produce in remote areas and raising bargaining power of producers.

One of the most effective ways of supporting marketing may be to invest in non-specific infrastructure, e.g., roads, communications. Some of the agricultural market reforms practised in India are as follows:

1. Loan provision to farmers at low rate of interest.
2. Provision of subsidized power supply.
3. Generation of new distribution network that connects the farmers directly to the consumers to get maximum returns.
4. Elimination of the existing loopholes in the present legislations is warranted.
5. Stringent action taken against black marketers and hoarders.
6. Creation of local outlets at each village where the farmers sell their stocks directly to the consumers on authorized buyers at fixed prices.
7. Village level counselling centres for farmers about the worth of their stocks—role of NGO's is or prime significance.
8. Provision of reasonable prices for the basic food commodities through Public Distribution System with a network of 350,000 fair price shops, monitored by state governments.

7.2 NEW APPROACHES TO AGRICULTURAL DEVELOPMENT

7.2.1 Participatory and Client-oriented Approaches

Although there are some contradictory trends, one of the most important recent innovations in development is the growth of participatory approaches, and a shift from supply-driven service delivery to demand-driven or client-oriented service delivery (although in some cases the rhetoric of this shift may be greater than the reality).

Participatory approaches share a number of common principles (Pretty and Chambers, 1994):

1. A defined methodology and systemic learning process, encouraging cumulative learning by all participants.
2. Multiple perspectives, which seek diversity rather than average conditions.
3. Group inquiry process, including people from different disciplines, different sectors and different backgrounds (outsider professionals and insider local people).
4. Context-specific approaches need to be flexible enough to be adapted to new sets of conditions and actors.
5. Facilitating experts and stakeholders.
6. Leading to sustained action – analysis defines desirable changes and also seeks to motivate people to undertake these actions themselves. Institution-building or strengthening are often required as a pre-requisite for action.

Participatory approaches have considerable potential in the area of developing agricultural technologies with and for resource-poor farmers.

Conventional research and extension systems have, however, not tended to follow participatory principles; instead, they have tended to be based on the following assumptions:

1. Real knowledge rests with the technical expert, and farmers' knowledge is given little value.
2. The farmer is to some extent a passive recipient of information and technologies.
3. Initiative for disseminating information rests exclusively with the communicator (e.g., extension agent).
4. Increased production is the main criterion for farming improvement.
5. Farmers' information needs are in the area of technical research results rather than in the area of management of livelihood systems.

—(Pretty and Chambers, 1994).

Pretty and Chambers note that:

> "*In group-based approaches, extension becomes facilitation, through using and developing farmers' knowledge, teaching observational skills and using adult education methods to develop joint decision making skills.*"

Chambers (1993, 1994 and 1997) has been writing for many years about the need for *reversals* in development work to ensure that poor people are the genuine beneficiaries of development. These reversals include a need for institutions and professional development workers to change attitudes and operational approaches in terms of how they relate to poor people.

These new approaches demand new ways of working and new attitudes from rural development workers. For example, whereas extension agents (development agents) have been accustomed to providing farmers with relatively standardised extension *packages* which have been developed on agricultural research stations, participatory forms of on-farm research and on-farm technology development require a different approach from the development agent, an approach which involves listening to farmers' views, respecting their knowledge, and working with them in mutual learning processes.

Client-oriented approaches require similar shifts in mindsets and attitudes. A client-oriented research and extension system, for example, would conduct research to identify suitable technologies to overcome constraints identified by farmers, rather than promoting standardised packages of technologies, which might not be appropriate, particular in diverse agro-ecological environments.

New approaches to agricultural and natural resource management, which are based on participatory principles and methodologies have been given below.

7.2.2 Participatory Watershed Development

Participatory watershed development (PWD) approach has become more widely used in recent years. It is a response to:

(a) failures of conventional approaches to soil and water conservation which often relied on building inappropriate structures which farmers rejected; and

(b) the realisation of the collective action nature of development at the watershed level, where local institutional development is required to overcome negative externalities (e.g., problems of deforestation upstream).

Participatory watershed development differs from conventional approaches in a number of ways:

1. Local communities are fully involved in analysis of their own soil and water conservation problems.
2. The role of the external support organisation is as a facilitator of analysis and catalyst for action, building on local knowledge, needs and opportunities of the communities. The support organisation can help form local institutions and groups to manage and protect the watershed.
3. Farmer-to-farmer extension is a key process for passing information to catchment inhabitants, for building closer collaboration between farmers, and for scaling-up watershed conservation in neighbouring areas.

4. Project staff do not take a blueprint approach; technologies selected and crops encouraged depend on needs of farmers.
5. The emphasis is on sustainability and equity of improvements rather than short-term benefits.

—(Hinchcliffe et al., 1995)

This approach has been pioneered and used most extensively in India, both by NGOs and under Government of India programmes.

Hinchcliffe et al. (1995) after reviewing a number of such approaches, drew some general conclusions on what is needed for successful participatory watershed development, focusing on five cross-cutting themes:

1. Technologies
2. Process and methods
3. Impact and indicators
4. Inter-institutional arrangements
5. Policies

1. Technologies

(a) Redirect incentives – away from financial inducements for standard conservation measures, towards institutional development and increased access to credit.
(b) Encourage innovation rather than pre-selection of specific technologies.
(c) More emphasis on biological measures.
(d) Promote participatory technology development and adaptive research as integral parts of watershed management programmes.

2. Process and methods

(a) Farmer-to-farmer extension and experimentation are important for sustainability and to promote scaling-up. The capacity of farmer and community-level organisations for experimentation and extension should therefore be strengthened.
(b) Flexible and responsive external institutions are needed.
(c) Confidence-building – the pace of programmes and projects must allow time to build confidence.
(d) Decentralisation – village-based management of programme funds and planning are important prerequisites.

3. *Impact and indicators*

(a) Adaptation versus adoption – impact indicators should focus on adaptation by farmers rather than adoption of technologies.
(b) Equity – much greater efforts are needed to address equity issues to ensure that the poorest and most marginalised are not left out.
(c) Self-evaluation enriches the learning process in institutions.

4. *Inter-institutional arrangements*

(a) Widespread training and competence building is needed to encourage and sustain a participatory approach, in particular there is a need to expand training in participatory methods that focus on joint learning for action.
(b) Joint approaches increase the contacts and linkages between farmers and external institutions, improving the likelihood of policies and practices emerging that satisfy all stakeholders. Many creative approaches to developing partnerships have been developed between farmers and extensionists, researchers, markets, private companies, etc.
(c) Clear roles of different institutions need to be clarified, e.g., roles of Government and NGOs.
(d) Inter-village federations required for sustainable PWD; such institutions can then manage a range of activities such as credit, marketing and protection of common lands.

5. *Policies*

(a) Policy reform – most policies are not supportive of PWD
(b) Appropriate support – Government authorities must provide appropriate financial and institutional support to local institutions if the latter are taking control of watersheds.
(c) Equity and livelihoods – the policy focus should be not just on natural resource management, but also on livelihood security, equity, and institutional development.

Participatory watershed development clearly involves a different approach compared with conventional methods of catchment conservation. The focus is on a combination of conservation and production measures, where both are identified through joint approaches where farmers and support agencies operate on an equal level; and again institutional development is a key element of the approach.

7.2.3 Farmer Participatory Research and Extension

> "*In most development farmers are informants or at best data collectors. They do not participate in analysing data and taking decisions based on the analysis. This process loses the use of inherent analytical capacity of the farmers. The resultant development process although [it] may lead to tangible development results in the short run does not lead to a sustained innovation by the local villagers and also does not lead to institution building at the village level. This does not lead to building of an enabling environment in which innovations are encouraged from local people*".
>
> —Shah, Baradwaj and Ambastha 1995

Participatory research and extension approaches aim to change the way in which research and extension are carried out, and in particular they aim to put the farmer at the centre of research and technology development activities. In fact there is a strong viewpoint that the term *extension* is obsolete. It denotes a one-way flow of information and technology, from the extension agent to the farmer, who passively receives the technology. Participatory approaches involve the farmer from an early stage in the development of new technologies, which is why the term *participatory technology development* is increasingly used.

There are many examples of participatory approaches. Because of the tendency for State research and extension systems to use relatively bureaucratic and top-down processes, much of the pioneering work on participatory research and extension has been done by NGOs, and sometimes by farmers groups themselves.

Participatory Plant Breeding and Varietal Selection

Conventional plant breeding methods produced the high-yielding varieties of the *Green Revolution,* which contributed to a significant increase in aggregate food output from favourable areas, but which did not produce varieties of relevance to the risky and diverse conditions characterising different parts of Asia. Rural poverty has persisted in most of these areas, and there has been a realisation that *Green Revolution-type* standard packages of inputs generally do not suit the micro-environments which make up risky and diverse areas.

Similarly, there is a growing acceptance, including in much of the CGIAR (Consultative Group on International Agricultural Research) system which developed the *Green Revolution* technology, that farmers' knowledge is critical in these complex areas, and that farmers have been making adaptations for centuries to produce crop and livestock varieties well attuned:

(a) to specific micro-environments; and
(b) to farm households' priorities, which in many areas will emphasise food security through growing drought-resistant varieties, rather than maximising potential food output and/or income.

In order to address these kinds of concerns, the CGIAR system, as well as a number of NGOs, agricultural research institutes and, to a lesser extent, Government research systems, have developed a range of farmer-centred, research approaches known as participatory plant breeding (PPB). CGIAR (1999) noted that:

> "PPB covers the full range of genetic improvement activities: setting breeding goals, creating genetic variability, selecting within variable populations, evaluating experimental varieties, releasing and popularising new varieties, and producing seed. Farmers can take part in any of these phases and in varying degrees."

CGIAR noted that PPB appears to have a number of advantages over conventional breeding:

- PPB may cut research costs: farmers and scientists share key tasks, thereby reducing some on-farm trial costs normally borne by the formal research system.
- PPB leads to more accurate identification of varieties farmers prefer which are adapted to local conditions.
- PPB leads to faster release and dissemination of locally accepted varieties: since trials are conducted on-farm, farmers see the results quickly and may then do their own tests and start multiplying and distributing improved seed.
- PPB gives formal research programmes the means to help farmer-breeders acquire knowledge they need for better plant breeding.
- PPB provides a rationale for farmers to conserve genetic material on-farm, thereby contributing to the maintenance and enhancement of genetic diversity, whereas conventional breeding has tended to reduce such diversity.

In addition, and critically, PPB can be particularly effective in targeting poor rural women and other often marginalised groups. CGIAR noted that:

> "PPB is particularly effective in targeting poor rural women, who are key players in managing plant genetic resources... Women can play an especially

important role in plant breeding when its objectives need to take into account the many purposes that a single crop may serve in the rural household."

Farmer-led and Participatory Extension

As with the move towards decentralisation and partnerships with farmers in research, so in the area of extension there has been a shift, at least in thinking, towards a *farmer-led* approach. This has in part been because of the inherent desirability of such an approach, as the limitations of rigid, one-way *transfer of technology* models became apparent. These limitations are partly consequent on the methods used in *pushing* technologies, and partly because there were few useful new technologies to push once the limits of *Green Revolution* technologies were reached. However, in addition to this, there has been the preoccupation with decentralisation and, in some areas, privatisation, which we discussed earlier.

Scarborough et al. (1997) discuss some of the concepts behind farmer-led extension. In fact they point to a difference between farmer-to-farmer extension (an approach which has developed particularly in Latin America) and farmer-led approaches. Whereas farmer-led extension tends to imply farmers seeking a stronger voice in partnerships with the agencies – generally the public sector – responsible for delivery of extension services, farmer-to-farmer extension is a more self-reliant approach characterised by:

1. The emergence of a "movement" initiated and sustained by farmers.
2. The generation of most innovations by farmers themselves, with occasional external support (e.g., from an NGO).
3. The provision of training by farmers to other farmers.

One of the key issues in relation to the evolution of extension approaches is the link between research and extension. The *old* model, as portrayed in Figure 7.1, can be characterised as one where new varieties were developed through on-station research and *pushed* down to passive farmers who received extension messages (along with other inputs). This method may have been reasonably effective where a uniform technology was to be delivered in uniform growing conditions — conditions which rarely prevailed outside the irrigated *Green Revolution* heartlands – but is generally ineffective in other circumstances. Public extension systems often do not know any other model however, which is one reason why there is a presumption that private systems might be more effective.

However, one danger of moving to a private, or contract-based, system, is that there are potentially major economies of scale and scope in combined research and extension which might be lost through relying on contractual arrangements which would often be geared to shorter-term paybacks. This danger is likely to be greater, the smaller (and poorer) the farmers are and the more diverse their cropping systems – which small holders' cropping systems tend to be, as a means of livelihood security.

Therefore alternatives to contracting-out lie in the development of partnerships which bring together farmers, support agencies (public, NGO, and/or private), and often research institutes, in approaches which focus on farmers needs and which may combine research and extension elements.

A number of key issues come up constantly in discussions of more farmer-based approaches, including:

1. Cost-effectiveness – since these approaches are generally time-consuming and locally-based, questions are raised about their sustainability and cost-effectiveness.
2. The role of professionals – generally *professionals* (researchers, extension agents, etc.) need to play more of a facilitatory role in all farmer-based approaches. Many existing staff in the public system are ill-equipped to play such a role without considerable training and capacity-building.
3. The role of partnerships – generally partnerships (between farmers, the public sector, NGOs, possibly the private sector, etc.) are seen as critical for linking different skills and knowledge by which the system as a whole can be more responsive to the needs of farmers in diverse environments.

7.3 NEO-INSTITUTIONALISM AND THE ROLE OF ORGANISATIONS

7.3.1 New Institutional Economics

This is an increasing focus on the essential role of institutions and organisations in development. From a theoretical perspective, this issue has been addressed through institutional analysis. More recently the focus on the role of institutions has been extended through what is termed *neo-institutionalism*. Neo-institutionalism is a theory that focusses on developing a sociological view of institutions—the way they interact and the way they affect society. It provides a way of viewing institutions outside the traditional views of economics by explaining why so many businesses end up having some organizational structure (isomorphism) even though they evolved in different ways, and how the institutions shape the behaviour of individual members.

Two weaknesses in the theoretical basis for neo-classical economics provide much of the basis for the development of *the new institutional economics*. These are the recognition of the importance of transaction costs in *real* firms and economies and the more general recognition of the pervasiveness of a whole range of market failures, particularily in relation to:

(a) the analysis of environmental externalities; and

(b) broad areas of analysis in developing economies.

The new institutional economics, as the term suggests, emphasises the important role of institutions, in the first instance to reduce transaction costs, but more broadly as non-market mechanisms to overcome market failures.

The new institutional economics is generally seen as an extension of neo-classical economics rather than as a radical departure from it. Rational agents are seen as demanding and supplying institutions, which help them to overcome the consequences of market failure. Viewed more broadly, however, the focus on institutions has:

(a) drawn attention to the fundamental role of institutions in the process of development; and

(b) prompted analysis and policy-oriented work on the specific nature and characteristics of institutions which are neither market nor State.

These analyses, applied particularly to problems of development, have underlined the potential of such institutions in the development process.

7.3.2 Managing Common Property Resources

One of the most important areas of application of the new institutional economics is in the area of management of common property resources. Common property resources are those natural resources – grazing lands, forests, rivers, etc. – that are managed in common by a group of users. Examples of common property resources include fishing grounds, pastures, irrigation systems, forests, water or the atmosphere. Due to overuse, their common property resources are generally subject to the problems of congestion, pollution, etc. It has been observed in many situations that common property resources can be managed effectively and sustainably by local communities – and yet, in other situations such resources are often degraded and people's livelihoods are negatively affected as a result.

Ostrom (1990) questions how some communities are able to develop successful institutions, which help them to manage such resources effectively, while other communities cannot do so. One point which is clear is that without such institutions, these resources would become degraded because of the problem of the *tragedy of the commons* (Hardin 1968). This problem was identified by Hardin, who gave as an example herdsmen using a common grazing land.

Hardin's argument rests on a number of assumptions:

- It assumes that there is no authority, either local or State, regulating the decisions of individual herdsmen and restricting their decisions in regard to use of the commons; essentially he is confusing common property with open access.
- It assumes that individual herdsmen make decisions purely from a short-term, self-interested perspective.
- It assumes that individual herdsmen are in some sense ignorant of the dangers of over-use of grazing resources.

There is another possibility, not clearly spelt out by Hardin but consistent with his argument. Individuals may have made a calculation that, if they do not exploit these resources, another user will, and therefore they will suffer the losses imposed by the second user without gaining any of the benefit accruing in the short-term from using the resource. This is a problem of lack of assurance. In such circumstances each user may indeed be compelled to *rush towards ruin* – but may be doing so in the full knowledge that such a strategy is not in their best long-term interests. This situation does indeed occur, but such circumstances are more typical of discontinuities in the property system, i.e., where property rights become uncertain.

7.3.3 Institutional Arrangements

In view of the *tragedy of the commons,* one can see that an effective institution could address all of them. An effective institution could:

- set rules which govern use of the resource;
- encourage long-term co-operative behaviour; and
- provide information on the risks of overuse of a resource; and provide a stable environment where people could have assurance that their restraint in using resources would be matched by the restraint of others.

These actions illustrate the importance of institutional arrangements. They provide a reasonably predictable framework within which individuals can conduct productive activities securely. Without such a framework, insecurity sets in and creates the environment within which people take a short-term, self-interested view. The result tends to be over-exploitation and degradation of resources, and the consequent impoverishment of people dependent on those resources.

In relation to the management of common property resources, the kinds of institutions/organisations which have been observed to work most effectively are community-based organisations of resource users. In other words, the resource users self-organise and self-regulate.

In short, according to Burns and Admassie (1994), "...***the institution consists of a system of authority and power.***"

7.3.4 Institutions, Poverty and Community-Based Property Resources

The issue of the sustainable management of common property resources (CPR) is complex and requires much more detailed study. It is important to be aware of the importance of institutions and organisations at different levels, as critical elements of the development process.

Secondly, the nature of institutions and organisations is important in terms of impacts on poverty. For example, community-based common property resource management systems tend to permit inclusion of a well-defined group (and exclusion of others), compared with the alienation and more extensive exclusion processes that would result from privatisation of a resource. This inclusion tends to promote relative equality in income derived from a common property resource, and also tends to provide a valuable source of income and/or produce for poor households.

Dasgupta and Maler (1993) noted from their studies in India that:

(a) Income inequalities are less where CPRs are more prominent (although average incomes also tend to be lowest in such areas).

(b) The proportion of income of poor households derived direct from CPRs in certain areas is high (15–25 per cent).

(c) CPRs are particularly important for poor households in times of unusual economic stress (for example, a drought).

Dasgupta and Maler suggest that

> "It is not difficult to see why common-property resources matter greatly to the poorest of the rural poor in a society, or therefore, to understand the mechanisms by which such people may well get disfranchised from the economy even while in the aggregate the society enjoys economic growth. If you are steeped in social norms of behaviour and understand community contractual obligations, you do not calculate every five minutes how you should behave. You follow the norms. This saves on costs all round, not only for you as an "actor", but also for you as "policeman" and "judge". It is also the natural thing for you to do if you have internalised the norms. But this is sustainable so long as the background environment remains pretty much constant. It will not be sustainable if the social environment changes suddenly.

> You may even be destroyed. It is this heightened vulnerability, often more real than perceived, which is the cause of some of the greatest tragedies in contemporary society. They descend upon people who are, in the best of circumstances, acutely vulnerable". —DASGUPTA AND MALER (2000)

CPRs are therefore important to the survival of poor households, and the destruction of a CPR can be, and historically has been, a major source of socio-economic tragedy. Also, we can note that, given a recognition that a CPR is important to the survival of a group of households, it is *collectively rational* for those households to stick to the norms. Any deviation from the norms is not therefore likely to occur instantaneously, let us say due to a change in relative prices of commodities which can be produced from a CPR: it needs a more fundamental shock to the system to promote such change. Dasgupta and Maler (1993) suggest some possible causes of the erosion of CPRs:

> "...shifting populations (accompanying the growth process itself), rising populations and the consequent pressure on these resources, technological progress, unreflective public policies, predatory governments, and thieving aristocracies."

How can successful institutions be developed to manage common property resources? Ostrom identifies what she terms eight "design principles", by which she means "an essential element or condition that helps to account for the success of these institutions in sustaining the CPRs and gaining the compliance of generation after generation of appropriators to the rides in use" (Ostrom, 1990).

These design principles are given in Table 7.1. Although the design principles in Table 7.1 are at a somewhat general level and therefore lack some explanatory power, they nonetheless provide a good basis for the identification of key factors influencing the effective functioning of CPR institutions.

Table 7.1: Design principles illustrated by long-enduring CPR institutions

	Design principles
1.	Clearly defined boundaries Individuals or households who have rights to withdraw resource units from the CPR must be clearly defined, as must the boundaries of the CPR itself.
2.	Congruence between appropriation and provision rules and local conditions. Appropriation rules restricting time, place, technology, and/or quantity of resource units are related to local conditions and to provision rules requiring labour, material, and/or money.

Contd...

Contd...

3.	Collective-choice arrangements Most individuals affected by the operational rules can participate in modifying the operational rules.
4.	Monitoring Monitors, who actively audit CPR conditions and appropriate behaviour, are accountable to the appropriators or are the appropriators.
5.	Graduated sanctions Appropriators who violate operational rules are likely to be assessed graduated sanctions (depending on the seriousness and context of the offence) by other appropriators, by officials accountable to these appropriators, or by both.
6.	Conflict-resolution mechanisms Appropriators and their officials have rapid access to low-cost local arenas to resolve conflicts among appropriators or between appropriators and officials.
7.	Minimal recognition of rights to organise The rights of appropriators to devise their own institutions are not challenged by external governmental authorities.
8.	For CPRs that are parts of larger systems Nested enterprises Appropriation, provision, monitoring, enforcement, conflict resolution, and governance activities are organised in multiple layers of nested enterprises.

Source: Ostrom 1990.

CHAPTER 8

Linkages between Agriculture and Rural Development

CHAPTER OUTLINE

- Trends in rural/agriculture thinking
  - 1950s – Emphasis on Economic Growth through Industrialization
  - 1960s – Emphasis on Industrial and Agricultural Growth through Green Revolution
  - The Green Revolution
  - Criticism of the Green Revolution
  - 1970s – Redistribution through – Integrated Rural Development Programmes (IRDP)
  - 1980s – Structural Adjustment through NGOs and Emergency Relief
  - 1990s – Poverty Reduction Gains Prominence Again
  - 2000s – Current Viewpoints
- Agricultural Development vis-a-vis Rural Development
  - Rural Diversification
  - Scope of Rural Development
- The Role of Agriculture in Economic Development
- Linkages between Agriculture and Non-Agriculture Sector
- Geographical Classification of Potential Agricultural Areas
- Environment and Development

8.1. TRENDS IN RURAL/AGRICULTURE THINKING

Generally, thinking about rural and agricultural development reflects thinking about development. Traditionally, agriculture was seen as playing a passive and supportive role in achieving development aspirations that rested on rapid industrialization. Agriculture's role was to supply food, labour and surpluses to facilitate the expansion of the industrial and urban sectors. However, a new view has emerged that sees rural and agricultural development playing a dynamic role in a country's development. This view acknowledges the importance of agricultural development in:

- Driving economic growth
- Reducing poverty
- Providing employment
- Ensuring food security.

In parallel with development thinking, rural development has witnessed shifts between the relative importance of the market and the state; and between the productive and social sectors over time.

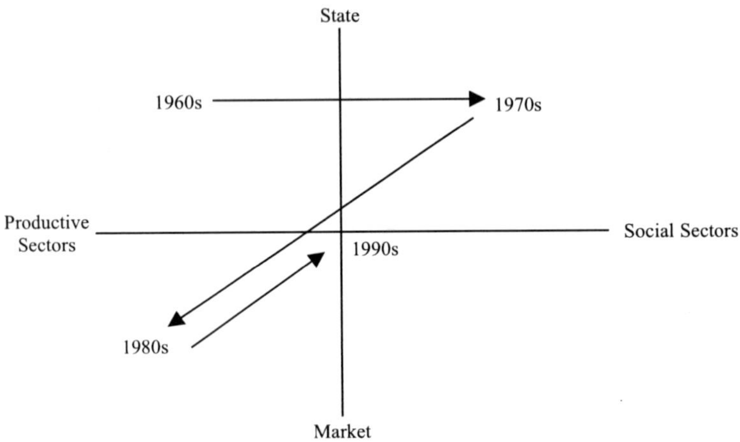

Fig. 8.1 Rural development thinking (1960s–90s). *Source:* ODI (2002)

In Figure 8.1, ODI (2002) illustrates the shifts in priorities in rural development models over time. In the 1960s, the *Green Revolution* was characterised by large-scale State investment in infrastructure, research, and support for the adoption of new technologies with the productive sectors being prioritised. In the 1970s priorities shifted to social investments in the context of IRDP, and the State continued to play a leading role. The 1980s saw the State being rolled back and markets being prioritised, while the 1990s witnessed increased interest in poverty reduction, sustainable livelihoods and a more balanced approach between the State and the market and between the productive and social sectors.

There are a number of schools of thought/ideas in relation to agriculture and rural development. Models focussing on small farm development have been put forward since the 1950s and have been allied to community development, intensive agricultural development, integrated rural development, participatory approaches, sustainable agriculture and livelihood approaches all of which have been competing for policy space. Different models have existed and continue to exist simultaneously, have fallen out of favour and subsequently been reworked and adapted. In

Table 8.1 Maxwell and Percy (2001) outlined the evolution of development thinking and its relation to the predominant agriculture and rural development thinking over decade-long periods.

Table 8.1: Evolution of thinking about agriculture, 1950s–1990s

Period	*Dominant Development Paradigm*	*Agricultural Strategy*
1950s	Growth through industrialisation	Community development
1960s	Growth through industry and agriculture	Green revolution
1970s	Redistribution with growth and basic needs	Integrated rural development
1980s	Structural adjustment	NGOs/emergency Rrelief
1990s	Poverty reduction	Small scale credit/linking relief and development/sustainable livelihoods/participation

Source: Maxwell (1998) in Maxwell and Percy (2001).

8.1.1 1950s Emphasis on Economic Growth Through Industrialization

The primary emphasis during this period was on economic growth to be achieved through industrialization. The rural sector was largely neglected and its function was to provide labour, food and finance to facilitate industrialisation. Most interventions were primarily community based investments and welfare. Interventions included public irrigation, land reforms, promoting co-operatives and community development projects.

8.1.2 1960s Emphasis on Industrial and Agriculture Growth Through Green Revolution

While the emphasis was still very much on economic growth a more positive predisposition developed towards agriculture, as it was increasingly recognised that agriculture could contribute to growth. This view was supported by the productivity gains that resulted with the spread of the Green Revolution in India, Mexico and South Asia. Also, increasing agricultural output was essential to provide food for a rapidly growing population. The priority was therefore one of increasing productivity in high potential areas.

8.1.3 The Green Revolution

Essentially, the Green Revolution consisted of increasing the output of farmers through the provision of a package of biochemical inputs that included high yielding varieties, fertilisers and water. Output was increased through increasing yields, areas cultivated and the number of crops grown in a year. Intervention therefore focussed on research, agricultural extension, and provision of inputs, credit and infrastructure in high potential areas.

The Green Revolution offered a number of attractive features as an agricultural development policy. Principal amongst these was that the technology was said to be scale-neutral. This meant that large landholdings were not needed for the technologies to be economically viable, as in the case of mechanisation. It promised equal access to the benefits and was thereby seen as a possibility to compensate for inequalities in land distribution and to counter pressure for land redistribution. As industrialisation dominated the development paradigm at the time, the other attractive feature was that it provided a strategy for providing cheap food to growing urban populations.

While the applicability of the Green Revolution may have been scale-neutral it was not resource-neutral. To benefit from it required access to irrigation, good soil, technical assistance, credit and infrastructure and institutions such as roads and markets. The main critiques of the Green Revolution are broadly based on the fact that it did not address the plight of those who lacked these resources.

The uncontested achievement of the Green Revolution was that it was effective in increasing agricultural productivity and output, but it has been criticised for a number of reasons as given below:

8.1.4 Criticism of the Green Revolution

Geographic inequalities

As a strategy that focused principally on high potential areas it led to inequality between countries and within countries. Countries in South and South-East Asia benefited most. Within countries intervention was focused on high potential areas. This resulted in those living in low potential areas, where poverty was concentrated, being neglected.

Socio-economic inequalities

Rich farmers and those that had better access to resources benefited more than poor farmers so it led to rising inequalities between rich and poor peasants. Rural poverty still remains extensive in areas that adopted the *Green Revolution*.

Health effects

The use of pesticides and herbicides and their poor management has had negative health impacts. Also it has been argued that since research favoured certain crops, primarily wheat, rice and maize, this led to a bias against crops such as sorghum and millet, which are widely grown in low-potential areas.

Environmental effects

It has also been criticised because of the loss of genetic biodiversity resulting from widespread use of high yielding varieties and a bias towards monoculture, as well as causing pollution and damaging wildlife through the use of chemical inputs.

8.1.5 1970s Redistribution Through Integrated Rural Development Programmes (IRDP)

In the 1970s, there was increasing disillusionment with the pursuit of economic growth as a development strategy because poverty, inequality and unemployment persisted. This led to increasing attention being given to basic needs, redistribution and poverty reduction. The counterpart of this was found in the expansion of *Integrated Rural Development Programmes* (IRDP).

Integrated Rural Development has been defined as:

> "A comprehensive and coordinated approach of all persons and agencies concerned, aimed at involving rural people in determining policies and planning and implementing programs that are designed to improve their economic, social and cultural conditions and enable them to make a positive contribution to national development."
>
> —Abasiekong, E (1982)

The underlying premise of IRDP was that rural poverty could be combated by supplying the poor with a broad based package including credit, extension services, green revolution technology, water, roads, health, education and non-farm sources of employment. As such it focussed on investments in production, production support and social infrastructure in defined geographic areas, and intervention through a multi-sectoral and multi-agency approach. Fundamental to the approach, was that beneficiaries were to be active participants in the planning and implementation of the programmes and the package of inputs adapted to local conditions. It differed from the *Green Revolution* approach to the extent that it was intended to target poorer areas and the rural poor and placed greater emphasis on social investments.

According to Grindle (1982) the *Integrated Rural Development* approach was attractive for a number of reasons. It allowed public policies to work with two sectors of the agricultural economy with different types of policies. One sector was promoting the expansion of commercial agriculture and the other responding to poverty. The approach also reaffirmed previous experience from expanding the agricultural frontier, agrarian reform and agricultural modernisation, which indicated that increasing production required inputs in addition to land. Politically, it was attractive as it proposed to diminish rural poverty without requiring land redistribution and would counter rural unrest. Overall Grindle argues that these programmes have been effective in delivering public goods and services to the needy rural areas.

However a number of concerns/limitations have been identified by Grindle (1982) and summarised from other sources by Norton (2004). These include both context issues and implementation problems:

- The policy of environment
- Expensive
- Organisational problems
- Beneficiary participation
- Lack of appropriate research

Policy of environment

Grindle (1982) identified both political and economic constraints in achieving the objectives of the programmes in the case of Mexico and Colombia. She argues that the main priority of the governments continued to be growth and industrialisation and policies maintained an overall urban bias. As such IRDs were an add-on to this paradigm and did not mark a reorientation of national development policy. Their conceptualisation tended to be more palliative than addressing the contentious underlying issues of poverty and under-productivity such as land reforms and access to water. Therefore, the overriding commitment to the objective of achieving rural development and reducing rural poverty was lacking.

Expensive

Such programmes were expensive and this became problematic at the beginning of 1980s with the emergence of the debt crisis and associated financial austerity. With a reduction in the availability of public resources and increased competition from different sectors it became difficult to continue funding large public programmes. Again growth became the dominant development mantra and emphasis was placed on commercial export-oriented agriculture.

Organisational problems

Coordination and cooperation amongst national, regional and local agencies became the main stumbling block with the process becoming extremely bureaucratic. Often the result was a scatter of projects and interventions that lacked a coherent local development strategy. Institutional capacity-building was often overlooked as special coordination units, often staffed by outsiders, were established to coordinate the projects thereby limiting the development of local capacity.

Beneficiary participation

While beneficiary participation was to be fundamental to the approach, a top-down centralised approach would more accurately describe the reality of projects. Grindle (1982) believes that the empowement of local population was hindered because it was seen as a direct threat to the status quo.

Lack of appropriate research

This proved to be a special problem for African countries where there was little commitment and a failure to develop improved technologies that were applicable to rain-fed areas and of benefit to the rural poor.

8.1.6 1980s – Structural Adjustment – Through NGOs and Emergency Relief

The 1980s was dominated by structural adjustment. Both the predominance of neo-liberal thinking and the debt crisis resulted in the rolling back of the State and increasing reliance on the market. The implications for the rural sector were large cutbacks in development programmes such as IRDP and the services offered by the State such as agricultural extension, credit, inputs, subsidised fertilisers, etc. To a limited extent NGOs began to fill the vacuum left by the State and donors in the provision of services. The predominant paradigm again was growth, which prioritised market forces and productive sectors with support to smaller, traditional producers being severely curtailed. The need to generate foreign exchange earnings to meet debt repayments would place increasing importance on export-oriented agribusiness, high potential areas and cash crops.

As the 1980s advanced it became clear that the impact of structural adjustment was being associated with growing poverty and development reversals, which led to increased questioning of this approach. Another important feature of the 1980s was the impact of drought and famine in Africa, leading to increasing reliance on emergency relief. This highlighted the importance of food security and raised the issues of tackling poverty, looking at low potential areas and food crops.

Debate on Cash and Food Crops

There are arguments for and against cash crops especially in countries that are in food deficit. Those in favour of cash crops see it as a route to growth, diversification and prosperity. Those against see them as creating dependency and poverty. Table 8.2 summarises the arguments outlined by Maxwell (n.d.) for and against cash crops.

Table 8.2: Arguments for and against cash crops

Areas	*For*	*Against*
Growth	Cash crops allow farmers and countries to exploit comparative advantage, increasing individual incomes and promoting economic growth	Comparative advantage is not a good guide because it can change quickly
	Upstream and downstream linkages promote growth	Benefits leak from the economy
Income distribution	Cash crops can promote small farm development	Cash crops are mostly associated with plantations and large farms

Food security	By increasing the incomes of the poor cash crops allow them spread their production and marketing risks thereby improving their food security	Depending on who has control over cash it can affect allocation of food within households. It is often stated that access to food for women and children may become worse as cash crops substitute food crops
Dependency		Reliance on market makes producers vulnerable to competition and price changes
Environment	Improves tree cover, promotes more appropriate use of technology and land	Results in monoculture, reduces biodiversity, increases use of pesticides and herbicides

With respect to the evidence of the impact of cash cropping Maxwell (n.d.) reviews a number of studies that show that cash cropping can be of benefit to the poor. These studies show that increased cash cropping had no significant impact on subsistence food production, and generally led to increase in employment and income. Though income led to increases in nutrition this effect was modest because of a number of leakages such as non-food expenditure, changes in distribution of food within the households, changes in composition of diet and constraints of the general health care environment. Overall Maxwell is optimistic about the potential of cash crops but suggests a set of strategic guidelines for policy to maximise the benefit of cash crops for the poor.

8.1.7 1990s Poverty Reduction Gains Prominence Again

The 1990s led to poverty reduction once again being placed centre stage. Since the majority of the poor live in rural areas there was renewed interest in agriculture and rural development. However, unlike the large integrated rural development and government interventionist programmes of the 1970s, this time there was more interest in smaller market-led rural credit programmes and demand-led agricultural extension services. In relation to production, sustainable agriculture gained prominence. Debt relief also created a greater incentive for increased social investments in areas such as health and education.

(a) Sustainable Agricultural Development

Sustainable agriculture also needs to be viewed within the broader context of concerns to promote sustainable development, as formally laid down at the United Nations Conference on Environment and Development (UNCED) in 1992.

Sustainable development as a goal has many dimensions, and given the continued importance of agriculture as a source of livelihood for a majority of people in a majority of developing countries, there are many ways in which agriculture and sustainable development interact.

One element of the *Agenda 21* programme is a broad range of actions for conservation and management of resources for development, including promoting sustainable agriculture and rural development, and actions for the management of fragile ecosystems, combating deforestation and rational management and use of fisheries resources. All of these areas are relevant to agricultural development, broadly defined, and are essentially concerned with the sound management of natural resources in ways that: (a) contribute to livelihoods; and (b) do not deplete the underlying resource base.

Box 1: Relationships between agricultural growth, poverty alleviation and environmental sustainability

How to Win-Win-Win: virtuous relationships between agricultural growth, poverty alleviation and environmental sustainability

Hazell (1999) notes that there is a continued need for agricultural growth in developing countries which must be equitable – to alleviate poverty and address food insecurity issues – and must sustain the natural resource base. These triple aims are not necessarily complementary, but are more likely to be so when agricultural development is (a) broad based, involving small and medium farmers, (b) market driven, (c) participatory and decentralised, and (d) driven by technological change which enhances factor productivity but does not degrade the resource base. Hazell proposes some key points to address each of the three key issues:

Agricultural growth

Conventional development thinking on the requirements for agricultural "transformation" focussed on the five I's, which are still seen as relevant:

1. Innovation – through agricultural research and extension
2. Infrastructure
3. Inputs
4. Institutions
5. Incentives.

Poverty reduction

In terms of the ways in which agricultural development can contribute to poverty reduction, Hazell terms these the "equity modifiers":

- Promote broad-based agricultural development, with priority given to small and medium farms in terms of publicly-funded agricultural research and extension, and in marketing, credit and input supplies

- Undertake land reforms where necessary. Invest in human capital (e.g. education, clean water, healthcare and nutrition, support to family planning services, etc.)
- Ensure all agricultural supports as well as human capital programmes reach rural women
- Involve all rural stakeholders in setting priorities for public investments
- Actively encourage the rural non-farm economy.

Environmental sustainability

In order for equity-oriented agricultural development to be environmentally sustainable, Hazell proposes the following *environmental modifiers:*

- Give higher priority to less favoured ("low potential") areas even though they may be resource-poor
- Pay more attention in agricultural research to sustainability aspects of recommended technologies, to broader natural resource management issues (e.g. at watershed level), and to specific problems of resource-poor areas
- Ensure that farmers have secure property rights (which can be based on indigenous tenure systems)
- Strengthen community management systems on common property resources (or privatise if there are no negative externalities or equity factors involved in doing so)
- Address externality problems through a variety of instruments
- Improve the performance of relevant public institutions involved in managing and regulating natural resources, and devolve management to resource users where possible
- Correct price distortions which encourage excessive use of modern inputs in intensive agriculture, for example, by removing subsidies on fertiliser and pesticide use (fertiliser subsidies might still be justified in low-productivity areas)
- Establish resource monitoring systems and environmental education programmes.

Source: Hazell 1999

The link between sustainable livelihoods and sustainable resource management, and the possibilities for *win-win* developments addressing both issues simultaneously, is one of the key areas of focus of current development policy and practice, essentially because it addresses the two key development priorities of alleviating poverty and reversing environmental degradation. In fact there is a broad consensus on the need to focus on the "critical triangle" (Scherr, 1999) of the poverty-agriculture-environment nexus, although that still leaves many questions open on how to proceed and prioritise. Ideally, the aim is to find *win-win-win* approaches (Hazell 1999, see Box 1) in terms of agricultural growth, poverty alleviation and environmental sustainability.

(b) Consensus on Sustainable Agricultural Development

Box 1 provides a basis for prioritisation at a broad level. However, there are still many different views on what sustainable agricultural development is, and what are the specific implications in terms of livelihood outcomes, levels of input use, research priorities, etc. For example, some researchers and analysts tend to equate sustainable agriculture with low external-input approaches and an emphasis on *agro ecological technologies* as a means to sustainable natural resource management (e.g., Altieri, 2000). Other researchers note that inorganic input use in sub-Saharan Africa is at extremely low levels compared to other developing countries (on average 9 kg/ha, compared with over 50 kg/ha in Latin America and over 80 kg/ha in Asia, Kelly et al., 1998), and that "*outside Africa, as much as 75 per cent of crop yield increases since the mid-1960s are directly or indirectly attributable to fertiliser use*" (Reardon et al., 1999). Lack of consensus is even more clear-cut in the case of the potential for biotechnology.

What is generally agreed on is the need for increased yields, for sustainable agricultural intensification. The issue is how to intensify production sustainably. There is a need for diversification in terms of agricultural development strategies. For example, whereas previously there was an emphasis on the need to increase aggregate food output by focussing on high potential areas (the *Green Revolution* approach), there is now a general view that agricultural development efforts should also focus on low potential areas which, it turns out, also have agricultural potential, as well as being the areas where the majority of the rural poor live.

Whereas previously there was a tendency to focus either on export-oriented cash crop production (to earn foreign exchange) or on food crop production (to meet local food needs), there is now a greater appreciation of the need for more differentiated approaches which support both cash and food crop production and seek potential complementarities in doing so. Agricultural development strategies therefore tend to have a greater focus on:

- The complexities involved in promoting agricultural development within the framework of poverty reduction and environmental sustainability; and
- The need for approaches stratified by agro-ecology, food security status, levels of degradation, degree of market and institutional development, etc.

In more narrowly focused discussions of sustainable agricultural intensification, there are a number of critical debates on pathways to sustainable agricultural development. Reardon (et al.) distinguish between capital-led intensification and labour-led intensification. They suggest capital-led intensification is necessary for sustainability, and involve substantial use of non-labour variable inputs, which enhance soil fertility (e.g. organic and inorganic fertiliser) and investment in quasi-fixed capital (particularly land and water conservation infrastructure), which increases labour productivity. Labour-led intensification is defined by high levels of dependence on labour as a variable production input, with little augmentation by other inputs. Ultimately, Reardon (et al.) note that a combination of intensive land use and insufficient use of quasi-fixed and variable capital, results in soil mining and degradation — *non-sustainable intensification.* They also note that abolition of fertiliser subsidies has in some areas caused a switch from a sustainable intensification to a non-sustainable intensification path where both farm incomes and soil fertility are likely to be reduced (Reardon et al., 1999).

However, advocates of agro-ecological approaches do not necessarily agree that substantially increased use of inorganic fertiliser is essential to increase yields and output. Agro-ecological approaches provide *"ecological principles for the design and management of sustainable and resource-conserving agricultural systems"* (Altieri, 2000). They involve integration of biophysical processes to minimise use of external inputs and increase output; agro-ecology usually implies the use of multifunctional technologies such as use of cover crops, intercropping, agro-forestry, and integrated crop-livestock systems including aquaculture. Agro-ecological approaches generally start from existing systems and make use of farmers' local knowledge. Therefore, they generally involve the use of a variety of techniques for participatory technology development. They also tend to be labour-intensive, involving considerable labour input for organic soil fertilisation and other processes. However, advocates of agro-ecological approaches see increased labour use as an efficient and productive use of underemployed labour, not as an example of non-sustainable intensification.

Altieri notes that NGO-supported projects to promote agro-ecological approaches have had notable successes, increasing yields in some marginal lands from 0.4–0.6 m.t./ha to 2–2.5 m.t./ha; maize yields can reach 3–4 m.t./ha where organic management techniques are emphasised. There are also other benefits in terms of enhanced general agro biodiversity. Pretty (1995) provides many examples of success stories, some at quite a large scale, where a combination of the use of resource-conserving technologies and the development of effective local institutions resulted in significantly increased yields. In all such cases there were technological and/or institutional innovations, which were key to the increased output.

Two key points in relation to the development of agro-ecological approaches are:

- their site-specificity; and
- the importance of local institutional development.

The issue of site-specificity is evident enough, but it runs counter to the aim of much previous – and still current in some areas – agricultural research and food self-sufficiency approaches which sought growth in output through a move towards high-yielding monocultures. There is tension between the two approaches, although there may be some *high-potential* areas where the latter approach might have a greater prospect of success.

(c) Role of Local Institutions

The importance of local institutional development follows from the fact that many agro-ecological techniques imply:

(a) Learning between farmers at local level;

(b) Co-operation/collective action to maximise the benefits of such techniques, for example, the benefits of Integrated Pest Management (IPM) or soil and water conservation structures on a catchment can only be realised through collective action.

Local institutional development is more widely needed, and may need to be facilitated since it may not emerge automatically. This partly depends on the *enabling environment.* However, this collective action has needed subsidisation (through *Food or Cash for Work)* since, as a result of chronic food insecurity, farmers might migrate to find seasonal work rather than engage in non-subsidised conservation work. This is what Reardon (et al.) refer to as the need to invest in quasi-fixed capital.

Most interpretations of sustainable agriculture feature the reduction of external inputs and optimising locally available resources while also looking at the enhancement of natural and socio-cultural resources. Other interpretations place greater restrictions on the type of external inputs which can be used such as organic farming which prohibits the use of artificial fertilisers and agrochemicals; while others look at addressing environmental degradation while remaining open about the use of external inputs.

Sustainable agriculture has been useful in promoting broader thinking about agriculture and its role in development as well as highlighting the complexities of promoting agriculture development while simultaneously looking at poverty reduction and environmental sustainability.

8.1.8 2000s, Current Viewpoints

In its paper *Rethinking Rural Development* the Overseas Development Institute (ODI, UK, 2002) outlines a view of current thinking on rural development. While acknowledging the role of small farm agriculture, it suggests that the importance of this is lessening and that diversity and differentiation of rural situations needs more attention. This therefore requires strategies linked to the non-farm rural economy, employment creation in commercial farming and welfare strategies. It also argues for a larger role for the State than it currently has. While there is consensus about the need to take a diversified approach by looking at the social sectors, rural employment creation and non-farm rural economy, the debate on the relative importance of the small farm model is likely to continue.

Box 2: Consensus on rural development

The ODI paper identifies four principles for a successful rural development strategy, and 11 more specific recommendations. A successful rural development strategy should:

- recognise the great diversity of rural situations;
- respond to past and future changes in rural areas;
- be consistent with wider poverty reduction and decentralisation policy;
- make the case for the productive sectors in rural development, as a strategy both to maximise growth and to reduce poverty.

Specifically, a rural development strategy should aim to:

- offer different options for peri-urban, rural and remote locations;
- invest in agriculture, non-farm rural enterprise, and linkages between them;
- expand diversification options for multi-occupational and multi-locational households;
- recognise that market institutions need to be in place before liberalisation, and that states have a key role to play, for example, in supplying (national and global) public goods;
- include explicit measures to address inequality in assets and incomes;
- counter the anti-South bias of technical change, and include public support to research;
- promote agricultural strategies consistent with natural resource protection, including water management;
- increase investment in infrastructure and human capital;
- respond to the 'obligation' to protect the poor, with new social protection measures, including for people in conflict areas, and with HIV/AIDS;
- propose pragmatic steps for democratic deepening in rural areas; and
- identify the place for agriculture and rural development in PRSPs and sector programmes.

Source: ODI (2002)

8.2 AGRICULTURAL DEVELOPMENT VIS-A-VIS RURAL DEVELOPMENT

In countries (such as India) where the majority of the population lives in rural areas, and particularly where there are problems of food insecurity and poverty, it is not surprising that the main focus of policy in rural areas is on agriculture. The stress is usually on how to increase agricultural production. It often appears that agricultural development policy and rural development policy is essentially the same thing.

This experience is not limited to developing countries. In Ireland, for example, from the early 1970s until the late 1980s, rural development policy and agricultural policy were more or less synonymous. Agriculture was still a very important component of the economy. In fact, farm households made up the majority of the rural population, and a significant percentage of the total population. Only from the late 1980s onwards and influenced by policy in the European Union did a distinctive rural development policy emerge in Ireland which clearly went beyond agriculture.

Rural development goes beyond a focus on agriculture. However, agricultural development will generally be an important component of rural development. There is increasing evidence that many rural households gain a livelihood partly by engaging in activities outside agriculture.

8.2.1 Rural Diversification

Many studies of rural households in developing countries have shown a high level of rural diversification. For example, Reardon et al. (1999) found, in a review of 28 field studies, that the average share of non-farm income in total income (measured in cash and kind) was 45 per cent. Other studies quoted in Delgado (1999) show non-farm income in a range of 25–50 per cent of total income, while Ellis (1999) notes that in southern Africa non-farm income might comprise 80–90 per cent of total income. This is an indication of the need to focus beyond agricultural elements of rural activities.

There is some disagreements on whether high levels of diversification are likely to contribute positively to development and household livelihood security, or not. Two opposing views are as follows:

- Reardon et al. (1999), for example, note that, particularly in the absence of reliable rural financial systems, non-farm income sources might provide the necessary financial resources required for capital-led agricultural intensification.

- Delgado (1997) however suggests that the high levels of diversification are essentially part of small holders' risk management strategies, and that increased specialisation will ultimately be required to make the productivity gains needed for sustainable agricultural intensification, which will ultimately contribute to broad-based economic development.

Both of these analysts focus on the need for sustainable agricultural intensification, which they equate with increased specialisation and higher yields of the main food and cash crops. Other analysts are more inclined to believe that diversification is a long-term feature of the rural economy and in many respects desirable. Diversification is currently important for African small holders.

Ellis (1999) discusses a number of positive benefits of diversification.

- **Seasonality effects**–i.e., the fact that agricultural income is lumpy while consumption requirements are continuous – this can be mitigated through diversification, which provides alternative and more continuous sources of income.
- **Risks of income failure**– e.g., due to drought, which can be minimised by having an additional income source, e.g., wage labour.
- **Higher income** – if labour is underemployed on-farm, higher total incomes can be achieved through diversification.
- **Asset improvement** – cash resources generated by diversification can be used to build up assets, which are fundamental to sustainable livelihoods.
- **Environmental benefits** – these can result either through diversification generating assets which are used to upgrade the quality of natural resources (e.g., tree planting), and/or by providing alternative income sources which reduce the pressure on natural resources.
- **Gender benefits** – diversification may improve the independent income-generating capability of women, which also has a positive spin-off for children's welfare.

However Ellis also cites some observed negative effects of diversification.

- **Income distribution** – the better-off are often more able to diversify into more remunerative activities, thereby increasing the gap between better-off and poor households.
- **Farm output** – diversification which results in depletion of on-farm labour resources can be detrimental to farm output, as has happened in southern Africa.
- **Adverse gender effects** – if men are best placed to take advantage of diversification opportunities, this may result in women being exclusively confined to the domestic sphere.

In terms of securing livelihoods, it is clear that non-farm income is increasingly important, and therefore part of policy needs to be geared towards recognising, and then enhancing the opportunities for, diversification. However, in some respects the extent of off-farm diversification also indicates the failure of agriculture to ensure adequate livelihoods for large numbers of rural households in India (and elsewhere). Therefore, it remains valid to seek to enhance productivity and incomes in agriculture as a major component of broader livelihood strategies.

It has been shown that a focus on productive sectors involves more than just a focus on agriculture, although agriculture is very important. Rural development also involves going beyond the productive sectors, as we have discussed.

8.2.2 Scope of Rural Development

There are different ways of thinking about rural development, and of categorising the key activities that it comprises. One way is to think in terms of core productive activities, enabling activities, and broader activities. Another way is to think of key productive sectors, the enabling environment, and social sectors. A third way is to think in terms of the different types of capital required for rural development.

The first two categories are essentially similar, varying mostly in terminology. (Table 8.3)

Table 8.3: Rural development: scope and examples

Activity/sector	*Examples*
Productive activities/ sectors	Agriculture, small-scale enterprise, mining, etc.
Enabling activities/ enabling environment	Rural infrastructure, market development, financial support, legal framework, responsive governance system, active gender and environment policies, etc.
Broader activities/social sectors	Health, education, water and sanitation, literacy, etc.

There is no attempt here to suggest any particular sequence in which these activities should occur. In general they are mutually reinforcing, so that in principle there is logic in pursuing them simultaneously. In reality however, financial and other resource constraints (e.g., shortage of skilled technical manpower in some areas, lack of or high price of construction materials, etc.) will force development agencies to prioritise. In such a situation, support to basic infrastructure development, to the core productive sector(s), and to the core social sectors of primary healthcare, primary and secondary schooling, and basic village water supply, are probably the priority areas.

Table 8.4: Five types of capital required for rural development*

Capital	*Characteristics/areas of deficit*
Human capital	Low education levels, inadequate relevant training
Social capital	Low levels of community organisation
Physical capital	Inadequate physical infrastructure (roads, communications, irrigation water, etc.)
Institutional capital	Weak agricultural research and extension poorly developed rural financial systems, unclear tenure rules over common resources, weak contract enforcement, etc.
Private physical capital	Inadequate land availability or on-farm investments.

**Table is based on discussion in Norton (2004).*

In Table 8.4 the focus is on building up capital – which is seen as a pre-requisite for a process of sustained development.

It is imperative to look a bit more closely at some of these components of rural development approaches, and has been done in the following sections. Table 8.5 summarises some of the key intervention areas in agricultural and rural development, and measures the strength of their impact on key development goals of poverty reduction, food security, sustainable management of natural resources, and gender equity.

Table 8.5: Key intervention areas for rural development

	Poverty reduction	*Food security*	*Sustainable NRM*	*Gender equity*
Physical infrastructure. (roads, etc.)		x		
Short-term food access (cash-for-work, etc.)	x	xx		x
Agricultural research	x	x		x
Agricultural extension	x	x		x
Market information and market development	x	x		x
Rural finance	xx	x		xx
Partnership development	x	x		x
Local institutional development	x	x	x	x

Contd...

Contd...

Livelihoods analyses	x	x	x	x
Capacity-building support (participatory methods, etc.)	x	x	x	x
Support to land reform/land tenure reform	x	x	x	xx
Support to women's groups and gender approaches of service organisation	x	x	x	xx
Promoting win-win solutions to NR degradation	x	x	xx	x
Support preventative veterinary services and animal feed issues		x		x
Support co-management of NR (including forest and fishing areas)	x	x	xx	x
Support for micro-enterprise development	x	x		x
Irrigation development	x	x	x	x
Development of primary healthcare, primary education and local water supply	xx	x	x	x
Electrification & communications	x			
Regional balances in development	x			

The assessment of impacts in Table 8.5 is not absolute. For example, most of these interventions are capable of having positive impacts on gender equity, but will not necessarily do so unless there is a strong policy commitment to it. Similarly, some may disagree with the assessment that infrastructural development contributes to poverty reduction — but it does so indirectly by providing basic facilities to stimulate economic development. Table 8.5, however, shows the scope of rural development actions required to address problems of poverty and development in a comprehensive manner.

8.3 THE ROLE OF AGRICULTURE IN ECONOMIC DEVELOPMENT

> *"It is in the agricultural sector that the battle for long-term economic development will be won or lost."*
>
> —Gunnar Myrdal
> Nobel Laureate in Economics

Although the role of the agricultural sector has been declining, it continues to be a critically important sector in the economies of developing countries. Over 58% of the rural households depend on agriculture as their principal means of livelihood. Agriculture, along with fisheries is one of the largest contributors to the Gross Domestic Product in India. Agriculture exports in India constitute 10% of the exports and is the fourth largest exported principal commodity. Indeed, for a number of countries, such as Ethiopia, Myanmar, Democratic Republic of Congo and the Central African Republic it accounts for over 50 per cent of GDP. Table 8.6 chart changes in:

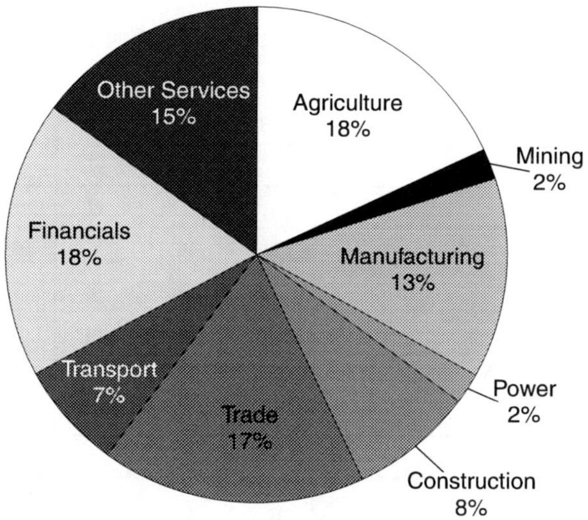

Fig. 8.2 Agricultural share of GDP

(a) agriculture as a share of GDP;

(b) the share of labour force in agriculture; and

(c) primary commodities as a share of merchandise exports, for the main developing regions and the world from the 1960s through to the 1990s.

Although there are variations in the regions, the overall trend shows that the contribution of agriculture to GDP and exports has declined, as has the labour force involved in agriculture. This decline has been more in areas such as South Asia and East Asia.

Table 8.6: Main changes in the agricultural sector 1960–1997

(a) Agriculture (% GDP)	*1965*	*1970*	*1980*	*1990*	*1997*
Sub-Saharan Africa	24	21	18	18	18
South Asia	43	43	37	30	25
East Asia & Pacific	39	35	28	24	18
Latin America and Caribbean	17	12	10	9	8
Europe and Central Asia	-	-	-	17	12
World	11	9.1	6.6	5.6	-
(b) Agriculture Labour Force (%)	*1960*	*1970*	*1980*	*1990*	
Sub-Saharan Africa	82	78	72	68	
South Asia	75	71	69	63	
East Asia and Pacific	82	76	72	69	
Latin America and Caribbean	48	41	34	25	
Europe and Central Asia	46	33	27	23	
World	61	55	52	49	
(c) Primary Commodities (% of exports)	*1965*	*1970*	*1988*	*1992*	
Sub-Saharan Africa	58	46	38	32	
South Asia	57	44	24	21	
East Asia & Pacific	58	45	16	15	
Latin America & Caribbean	50	45	29	30	
Europe and Central Asia	27	20	14	13	
World					

Source: Maxwell, S. & Percy, R. (2001)

Traditionally, development thinking has considered agriculture as playing a supporting role to industrial development. Agriculture was seen as the provider of surpluses, such as labour, foreign exchange and savings, necessary to fuel industrial development. Such a view of agriculture's role in economic growth resulted in policies that were biased in favour of industrialisation and against agriculture.

However, more recently evidence is emerging to support the theory that agriculture can be the engine of economic growth. This has been acknowledged in the policy priorities of a number of low-income countries. Many developing countries define agriculture as the priority sector for stimulating economic growth while other countries list the agriculture sector amongst their key priorities.

A number of reasons are put forward to explain how agriculture can form the basis of economic development, especially in the case of *early development* economies, where a high percentage of the population is living and employed in the rural sector and where agricultural commodities are an important source of foreign exchange earnings. These arguments are based on a relatively higher multiplier effect of agricultural growth and strong linkages with other sectors. When agriculture prospers, farmers and farm labourers benefit and so do those employed both upstream and downstream from fanning. Since rural populations tend to be poorer, on average, than urban dwellers, they have a higher propensity to spend additional income. Also, their expenditure patterns tend to favour domestic goods and services. Because of this, the multiplier effects of increasing incomes in agriculture tend to be higher than in other sectors.

How does agriculture contribute to overall economic development? Maxwell identifies six different contributions that agriculture can make to growth and food security.

(a) As a supplier of food – despite rising cereal imports in many countries, the import dependency ratio remains below 15 per cent
(b) As a source of livelihood – agriculture generates employment for over two-thirds of the workforce in India.
(c) As a market – both directly for inputs, machinery and processing equipment, and indirectly as a result of the expenditures of agricultural workers.
(d) As a supplier of raw materials to domestic food and fiber processing industries.
(e) As a generator of foreign exchange.
(f) As a source of savings or surplus that can be invested, which can be used for further growth.

8.4 LINKAGES BETWEEN AGRICULTURAL AND NON-AGRICULTURAL SECTORS

Studies in *Green Revolution* areas of Asia have shown that an additional US$1 of agricultural income is typically associated with a further US$0.80 of non-agricultural income from local enterprises stimulated by the spending of farm households (Delgado, 1997). A number of studies cited in Delgado (1997) show a US$1 increase in tradable (usually exportable) agricultural commodities leads to a US$1 or more of additional income due to new production of non-tradable goods and services and intermediate inputs purchased by farm households. Delgado concludes that:

> *"Growth in the production of tradable agricultural commodities, such as export crops, livestock, and some cereals, appears to be the most feasible way to sustainably boost the incomes of large numbers of rural people ...growth ultimately must come from technological progress that lowers unit costs of production in agriculture."*
>
> —DELGADO, (1997)

In an analysis of the potential of the *Agricultural Development-led Industrialization* (ADLI) strategy to stimulate economic development in Sub-Saharan Africa, Adelman and Vogel (1992) estimate, on the basis of data from six African countries, substantial multiplier effects as a result of growth in agricultural output, particularly in terms of backward linkages. A US$1 increase in non-agricultural production results in US$0.70 increase in derived demand for agricultural output (forward linkage), while a US$1 increase in agricultural production results in almost US$4 increase in induced demand for non-agricultural inputs. Furthermore, this backward multiplier rises rapidly as per capita income rises. From a demand-led perspective, therefore, ADLI appears to be a highly appropriate strategy for Sub-Saharan African countries, which have large agriculture based populations. However, there are two serious limitations.

(i) **Supply-side constraints:** The first limitation, supply-side constraints, implies the inability of domestic industries to respond to the increased demand from agriculture, meaning a greater propensity to import and/or generate inflationary pressures. Adelman and Vogel advocate import-substitution approaches to address the supply constraint, but in the current liberalising climate the feasibility of such an approach is questionable.

(ii) **Environmental limitations:** The second limitation is environmental. The applicability of *Green Revolution-type* technologies to African ecological conditions is very much open to question. The current implementation of this approach through the Global 2000 programme in a number of African countries provides interesting evidence of both the potentials and the constraints. Where *Green Revolution-type* technologies cannot safely or economically be applied, there is a need for different technologies to be used. Agro-ecological approaches, for example, might combine increased sustainability with smaller growth multipliers.

Despite a general perception that agriculture in India is not making the major productivity gains that are needed to (a) provide adequate food security for the millions directly involved in it, and (b) to enable these growth linkages to be achieved in a way that will contribute to broad-based development, a number of studies indicate that in some areas, and for some crops, there have been impressive gains. Delgado (1997) notes that, considering the burdens faced by African small holders, they have shown considerable resilience and have been able, albeit slowly, to raise land and labour productivity. The burdens faced by African small holders include:

- Rapid population growth rates putting pressure on resources.
- 50 per cent secular declines in prices of major export crops.
- Economic distortions due to policies of national governments and the impact of food aid and other elements of foreign assistance.
- The burden of taxation in the form of forced deliveries to State Marketing Boards.
- Overvalued exchange rates, etc.

African economies are still in large measure dependent on the performance of small holders. Small holder farming is estimated to account for about 70 per cent of total employment, 40 per cent of total merchandise exports, and on average some 33 per cent of GDP (Delgado, 1997).

In a review of empirical studies on the contribution of agriculture growth to overall growth and poverty reduction, Mellor (2000) argues that it is the direct and indirect effects of agricultural growth that are key to the expansion of the entire economy and poverty reduction. The key points that the review of the empirical evidence illustrates are outlined below.

- Increases in agricultural productivity play a major role in reducing poverty, and the impact is relatively greater on the poorest and on the distribution of income amongst the poor. In contrast, industrial growth has less, or even no effect in reducing poverty and service sector growth is positive where it is small scale but has no effect where it is large-scale.
- The impact of rural growth on poverty reduction is nearly three times as great as urban growth.
- The principal reason that overall economic growth and poverty reduction is driven by agricultural growth is because the income generated by this growth is spent on locally produced, labour intensive, non-tradable goods and services that drive employment creation, poverty reduction and economic growth.

Against the backdrop of this evidence in support of agriculture growth Mellor (2000) laments:

> "*It is ironic that just when so much more can be achieved in agriculture growth and at a time when its role in poverty reduction is understood, the foreign assistance community has drawn back from pressuring for and assisting agricultural growth*".

Aid to the agricultural sector has declined dramatically. As can be seen in Table 8.7 development assistance to the broad agriculture sector (including agro-industries, rural infrastructure, production, research, irrigation, etc.) has fallen from US$17 billion in the early 1980s to US$ 10 billion by the mid-1990s. An ODI report notes that USAID reduced its assistance to agriculture from US$1.2 billion in 1986 to US$240 million, an eighty percent reduction.

Table 8.7: Agricultural overseas development assistance

	Agricultural ODA, broad definition, US$ million, 1990 prices				
	1980-82	*1983-86*	*1987-89*	*1990-92*	*1993-95*
Total	17,168	16,433	16,845	13,299	10,038
Bilateral	6,415	6,020	7,510	5,394	4,035
Multilateral	11,283	10,413	9,335	7,905	6,002
Share bilateral	37	37	45	40	40
(%)					

Source: Matthews 1998 and FAO.

While the evidence cited by Mellor presents a compelling argument in favour of agricultural growth, there are a number of considerations to bear in mind. ODI (2002) cautions that natural resources are under pressure, and that agriculture everywhere may not have the same dynamics for growth and poverty reduction it once had. Additionally, the long-term decline in agricultural commodity prices has weakened the sector. Mellor acknowledges that there may be certain areas where agriculture may not be responsive to improved productivity and indicates that in such areas the focus should be on increasing education to facilitate migration. He also points out that in situations where incomes are highly skewed in favour of the rich, increasing agricultural growth may do little to reduce poverty and in such instances a more radical approach to asset distribution may be called for.

8.5 GEOGRAPHICAL CLASSIFICATION OF POTENTIAL AGRICULTURAL AREAS

In the previous section, on 'agriculture growth, the argument was made that increasing agricultural productivity drives economic growth and poverty reduction. A cautionary note was made that due to natural resource limitations it may not be possible to substantially increase productivity across all areas. This raises an important issue in relation to rural development, economic growth and poverty reduction. Should attention and resources be focused on areas which have a high potential to increase productivity, or on poorer areas where poverty tends to be concentrated or on achieving some balance between them?

Table 8.8 outlines the differences in characteristics between high and low potential areas.

Table 8.8: Characteristics of high and low potential areas

High potential areas	*Low potential areas*
Fertile soils	Poor soils
Dependable rainfall/irrigated tends to be flat	High variability in rainfall
Plots tend to be large and close together	Often steeply sloping
Good physical, social and marketing infrastructure such as roads, access to credit, seeds and access to technical assistance	Poor physical, social and marketing infrastructure. Area is remote, poor access to credit, seeds, and technical assistance. High concentration of poverty high dependency on agriculture

High potential areas are also variably referred to as high input agriculture, *Green Revolution*, advanced agriculture, irrigated and high production areas. Similarly, low potential areas are also referred to as low input agriculture, low resource/resource poor agriculture, and marginal, rain-fed, low production areas.

The argument in favour of focusing on high potential areas rests on the basis that it yields higher returns. Also, those who view the world food problem as the need to increase the quantity of food available to meet a growing population would tend to favour increasing investment in high potential areas. The argument in favour of focusing on low potential areas is that poor people tend to be concentrated there, there may be positive environmental externalities of such investment, such as protecting land and water resources, and tackling food insecurity needs to target rural poverty and hunger. Table 8.9 outlines the main arguments in the debate.

Table 8.9: Investment in high and low potential areas

Why invest in high potential areas?	*Why invest in low potential areas?*
1. Higher rate of return means more output, faster growth, more jobs, less poverty	1. Low potential areas can be transformed into high potential areas with the right investment and technology
2. Labour migration will reduce pressure in low potential areas	2. There are pockets of high potential even in otherwise low potential areas
3. Remittances will reduce poverty in low potential areas	3. Investment in low potential areas saves on relief costs
4. Greater tax revenues means better funding for social security programmes in low potential areas	4. Investment in low potential areas has environmental externalities
5. Poverty is also significant in high potential areas	5. It is more effective to tackle poverty in low potential areas directly

Source: Maxwell

Each side of the argument makes a strong case. Clearly, the debate should not be considered exclusively from an either/or perspective, but rather by striking a balance between investing in low and high potential areas. Maxwell suggests that the appropriate strategy is one that combines investment in both areas, but emphasises public investment in low potential areas where it is more difficult to mobilise private resources. He calls this "*walking on two legs, but with one leg longer than the other*".

Also, evidence is beginning to emerge that is challenging the bias towards high potential areas. According to Fan and Hazell (2000) a strong argument can be made for focusing again on less favoured areas because:

(a) Past patterns of agricultural growth failed to resolve growing poverty, food insecurity, and environmental problems in many less favoured areas.

(b) There is increasing evidence of stagnating levels of productivity growth and environmental problems in high potential areas.

(c) There is emerging evidence that the right kind of investments can increase agriculture productivity to much higher level in many less favoured areas.

Based on a study of returns to public investment in high, medium and low potential areas, undertaken in China and India, Fan and Hazell argue that greater levels of investment are warranted in less favoured areas on the basis of both growth and poverty alleviation. However, they caution against interpreting these results as meaning that investment in high potential areas should be reduced, or against extrapolating the findings to poorer countries, especially in Africa, that have not yet invested sufficiently in the high potential areas to encounter diminishing returns. Again it can be concluded from this analysis that it is important to strike a balance between the two areas, but not to neglect low potential areas which has tended to be the case in previous agricultural development strategies.

8.6 ENVIRONMENT AND DEVELOPMENT

The relationship between environment and development, and between poverty and environmental degradation, is an important area of study. This is especially the case in the context of a country such as Ethiopia which:

(a) has enormous environmental resources;
(b) has high levels of environmental degradation; and
(c) has high levels of poverty.

At an international level, the 1992 United Nations Conference on the Environment and Development (UNCED), and the associated plan of action, Agenda 21, focused attention on the need for sustainable development. Ten years later, the 2002 World Summit on Sustainable Development (WSSD), again brought this theme to the forefront of international discussion. *Sustainable Development,* which underpinned these conferences, is defined as:

> *Development that meets the needs of the present without compromising the ability of future generations to meet their own needs.*

This definition provides a positive view that development can be achieved while protecting the environment. This implies a *win-win* situation in relation to both environmental and poverty reduction objectives. This view challenges the traditional view of development, which has tended to involve exploiting and consuming the environment, and contrasts with the perception of a downward spiral between poverty and the environment, population growth and the environment, and development and the environment. While there is broad consensus on the desirability of poverty reduction and protecting the environment, how these are to be achieved is more problematic.

Environmental concerns in developing countries can generally be viewed according to the following three aspects:

(a) The negative effects of degradation of international public goods such as the loss of biodiversity and of the rainforest for purifying carbon dioxide emissions.
(b) The potential for future industrialisation and urbanization to lead to pollution and increase pressure on water and sanitation resources within countries.
(c) Environmental degradation associated with agricultural including the loss of biodiversity, water contamination, degradation of soils and desertification, which puts at risk the food security and livelihoods of the people who live in these areas.

Following the previous discussion on the role of agricultural growth in poverty reduction, and the relative merits of focusing on high and low potential areas, it is worth looking briefly at the nexus between agriculture, poverty reduction and the environment. This is illustrated in Figure 8.3. In relation to the interaction between agricultural growth and poverty alleviation, it was mentioned that agricultural growth led to poverty reduction due to the forward and backward linkages that emanated from agricultural growth.

Viewpoints on the interaction between agricultural growth and the environment have been influenced by both the experience of the *Green Revolution* in developing countries and increasing agricultural intensification in developed countries. In both cases, increases in productivity have been associated with environmental problems. By the late 1980s a consensus was emerging on the need to use technology to increase production while simultaneously protecting the environment. This challenge has become known as the *Doubly Green Revolution,* which is hoped to yield similar results in productivity terms as the original *Green Revolution* yet is environmentally benign. Proponents of this approach point to using agro-ecological approaches, such as integrated pest management, that underpin sustainable agriculture, and developing participatory approaches to strengthen farmers' own experimentation and decision making.

Some analysts – although this is contested by ecological proponents – advocate that biotechnology is going to be important, if yields are to be raised, if crops are to be grown without excessive reliance on pesticides and herbicides, and if farmers on less favoured lands are to be provided with crops that are resistant to drought and salinity. While there is widespread agreement on the need to increase yields through increased intensification there are major differences of opinion on how this will be achieved, with the agro-ecological approach favouring a reduction in external inputs, while others argue that genetically modified organisms (GMOs) and inorganic inputs must play a substantial role in increasing productivity.

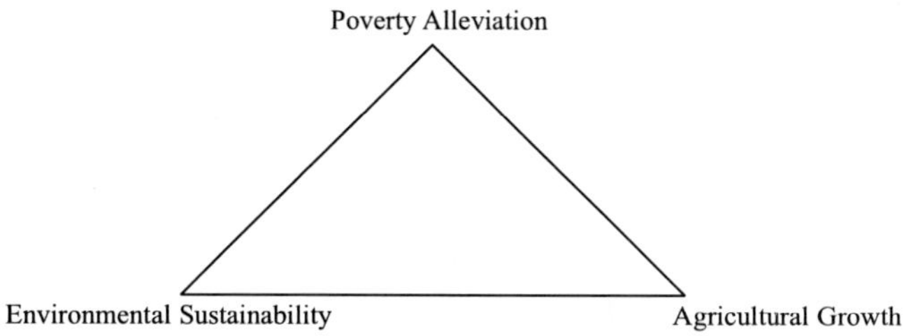

Fig. 8.3 Criticial triangle of development objectives

Scherr (1999) points out that the most controversial area has been the interaction between the environment and poverty. Much of the literature talks of a *downward spiral* of poverty and environmental degradation. The poor put increasing pressure on natural resources and, in turn, suffer from lower consumption, poor health and food insecurity due to environmental degradation. Scherr contests this analysis and argues that the rural poor have considerable capacity to adapt to environmental degradation by either mitigating its effects or rehabilitating degraded resources. The implication for policy makers is that they need to understand the factors that influence poverty-environment outcomes. Policy makers need to develop programmes and policies that can jointly address rural poverty and environmental objectives.

CHAPTER 9

Planning Issues in Agriculture and Rural Development

CHAPTER OUTLINE

- Support to Agriculture
- Major Issues in Agricultural Development
  - Land and Labour Productivity
  - Land Tenure and Common Property
- Broader Scope of Rural Development

9.1. SUPPORT TO AGRICULTURE

The scope of what is termed *agriculture* is enormous, and therefore so too are the range of activities involved in agricultural development.

Support to agriculture comprises all those activities that are involved in the sustainable production of, and realisation of value from, the basic commodities of crops, animals, trees and fish. This definition means that support could focus on:

- Production – of crops, livestock, tree products, fish
- The means of production – land, productive assets, inputs, finance
- Supports to production – research, extension, veterinary services, etc.
- Realisation of value – processing, marketing, storage
- Sustainability – the sustainability of the natural resource base.

In addition, there is a need to focus on the institutional supports for sustainable production and marketing (farmers groups, etc.), the policy environment and specific agricultural policy issues, broader issues related to food security (e.g., development of the capacity to address sudden food crises), and gender-specific issues (e.g., issues of women's rights to land, organisation of women farmer groups, etc.).

The wide scope of agricultural development is a reflection of the reality in India and other developing areas, of complex natural resource-based livelihood systems, partially market-oriented, where adequate support systems to raise productivity and value-added have generally not been well developed. It is also clear that support to agriculture is not just about how to increase crop production, but is rather about how to develop systems which support a broad-based and sustainable enhancement of livelihood systems, which are to a substantial extent based on production of crops and other agricultural products.

9.2 MAJOR ISSUES IN AGRICULTURAL DEVELOPMENT

9.2.1 Land and Labour Productivity

Intensification

One of the key issues in sustainable agricultural development is the need to increase productivity. If farmers continue to expand their land area, they will usually come up against constraints of land suitability or labour availability, and such expansion may also result in land degradation. Ultimately therefore it is desirable for farm yields to increase. However, strategies for increasing yields vary. Some analysts believe in *capital-led intensification* - in other words, that it is important to increase the use of higher-yielding seeds, inorganic fertilisers and pesticides if necessary; while others believe *in labour-led intensification* – in other words, farm families should make more use of labour, especially family labour, since the opportunity cost of such labour is often low.

The choice of the degree of intensity of production will generally be made by the farmer on the basis of different criteria. Such criteria include the household's preference for crops for own-consumption or for sale, land quality, availability of inputs and credit, labour availability, the extent to which the farmer is risk-averse, and so on.

One needs to be aware that different crop choices and levels of intensity will be selected even between neighbouring farmers, and it is not desirable to approach farmers with the view that they should all be producing in the same way — this tends to be the assumption when *package* approaches are being promoted. It is necessary to be aware of the diversity in agriculture, which can be an advantage to the farmer.

Farm size-productivity

Another issue which is relevant when we consider land productivity is the observation, which has been made through studies in many countries, that there is an inverse relationship between farm size and land productivity

— the smaller the farm, the higher the productivity. This seems unexpected, but there are a number of possible explanations:

(a) **Land use intensity** – i.e., declining land productivity as farm size increases is due to under utilisation of the total land area available.
(b) **Output composition** – output composition of larger farms may be oriented towards land extensive enterprises, e.g., livestock, or lower value crops compared with small farms
(c) **Double cropping** – smaller farms do more double cropping than larger farms, for the same crop in the same location.[1]
(d) **Soil fertility** – large farms may have on average less fertile soils than small farms.
(e) **Irrigation** – some studies show an inverse relationship between farm size and the proportion of total farm area under irrigation.
(f) **Labour intensity** – there may be an inverse relationship between farm size and the quantity of labour used per unit area: higher labour intensity also explains other factors, e.g., higher double cropping on small farms.

These explanations suggest that, if small farms are more efficient, it is due to the higher intensity of land use as a resource, not due to differences in yields per hectare of the same crops.

If the inverse relationship exists in a particular area, it provides a strong reason for the kind of policy that would support small family.

More generally, there are other possible objections to the relationship:

(i) Size class averages can obscure issues and may result in spurious findings. It is important to show the standard deviations of yields around means in each size class: large standard deviations imply that yields vary randomly over the whole range of farm sizes.
(ii) The area ranges of size classes can be manipulated to show declining yields when alternative ranges could show different patterns.
(iii) Scale may be important. Yields may not decline with farm scale: size and scale may not be related.
(iv) Partial productivity measures, e.g., yields or labour product, result in ambiguity on the relative efficiency of farms of different sizes. Land productivity is low when labour productivity is high (e.g., on mechanised farms) and vice versa. Farm efficiency should be compared using total factor productivity, not land area alone. This

[1]There is a difference between net sown area (where a given amount of land is counted only once in yield calculations) and gross sown area (where double cropped land is counted twice).

is difficult to measure since it has to be based on monetary values, and there can be problems with prices and the measurement of fixed capital.

Ultimately, this is an empirical issue, which has to be measured carefully. It may be that the important characteristic is whether the farmer is a family farmer mostly making use of own family labour. Family farmers are said to have more motivation, more local knowledge, more flexible labour deployment, and so on, and this might provide a reason for the inverse relationship.

Sharecropping

Sharecropping is quite commonly found in developing country agriculture, and the productivity implications of sharecropping arrangements have been explored both theoretically and empirically. In theory, since the tenant only receives (1–X) of the total product X, the tenant will reduce labour input below the optimal level and sharecropping will be inefficient, in the sense that land and labour productivity will be less than the case of owner-cultivation.

Many sharecropping agreements follow a 50 : 50 split, where the landowner provides the non-labour inputs and receives 50 per cent of the product, and the tenant provides labour and receives the remaining 50 per cent. Given that labour input is expected to be less than for owner-cultivators, yields should also be less. Does this happen? Again, it is an empirical issue that can be explored through surveys. One question that can be asked is if yields are lower on sharecropped land than owner-cultivated land, why does sharecropping happen? Another way of looking at the issue is since sharecropping exists, does that imply that there is no systematic difference in yields?

We can outline some of the reasons why sharecropping does occur.

Women, particularly in female-headed households, find it difficult to cultivate land themselves, due to labour shortages, cultural restrictions on ploughing, etc., and tend to rent-out their land.

There are increasing incidences of landlessness, where the only access that some households have to land is through the rental market. This is likely to become an increasing issue in many countries as regional governments try to provide security to existing landholders by developing policies that preclude further land redistributions.

Some farmers may want to increase their scale of operation but, due to the Constitutional ban on land sales, can only obtain more land through renting-in.

There may be situations—perhaps more described in theory than observed in reality — where the phenomenon of *interlinked markets* exists. This refers to the fact that, because of limited development of certain markets, for example, for credit, that people enter into interlinked contracts where two needs are met simultaneously from the same source. For example, a poor landless household may enter into a sharecropping agreement and simultaneously obtain credit from the landowner.

The latter situation is an example of differentials in power. This is often a factor in rental markets.

One point that should be remembered is that, whatever the efficiency implications of sharecropping, there are clearly distributional implications, which have a direct impact on poverty and food security. If resource-poor households rent-out land, they will only receive (at most) 50 per cent of the total output, which in low-potential areas will rarely be enough to meet domestic consumption needs. Therefore, households which rent-out land may be doing so out of necessity rather than out of choice.

9.2.2 Land Tenure and Common Property

Land is central to the livelihoods of millions of rural households. Land issues are highly complex and involve political as well as economic and social factors. However, in countries with highly unequal land ownership structures, land reform is a policy response, which cannot be excluded. Key recent debates in relation to land tenure have centred on issues such as:

- Comparative advantage of formal and informal tenure systems
- Assessing economic efficiency of small versus large landholdings
- Effects of different tenure systems on NRM
- Defining preconditions for effective management of common resources and seeking co-management options
- Continuing marginalisation of certain groups due to lack of access to land
- Market-based versus non-market-based approaches to land reforms.

In terms of actual policy measures to address land issues, two key areas are addressed here:

- Land redistribution
- Land tenure security.

Land Redistribution

For many years, land redistribution was dismissed as being politically infeasible and therefore beyond discussion. There is now an accumulation of evidence to suggest that redistribute land reforms can help and have helped to reduce poverty, increase efficiency and establish a basis for sustained growth. Deininger (2003) cites some of this evidence:

(a) There is general agreement that land reforms in Japan, Korea and Taiwan made a major contribution to the post-war and post-colonial development of those countries.

(b) There is aggregate evidence on the positive poverty impact of land reforms in India, and tenure reform in West Bengal is shown to have led to significant increases in productivity.

(c) In the Philippines, land reform beneficiaries have invested more in their children's education than non-beneficiaries, and increased their levels of assets at about three times the rates of non-beneficiaries.

(d) In South Africa, despite problems in implementation, there is no obvious conflict between equity and efficiency goals, and land reform offers key opportunities for the poor.

(e) In Brazil, land reform appears to have the scope to increase beneficiary income by up to 500 per cent.

(f) In Colombia, implementation of market-assisted land reform has potential to target the most unproductive areas, thereby leading to significant productivity increases.

(g) In general, Deininger and van den Brink note that greater equality in asset ownership is generally good for economic growth, contrary to some earlier assertions by economists. They also cite panel data studies of resettled households in Zimbabwe, showing, amongst other impacts, that their livestock wealth almost trebled, productivity has significantly increased, and their incomes are five times higher than incomes of communal households in similar areas.

There is therefore a new consensus that a well-designed land reform programme can have a major impact on equity as well as productivity. However, the question of what constitutes a *well-designed* programme has been brought into sharp relief by recent land invasions in Zimbabwe, and by the slow pace of land redistribution in South Africa. In the South African case, land redistribution is meant to take place through a *market-assisted* process involving willing buyers and willing sellers, the buyers being supported by grants from the State. The essential problems that have emerged with this process are:

(i) although there are willing sellers, in many cases they choose to sell off marginal land which is barely economically viable; and

(ii) land prices have risen beyond what would be merited from a pure calculation of economic value, and the size of the grant to assist *willing buyers* is hopelessly inadequate to allow significant amounts of land to be purchased.

It was expected by advocates of the land reform that it would help to release the *chains* binding peasant agriculture and result in a significant advance in production. This did not happen however. Clapham suggests that the land reform, and other policies towards agriculture introduced thereafter, ultimately contributed to further impoverishment. Certain aspects of the land reform did create new problems. Such problems included the prohibition on hiring labour and on informal land renting — given shortages of productive assets within some households — and, fundamentally, the right which the land reform gave to all peasants within their area to obtain land. Clapham suggests that:

> *"The result (in the absence of population control) was an increase in the pressure on land, with the inevitable decline in the size of plots, over-cultivation, increased environmental degradation, declining yields, and ultimately starvation. Land reform was certainly not the only factor leading to famine, as the experience of 1973 had showed [sic], but it was in pan responsible for a concentration of population on over-cultivated northern farmland, from which famine was the ultimate outcome".*
>
> —CLAPHAM (1988)

Clapham's conclusions with regard to the land reform per se are overstated. As noted above, the initial land reform was popular with most rural households, but there is little doubt that a range of related measures undertaken by the Government contributed to a disruption of production. These measures included:

(a) The prohibition on hiring/renting of factors of production as noted above.
(b) The establishment of a parastatal marketing agency with considerable, although not monopoly, influence over the domestic food market which consistently paid peasant producers at below open-market prices.
(c) The establishment (although not very successful) of producers co-operatives and State farms.
(d) Low producer prices paid for the key small holder export crop, coffee.
(e) The socially disruptive attempts in the mid-1980s at resettlement and villagisation.

Even though some of the pre-Revolution *package* interventions continued, the overall trend in per capita production was negative.

Source: Chisholm 2003.

Land Tenure Security

Whereas land redistribution is an issue of great contemporary importance in southern Africa due to the colonial and apartheid legacies of racially-determined major land inequalities, in other African countries the major movement is towards land tenure security. Land tenure security has its own complications. Currently, in eastern and southern Africa most countries are engaged in some form of land tenure reform (Alden Wily, 2000) but for a variety of reasons. One of the primary motives is to provide security of tenure to farmers to give them adequate incentives to make on-farm investments.

The second motive for addressing land tenure security, however, is in support of the broader trend towards commercialisation, liberalisation, and individualisation, in which case countries tend to move towards full freehold title. Kenya took such a step as long ago as the 1950s, which has given a good opportunity to observe the outcome of this process. Generally research in Kenya has drawn the following conclusions (Adams et al., 1999)

- land tilling did not give rise to a distinct *yeoman farmer* class as was originally intended, and impacts on production were less than anticipated.
- statutory registration of title weakened the rights of access to land for women and tenants; registration did not resolve land disputes.
- *English tenure* downplayed the status and role of women as actual land users.
- The land registration process marginalised pastoralists who lost access to key resources.

Other studies by the *Land Tenure Centre* (cited in Adams et al., 1999) have tended to find that land tilling as such has had little impact on productivity. However, this should not be taken to mean that tenure security is of no importance. In fact, the importance of tenure security is shown by the number of countries now engaged in it. However, the problem lies in a narrow view of what tenure reform should constitute. If, as in Kenya, it is seen as meaning a shift directly from colonial and/or customary forms to pure freehold tenure, then the results may be problematic.

However, there is now considerable evidence and a broader acceptance that customary forms of tenure can provide an element of tenure security, and that what is required, where land tenure reform is being undertaken, is an inclusive, consultative process of reform, and an outcome which provides for flexible tenure arrangements, for example, to deal with overlapping land uses (for example, where pastoralists might use cropland on seasonal basis for grazing), but which protects customary rights and affords them equal legal recognition alongside more *Western* concepts of land ownership which tend to come in with increasing commercialisation.

Major Concerns in the Land Tenure Reform Debate

- How far should land, and powers over land, be vested in the state?
- How far should a market in land be permitted and promoted?
- At what level of society should property relations be regulated and administered?
- How may land disputes be dealt with?
- How should unregistered, customary landholding and common rights be dealt with in the law?
- How should rights of women in land be handled?
- How far should rights of long-term farmworkers and tenants be made rights of ownership?
- How far should tenure regimes of pastoralists and others be recognised?
- How should the occupancy of urban poor "squatters" be recognised?
- How may all land rights be brought into a simple, efficient and accessible system of documentation and evidence?
- How may budgetary implications of tenure change be minimised?

Source: Alden Wily 2000.

Common Property Resources and Conflicts Between Land Users

The above discussion has already noted that there may be conflicting claims to land or overlapping traditional rights. This latter issue is becoming more critical as pressures on land resources increase, and as some forms of tenure reform and, sometimes, large-scale development projects or gazetting of land for National Parks or reserves, result in traditional rights being lost. The issue of pastoralist tenure, and the conflicts between pastoralists and settled cultivators, illustrates a number of points with respect to common property resources, which are also relevant to the broader discussion of tenure reform.

There are major issues in regard to the management of common property resources such as grazing lands, forest areas, coastal fisheries, etc. These issues are summarised below:

(i) These resources are often particularly important to the livelihoods of poor and marginalised groups.

(ii) Common property resource management, or collective action more broadly, may be important to allow flexibility in drought-prone areas, or to reduce transactions costs where a resource is being shared (e.g., a watershed or irrigation system being shared by upstream and downstream users), or to provide community-wide access to the multiple benefits of the resource (e.g., forest products).

(iii) It is often common property resources that are most at risk under poorly thought-out land tenure reforms with a bias towards individualised freehold tenure. Yet in the latter case Alden Wily (2000) points out that *commonhold* — property being held and managed by groups—is emerging as a new, legally recognised, form of tenure (in a similar manner as Communal Property Associations (CPAs) are recognised under new South African land legislation as legal entities in which land may be legally vested).

Common property resources, and the users of those resources, are at the interface between issues of resource tenure and of resource management; and a third part of this *triangle* is the local institutions which manage the resources. All of these interact to influence sustainability of the livelihoods based on the resource, and sustainability of the resource itself.

Natural Resource Management

Since all agricultural activities, (broadly defined to include production of crops, livestock, fish and forest products) in India are essentially dependent on the natural resource base, there is a clear correspondence between the aims of poverty-reducing agricultural development and sustainable management of natural resources. These issues are also bound up with the tenure arrangements governing the resource.

There is general acceptance that degradation of the natural resource base is a reality in much of India, and that this degradation is a clear threat to livelihoods. There are many differing estimates of the levels of degradation, with some researchers inclined to question the very high figures often quoted, although there are some clear environmental *hot-spots* where degradation is obviously at critical levels.

The central question in regard to natural resource management is not exactly how much degradation is taking place, but rather how sustainable management regimes can be developed which also form the basis for sustainable livelihoods. This issue has to be seen in a local context, and also needs to be viewed dynamically — i.e., it is not just a matter of how to reduce pressure on a resource — by, for example, reducing stocking levels to some notion of carrying capacity — but it is also important to develop approaches, with the community of users, to manage and to augment the resource, e.g., through grazing land enrichment, re-forestation, fish restocking, and/or the introduction of local bye-laws which regulate effort effectively. These approaches generally fall under the term *co-management,* which implies a collaboration between the resource users and an external agent(s), usually the State. This approach generally requires the existence of strong resource users organisations. Often such groups do exist. If not their emergence may have to be facilitated.

Beyond the issue of natural resource management, there is a need to recognise the importance of groups which often are neglected in development actions: pastoralists, fishermen, and forest dwellers. Delgado et al. (1999) refer to the *livestock revolution* in terms of the huge growth in demand for livestock products. Equally, however, the livestock sector in India has huge importance, both in pure pastoralist systems and in mixed crop-livestock systems. Furthermore, small livestock are particularly important as assets and means of income for women, and can form the basis for viable credit systems.

In regard to fisheries, there are many issues about the sustainability of coastal, offshore and inland fisheries, as well as the potential of aquaculture whether land-based or coastal. What is often not realised is the importance of fish as a source of animal protein in India. Furthermore — a significant export-oriented fish processing industry has developed in recent years which provides a major source of foreign exchange, but which also poses major sustainability questions.

In regard to forests, India's forest resources are being depleted at a relatively rapid rate, due to increased pressure on resources from population growth, increased commercial logging, and depredations occurring during civil conflict. Arnold (1998) notes that trees and tree resources can contribute to sustainable livelihoods, as follows:

- Increased incomes
- Increased well-being — a source of subsistence goods and materials particularly for the poor
- Reduced vulnerability — forest and tree stocks form a biomass reserve with people can fall back on to meet exceptional needs, e.g., during drought.
- More sustainable use of the natural resource base trees and woodland in agricultural landscapes (e.g., in agro-forestry) can help protect crops and soil and to maintaining site productivity.

There are fundamental issues of how to develop effective management systems and institutional arrangements to ensure (a) continued sustainability of the resource, and (b) the continuation and enhancement of livelihoods. Co-management arrangements in forest management have been tested in India (joint forest management) but are rare in the African context.

9.3 BROADER SCOPE OF RURAL DEVELOPMENT

Despite a number of success stories and the undoubted resilience of African small holders, macro-level data indicate that, on average, agriculture in sub-Saharan Africa has not expanded in the past two-three decades in comparison with other developing areas, hence the trends in rural poverty and food insecurity referred to above. The performance of agriculture is of course symptomatic of a broader economic malaise.

One strand of development thinking is concerned with the role of agriculture in contributing to *structural transformation*, defined as *"the process whereby a predominantly agrarian economy is transformed into a diversified and productive economy dominated by manufacturing and services"* (Gabre-Madhin and Johnston, 1999), as has been the historical experience in *more developed* economies. There has been some focus in this type of analysis on lessons learnt from countries which have relatively recently gone through this structural transformation.

The following section discusses the recent historical experience of East Asian development from the 1950s onwards. This period saw countries such as Taiwan and South Korea develop rapidly from least developed countries with high levels of poverty, to middle-income countries with highly developed economies, very high levels of education, and quite high levels of prosperity for the majority of their populations. It is the speed and extent of this transformation that has interested development analysts and policy makers in terms of the lessons to be learnt for the current set of least developed countries.

One of the clear lessons that can be learnt from this experience is that development in these countries resulted from a combination of actions of a structural nature. Such actions encompassed land reforms, enhanced agricultural productivity and institutional reforms, a strong focus on education, and promotion of non-farm rural enterprises. The multi-dimensional and multi-sectoral nature of the development process is important, clearly going beyond just agriculture, although agricultural development was of critical importance.

Agriculture and structural transformation in East Asia

Gabre-Madhin and Johnston (1999) provide some interesting evidence regarding *structural transformation* from Taiwan the main points of which are briefly summarised here. Important lessons are drawn from the Taiwan/ East Asian experience:

(a) Substantial increases in agricultural productivity are essential to transform the structure of a predominantly agrarian, semi-subsistence economy.

(b) The potential for positive interactions between agricultural and industrial development needs to be exploited, and depends on the expansion of the marketed share of agricultural output which allows farm cash incomes to rise.

(c) Demographic developments are important: increasing the growth of non-farm employment relative to the growth of the total labour force can accelerate transformation.

(d) Agricultural and rural development (including land reforms) was critical to the broader economic and social development of Taiwan. Key aspects of the agricultural and rural development strategies followed were:

(e) Increased agricultural output from productivity increases on small holdings supported by technological innovations and enhanced and farmer-managed productive infrastructure (particularly irrigation and flood-control). Particularly in the period 1952–66 (following land reforms), agricultural labour productivity increased at an annual rate of 3.3 per cent, associated with an expansion of fixed capital facilities (mostly irrigation and flood control) of 34 per cent, increased use of working capital of 140 per cent, and increased fertiliser use of 91 per cent.

(f) There was considerable expansion of the rural non-farm economy, primarily due to the "pull" factor of increased and broad-based rural demand consequent on rising farm cash incomes. This rural industrialisation was based on the rapid emergence of SMEs; some of these SMEs later developed into export-oriented firms.

(g) There was a rapid decline in fertility levels due to a combination of factors including the spread of education (primarily school enrolment was already 80 per cent by 1950 and reached 97.5 per cent by 1967) and rapid adoption of family planning practices.

There are, of course, huge differences in resource endowments, culture, historical experience, etc., which raise legitimate questions about the relevance of any lessons which might be learnt from the East Asian transformation process. However, it does demonstrate that relatively rapid transformation from a low-income, low-productivity economy is possible, and it provides some general pointers, which might be relevant from a strategic viewpoint. These include the following:

(i) Increases in agricultural productivity are essential to raise household incomes as well as to provide food (wage goods) for a growing non-farm population, notwithstanding the importance of diversification strategies followed by many African rural households.

(ii) Investments in fixed or quasi-fixed capital (including irrigation where relevant, but also water harvesting/soil conserving structures) and increased use of inputs (including use of organic and inorganic fertilisers) are means to increase labour and land productivity, as is land reform in some areas. Relevant agricultural research and extension can also contribute to enhanced productivity.

(iii) Rural infrastructure (support services) and institutions (including farmer based organisations), linked where necessary to land reform, can enable broad-based agricultural growth and therefore relatively equitable increases in farm cash incomes, which, in turn, stimulate demand for goods and services which could be supplied locally.

(iv) In response to rising local demand, the growth of rural non-farm enterprises can provide a means for non-farm rural employment growth.

(v) Commercialisation of agriculture can be based on both exports and on growth of the internal market, as non-farm rural employment expands; limitations on output expansion as a result of depressed local demand can thereby be overcome.

(vi) Human capital developments generally reinforce agricultural and rural development strategies.

Although there is a strong focus on broad development concepts and on agricultural development, it is important to also consider the other key components of rural development.

The scope of rural development can be divided into three broad categories:

(i) Productive activities/sectors
(ii) The enabling environment
(iii) Broader social-sector activities.

The enabling environment refers to a large range of policies and actions that promote sustainable rural development. These can include:

- The development of physical infrastructure — rural roads, electrification, telecommunications, markets, water and sanitation facilities, etc.

- Policy frameworks which provide support to the development of competitive market systems.
- Policy frameworks in key areas such as land tenure, the management of natural resources, etc.
- Policy frameworks promoting regional balance.
- Promotion of decentralisation and a parallel process of capacity-building.
- Financial systems which provide adequate financial resources at the appropriate levels where development activities occur.
- Support to processes of community development and participation.
- Policies addressing gender equality.

This is a large agenda which requires sustained support over the long term, and without which a focus purely on increasing production will be rendered ineffective by a variety of constraints.

With regard to social-sector activities, the key sectors are health and education (water and sanitation is also a key basic needs sector but in some respects can be treated as part of the development of rural infrastructure). Earlier, it was noted that the key role ascribed to education in the development of East Asian countries, and there is broad recognition of the fundamental importance of education as a foundation for broad-based development. In this section we discuss some of the key issues of relevance in regard to development of health and education facilities as a major component of a rural.

Access to health and education are basic human rights, which are too often denied to the poor. In addition, there is a clear gender bias particularly in access to education, and the benefits of correcting this bias are recognised as being substantial. The benefits of female education include:

- An increase in overall labour supply — greater female education increases their participation in the labour force.
- Positive effects on levels of agricultural productivity.
- Enhanced participation by women in civil society and the process of democratisation.
- Changes in household behaviour and practice – including improved health and nutrition of children, improved attendance of girl children at school, and impacts in terms of lowering birth rates, which, in turn, has a positive impact on dependency rates.
- Enhanced educational levels for girls also may contribute to a reduction in transmission of HIV/AIDS in the longer term.
- There is also a moral imperative to attain gender equality in education as a basic human right — but in doing so, the additional benefits outlined also accrue.

UNESCO 2003, Gender and Education for All: The Leap to Equality.

In relation to basic healthcare, least developed, countries are characterised by unacceptably high negative health indicators. Ten million children die from preventable diseases each year, and more than 600 million children live in poverty (UNICEF, 2002; quoted in Hall and Midgley, 2004). Less than 5% of children in least developed countries have access to routine immunisation services. The HIV/AIDS pandemic has added an additional enormous burden to already overstretched and vastly under funded health services.

In addition to the direct pain and suffering caused by ill-health, there are considerable broader development costs in terms of lost production and the added burden on health services. One measure of these broader costs is in terms of disability-adjusted life years (DALYs), which measure life years lost as a result of premature death and years lived with a disability. Table 9.1 shows DALYs by category of country.

Table 9.1: Mortality and burden of disease by income (1998)

Burden of disease	*High-income Countries, DALYs ('000)*	*%*	*Low and middle-income countries DALYs ('000)*	*%*
Infectious diseases	4,482	4.25	404,597	35.09
Maternal conditions	398	0.38	31,852	2.76
NCD	87,732	83.27	507,631	44.00
Injuries	12,739	12.09	208,934	18.10
Total	105,351	100.00	1,153,014	100.00

Source: WHO

Table 9.1 provides a very stark picture of the differences in burden of disease between high-income and low-income countries. The pattern of disease also varies significantly: in the poorest countries communicable diseases, maternal and perinatal conditions and malnutrition remain key causes of ill-health and mortality, accounting for two-thirds of DALYs in sub-Saharan Africa (Murray and Lopez, 2002. quoted in Hall and Midgley op. cit.). Similarly, within low-income countries, it is communicable diseases that have the greatest impact on health, suggesting that the focus of scarce health resources should be on this area.

Hall and Midgley point to analyses, which show how some poor countries or regions can improve health status significantly, even at low aggregate levels of national income. Although, in general, there is a negative relationship between national income and mortality, there are some low-income countries where vital health statistics more resemble those of high-income countries. These include China, Costa Rica, Cuba and Sri Lanka, and the Indian State of Kerala. Kerala, for example, has an infant mortality rate of below 20 per 1000 live births compared to 74 per 1000 for India as a whole. The factors explaining these atypical trends include effective health-promoting public policies such as preventive health measures, universal immunisation, food subsidies, educational programmes, and land reforms (Cadwell, 1985; quoted in Hall and Midgley, 2004). This evidence suggests that health prevention and improved public health services are key components of an effective health strategy for low-income countries.

There are many issues concerning the allocation of health and education budgets between different levels: primary, secondary and tertiary in the education sector, and primary health care or hospital-based care in the health sector. We will not address these issues in this Module, but we do need to look briefly at the issue of access to primary education and primary healthcare, since these are the levels of most immediate concern to the poor.

It has been observed that a key difference between poor rural households and the less poor is physical isolation, particularly distance from rural roads. This inhibits poorer households from being able to market produce and thereby increase incomes. These points emphasise the interconnectedness of rural development issues.

Secondly, the imposition of user charges on health and education facilities clearly reduces access for the poor, and therefore should not be part of policy, since:

(a) Health and education expenditures take up proportionately more of the income of poorer households than better-off households, such that the burden of user charges would fall disproportionately on the poor.

(b) Charges discourage poor households from using the services. Poor households are less likely to seek medical treatment than other households.

There is very clear evidence from countries where user charges and school fees have been abolished, that there is an immediate and massive increase in demand for the services. This has been observed in a number of Indian states that have abolished primary school fees.

To summarize, we can say that:

- There are clear differentials in access to basic health and education services between the poor and other rural households.

- These differentials have a reinforcing effect on poverty, and their reduction and eradication would have a strongly positive impact on rural poverty and rural development.
- Policies to address these differentials in access need to focus on a number of issues: there is some evidence that actions outside the health and education sectors — for example, increased access to rural roads, enhanced marketing of rural produce — contribute positively by enhancing incomes. Financial policies which include direct user charges on the poor have an adverse effect and should be avoided.

CHAPTER 10

Principles and Approach for Development Planning

CHAPTER OUTLINE

- Overview of Development Planning and Approaches
- Spatial and Sectoral Planning
  - Participation in Planning
  - Vertical and Horizontal Planning
- Macro-Level and Sectoral Planning Approaches
  - Poverty Reduction Strategies
  - Sector Programmes
- Participatory Development
- Sustainable Livelihood Approach
- Comparison between Sustainable Livelihoods and Integrated Rural Development Approaches

10.1 OVERVIEW OF DEVELOPMENT PLANNING AND APPROACHES

In the initial decades after World War II, the pursuit of development was reflected in a universal acceptance of development planning as the most effective way to achieve progress. Centralised planning was considered primary institutional and organisational mechanism for overcoming obstacles to development. A common feature amongst developing countries was the establishment of *Five Year National Development Plans.* Both India and China recently completed their ninth 5-year plan. The original rationale for establishing national development plans, with the government occupying a central role in its implementation, rested on a number of factors:

- Market failure
- Resource mobilisation and allocation
- Psychological impact
- Foreign aid

Market failure

It was argued that since markets in developing countries were imperfect they did not assign the real cost to society of goods, services and resources. This led to allocations that were not in the best interests of a country; this justified governments assuming a large and proactive role in the economy.

Resource mobilisation and allocation

Since developing countries had limited resources, government planning was seen essential to direct and prioritise investment in the interests of the nation. It was argued that markets would lead to less investment and would not direct investment to areas of national priority.

Psychological impact

It was felt that national plans played an important role in mobilising the population behind national governments' efforts.

Foreign aid

The formulation of detailed plans was important in securing development assistance.

Traditionally, plans tended to be very prescriptive and central government was responsible for their formulation and implementation. The approach to formulating and monitoring plans was technocratic with little involvement by actors such as civil society and the private sector.

The nature of development plans has changed. They now tend to be indicative frameworks for development. The process of formulation and implementation seeks to develop partnerships with civil society and the private sector. Also, through decentralisation, decision-making has been brought closer to the people it directly affects. Changes in circumstances and the political landscape led to this re-shaping of development planning.

The 1980s saw the State's central role in the economy being replaced by that of the market. This orthodoxy moderated somewhat in the 1990s and the State is once again seen as having an important role to play in addressing market failure but not to the same extent as it had previously. Planning has shifted from a philosophy of central planning to one of 'creating enabling conditions' for achieving development objectives and promoting partnership in the implementation of the plans. Also, whereas in the past there had been little civil society or private sector involvement, nowadays there is growing participation by different stakeholders in the formulation, implementation and monitoring of development plans.

The top-down approach is being supplanted by participative approaches and local level planning is emerging to complement national plans.

A broad range of development plans exist ranging from national, regional and local plans, to individual ministry plans, to sector-wide plans, to cross-sectoral plans. The time-frames covered in plans can also vary from short-term operational plans of one year's length, to medium-term 3 or 5 year plans, to longer-term strategic visions which may be framed for periods of up to 20–25 years. Amongst the different types of development plans a number of common characteristics can be identified.

Common characteristics in development plans:

(a) Starting by outlining the goals of development, planning attempts to define policy objectives for future development.
(b) The development plan sets out a strategy by which it is intended to achieve these objectives, which are normally translated into specific targets.
(c) The plan sets out co-ordination mechanisms for implementing and monitoring the strategy and guiding day-to-day decision making.
(d) The plan considers the role of different factors such as the private sector, NGOs, etc., in the achievement of the objectives.
(e) The plan will specify activities and resources required for its implementation.

There are a number of approaches to planning. Different types of planning reflect different ideas about development. Planning also reflects the ways in which responsibility for decision-making is distributed in the development process. Approaches to planning can be distinguished in a number of ways, as outlined.

10.2 SPATIAL AND SECTORAL PLANNING

Policy can be addressed either spatially or sectorally. Generally, governments have tended towards a non-spatial approach, organising government and policy along sectoral lines, e.g., ministry of agriculture, of tourism, of labour, etc. Rural development by its nature is more of a spatial concept crossing sectoral boundaries, therefore requiring spatial policy. Furthermore, as diversification and differentiation of rural livelihoods increases, and the relative importance of agriculture in the rural economy declines, there will be increased impetus for spatial planning. In reality a combination of both spatial and sectoral plans co-exist simultaneously.

Spatial plans can be federal, state, regional and sub-regional plans. Sub-regional plans might further distinguish between larger areas, such as the district, and smaller areas. Sectoral plans might seek to plan for a range of activities within a single sector, e.g., the health sector, the education sector, agricultural sector while a regional plan might seek to plan for the activities of a number of different sectors within a single region.

10.2.1 Participation in Planning

On the basis of who participates in the planning process it can be characterised as either:

- top-down planning; or
- bottom-up/participatory planning.

Top-down planning is used to refer to cases where planning is initiated by the government/state agencies. Plans are based on the assessments of those within the implementing organisations and little scope is allowed for participation by those outside them.

Bottom-up/participatory planning is where the local people are involved in the planning process, for example, members of voluntary organisations, specific interest groups or beneficiaries of the proposed programme. The involvement might be in the form of consultation, programme design, programme, delivery and/or programme evaluation.

10.2.2 Vertical and Horizontal Planning

A further distinction can also be made between *vertical* planning and *horizontal* planning. Vertical planning (Figure 10.1) happens within a single complex organisation. It links actions at different levels within an organisation. Horizontal planning links actions at a particular level across a range of organisations or sectors. For example, the ministry for agriculture might prepare vertical plans for its own operation, outlining the responsibilities and duties of different units within the organisation, from head office to the local branches. On the other hand, the plans of a number of agencies may be linked at regional level through horizontal plans that indicate how the actions of the different agencies can be co-ordinated.

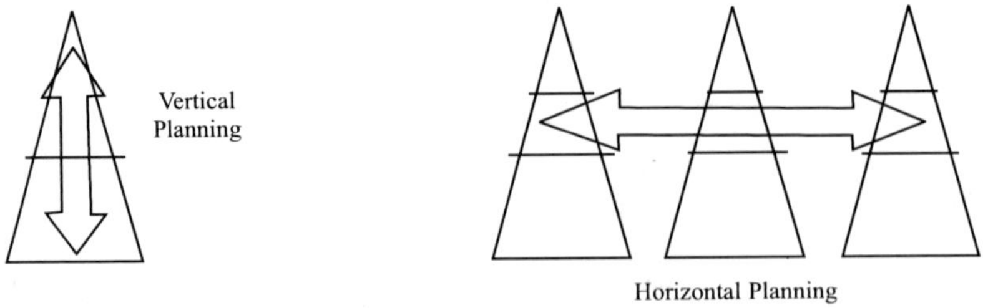

Fig. 10.1 Vertical planning and horizontal planning. *Source:* NUI (2002).

10.3 MACRO-LEVEL AND SECTORAL PLANNING APPROACHES

Many developing countries have a strong tradition of developing periodic national plans, often covering 5-year periods and setting out overall national objectives. Usually, line ministries prepare sector chapters for national plans following guidance by the government institution charged with planning, often the ministry of finance.

Planning at national level can be divided into comprehensive plans, which set targets for all major aspects of the national economy, such as in the case of a national development plan. Partial planning, in turn, covers only part of the national economy such as industry, agriculture, tourism, environment, etc. Two recent initiatives in the area of macro planning that look at comprehensive and partial planning respectively are PRSPs and SWAps. These are looked at in more detail here.

10.3.1 Poverty Reduction Strategy

The annual meetings of the World Bank and the IMF, in September 1999, marked the advent of the Poverty Reduction Strategy Papers (PRSPs). Here it was agreed that country poverty reduction strategies should form the basis for all World Bank and IMF concessional lending and for debt relief under the Heavily Indebted Poor Countries Initiative (HIPC). The impetus for such an approach was widely supported by other bilateral and multilateral donors. Currently, about 70 countries have developed or are in the process of developing PRSPs.

As an approach to development planning, the PRSP process was widely welcomed because of its promise of targeting poverty, promoting participation and allowing new approaches to development. The following five core principles underscore the approach:

- **Country driven** — involving broad-based participation by civil society and the private sector in all operational steps.
- **Results-oriented** — focusing on outcomes that would benefit the poor.
- **Comprehensive in recognising the multidimensional nature of poverty**.
- **Partnership-oriented** — involving coordinated participation of development partners (bilateral, multilateral, and non-governmental).
- **Based on a long-term perspective for poverty reduction**.

Though technically there was no suggested approach for developing PRSPs a number of core elements to be included within PRSPs were outlined:

- Description of the participatory process
- A comprehensive poverty diagnostic
- Clearly presented and costed priorities for macro-economic, structural and social policies
- Targets, indicators and systems for monitoring progress.

However, as PRSPs were rolled out there was increasing disillusionment as to whether the processes marked a fundamental departure in how development planning was approached and whether the range of policy options available to tackling poverty would be extended. Early on, expectations generated in relation to participation were frustrated. A Christian Aid (2002) survey of the PRSP process in Bolivia, Malawi and Rwanda outlined difficulties that ordinary people, marginalised groups and civil society organisations had in participating in the process. The survey concluded that participation was usually restricted to seeking information for the design of a country's PRSP, and did not extend to policy decision making, implementation and monitoring progress.

Civil society actors in many countries echoed this frustration at the limited scope of participation. Another critique of PRSPs by civil society was that alternative policy views were not open for discussion and the process was aimed more at promoting *buy in* for a set of predetermined policies rather than opening debate about different options and trade-offs between them. From a government perspective, the limited scope of policy options that would be supported by the World Bank and IMF, and the fact that HIPC debt relief and concessional lending was conditional on developing a PRSP, conflicted with the principle of country ownership. For example, Rwanda argued that a higher fiscal deficit (government spending) was both sustainable and necessary for poverty reduction but this conflicted with the IMF analysis. The result was that a significant rural public works programme, contemplated as a key component in the Rwandan PRSP, could not be implemented due to lack of resources.

Similarly, within the government, extending ownership for the policy objectives and priorities, contained within the PRSP, beyond the unit responsible for formulating the PRSP has proved challenging. With respect to content many PRSPs have been criticised as being overly reliant on social measures such as increasing health and education access for the poor while not paying enough attention to the productive sectors and measures to improve the livelihoods of the poor. Finally, in relation to aligning donor cooperation and support for the PRSP programme, this has tended to exist more in rhetoric than practise.

However, despite these limitations the PRSP has been recognised for placing poverty centre stage in development planning, increasing stakeholders' understanding of the multidimensional nature of poverty, and has contributed to opening space in relation to popular participation in policy dialogue. The World Bank's OED (2004) undertook an evaluation of the experience with PRSPs to date and some of its principal findings are outlined in Table 10.1.

Table 10.1: The OED findings on effectiveness of implementation of PRSP

Positive	*Negative*
• It has increased attention on poverty diagnosis	• It is often viewed as a condition of aid as opposed to being country owned/driven
• It has increased the number of stakeholders involved in programme design	• Participation has not been maintained through to implementation
• Resulted in better Government/ Donor dialogue	• Many groups still feel excluded from the process
• It is considered a relevant approach by different stakeholders	• Focus is more on the social sector with little attention paid to productive sectors

With respect to rural development, the *PRSP Sourcebook* devotes a chapter to guide policy makers in addressing rural poverty and developing pro-rural growth strategies. The approach outlined in the Sourcebook is closely related to the *Sustainable Livelihoods Approach* and highlights public actions to tackle poverty in the areas of human, physical, natural and social capital.

In practice the general limitations of the PRSP process resonate in how the issues of rural development are tackled. The priority accorded to the rural sector within PRSPs has been prominent, reflecting the fact that the majority of poverty is concentrated in rural areas. Also the poverty diagnostics in the PRSPs have been comprehensive and have been useful in identifying the causes and consequences of poverty, highlighting the inequality in incomes, asset ownership and public service delivery between urban and rural areas.

However, in certain cases the policies proposed to address rural development have been a continuation of existing policies, biases and vested interests. A study by Trocaire (2004) into the impact on rural development policy of the PRSPs in Honduras and Nicaragua concluded that the measures proposed for the rural sector were not sufficient to reduce the risks and vulnerabilities faced by rural families, to create opportunities for small producers to increase their income and standard of living, or to eliminate inequality in the distribution of income and productive resources. Public actions tended to focus on the social sectors, principally on expanding health and education coverage in rural areas. Attention to agriculture reflected the interests of commercial farming and emphasised improving the productivity and competitiveness of this sector with the objective of increasing exports and improving integration into global markets. There was little in the way of addressing traditional agriculture and small producers and tackling the contentious issues of access to assets such as land, even though the diagnostics had identified these as major issues to be addressed within the two respective PRSPs.

DFIL reviewed 12 PRSPs in relation to their rural development content. The main findings of this study were:

- Rural development is a priority sector in all the PRSPs.
- Rural poverty issues are clearly identified in the PRSPs.
- Most of the rural focus is on priority public actions, with less attention provided to rural issues in the participation strategy, poverty diagnostics, and targets and indicators.
- A limitation of the rural strategies in the PRSPs is the lack of a systematic and consistent approach to addressing core rural issues (building, for example, from a livelihood's framework).
- The priority public actions do not flow clearly from the poverty diagnosis and the participatory process and are not well linked to achieving the impact and outcome targets.
- Another concern is that almost all the strategies refer to the rural poor as a homogeneous group and the heterogeneity of the rural poor is not adequately recognised.

Notwithstanding the limitations of PRSPs, by focusing attention on poverty that is primarily located in rural areas, it provides an opportunity to redress past neglect of rural areas and the rural poor and for prioritising actions for rural poverty reduction.

10.3.2 Sector Programmes

Sector Wide Approaches (SWAps) are also known as *Sector Investment Programmes* and *Sector Programmes.* They were developed to overcome a number of problems in government/donor coordination. These problems included a large number of donor projects, poor coordination, lack of a common policy framework, high administrative and coordination costs resulting in poor sustainability and uneven service delivery. The response to this was to bring various activities under a common expenditure framework, negotiated between government and donors, based on agreed policies and priorities and common management procedures. More recently they are being linked to the operationalisation of priorities set out in PRSPs.

The common characteristics of SWAps are:

- Sector-wide in scope
- Development of a coherent policy
- Government leadership
- Common implementation approach
- Reliance on government procedures for disbursement and accountability of funds.

SWAps tend to be used more in countries and sectors where there is a high degree of aid dependency.

In a review Foster et al. (2000) outline both the positive and negative experiences with SWAps to date for both the social sectors (health, education) and the agriculture sector. These are summarised in Table 10.2. The case is made that SWAps have been more effective in the case of health and education and have encountered many limitations in the case of agriculture.

Table 10.2: Experience with SWAps

In the Social Sector	
Positive	*Negative*
Forum for policy issues to be discussed and problems jointly reviewed.	Some have proved difficult and time consuming to negotiate.

Increased focus on sector priorities and links between policy and implementation	Commitment and ownership has been fragile
Funding is increased and targets poverty reduction priorities	Donors still tend to micro-manage
Build government's management capacity	Participation by civil society has been very limited
Facilitates a long term view towards planning	Emphasis is on donor coordination rather than service improvement and poverty reduction
Improved balance between investment and operating expenditure	
In the Agriculture Secor	
Positive	*Negative*
Cooperation between government and donors has improved	Consensus on key policy issues is difficult
Some SWAps have stimulated consultation processes	Very limited participation of key stakeholders such as NGOs, private sector
Some progress towards harmonisation of donor procedures	Lack of institutional reform of agricultural ministries remains an obstacle
In some cases decentralisation has been strengthened	Sector programmes have not engaged in wider issues that affect agriculture policy and implementation
Sector goals for the poor have been identified	Link between policies and resources is quite weak
Some progress towards recognising cross sectoral livelihood security	

Overall, Foster et al. (2000) are sceptical of the role of SWAps in agriculture. They argue that agriculture is a very different case from the social sectors, which make it more difficult to successfully implement a sector-wide approach. The main differences they outline are as follows:

- Agriculture has a very large and diverse private sector. While the direct role of the State is important it is relatively smaller than in the case of health and education and moreover has been shrinking because of market based reforms.
- The role of the State in agriculture is contested both between donors and governments and within the government itself.

- Unlike in other sectors the most important actions are policy based as opposed to service delivery. This requires the cooperation of many ministries where agriculture may not normally be the lead ministry.
- Unlike health, education and infrastructure, where common technologies and approaches are more applicable given the relatively homogeneous nature of these sectors, agriculture and the intervention required is much more diverse.

10.4 PARTICIPATORY DEVELOPMENT

> *"Transformation is only valid if it is carried out with the people, not for them."*
>
> —PAOLO FREIRE

Participatory development is a philosophy of development that seeks to empower people in shaping their futures and overcoming their problems. The roots of participative development can be traced back at least to the 1960s. Paolo Freire did much work on developing the philosophy of education and development in late 1960s and early 1970s. This inspired many approaches to participative community development, empowerment and leadership training such as *Development Education and Leadership Training in Action* (DELTA) programme in East and Southern Africa. In the context of rural development practice, Robert Chambers has been a leading voice in promoting participatory development, wherein participation is viewed as empowering the marginalised.

By the 1990s, participation has become a mainstream component of development thinking, and it is a term used widely by government, development agencies and NGOs. Its appropriation into mainstream development thought coincides with the ascendancy of neo-liberal thinking and the consequent fall from favour of the interventionist State and top-down planning. Paradoxically, Mohan and Stokke (2002) point out that it is an approach that sits comfortably with both neo-liberal and radical approaches to development, though for different reasons. The neo-liberal view considers participation important for supporting democratic stability and good governance. Meanwhile, the radical view sees empowerment as necessary to empower the marginalised against the *disempowering* activities of the state and market.

Top-down approaches to development have been criticised for the following reasons:

- They overlook local knowledge and innovations.
- They fail to build local capacity to ensure the sustainability of interventions.

- A *one size fits all approach* tends to predominate which does not allow for modification to local conditions.
- As a process they tend to create and sustain unequal relations as power and knowledge are vested in a few people.
- They view people as passive objects in development and don't encourage ownership.
- Analyses and studies have shown that participation is a critical component in the success of projects.

In response to these limitations of top-down planning, participatory development has been advanced as an alternative approach. Participatory development seeks to incorporate local knowledge, local innovation, build local capacity and tackle unjust power relations, powerlessness and voicelessness, that are common characteristics of poverty.

Two views of the value of participation can be discerned. One views participation as a means to increase efficiency of development programmes, because if people are involved, they are more likely to agree and support new developments. The other view sees participation as an end in itself, it is an inherent right to be exercised, and empowerment of the marginalised reverses the powerlessness and voicelessness that they have been subjected to.

Participation as understood by different actors is subjective, ranging from mere passive involvement in a project/programme, to being actively involved in design, implementation and decision-making, to empowering people to take independent initiatives.

There has been a rapid expansion in participatory methods and approaches used in the design of agricultural and rural development programmes. These have built on approaches to participation, action research and adult education that have put empowerment centre stage. Increasingly, government and non-governmental institutions are involving local people in investigation and analysis rather than using traditional extractive approaches to research and analysis. There are many different terms and methods used in participatory development such as Participatory Poverty Assessments (PPA), Participatory Rural Appraisal (RRA), Rapid Rural Appraisal (RRA), Development Education and Leadership Training in Action (DELTA), to name a few. Despite the differences in methods and approaches Pretty (1995) outlines the following common principles:

- Focus is on learning by all participants.
- Multiple perspectives and diversity are represented.
- Approaches can be adapted to local situations.

- The function of external *expert* is to facilitate the group.
- Process leads to debate about proposed changes and the development of action to accommodate different conflicting views.

Four broad classes of participatory method can be identified:

- Group and team dynamic methods
- Sampling methods
- Interviews and dialogue
- Visualisation and diagramming methods.

However, a number of difficulties are associated with the practice of applying participative techniques:

- It is not realising its promise for empowering people and in some cases has just become another means/tool of pursuing the traditional top-down development approach while giving the impression that it is empowering the marginalised. Such implementation of participatory methods reflects little commitment by those employing the methods to its underlying philosophy.
- Even with the use of the techniques a bias can still persist in representing the interests of men and elites while the very poor and women can continue to feel alienated.
- Often, while local knowledge is elicited using these approaches it subsequently is not transferred into action because the emphasis of the technique is often to get *buy-in* by the communities of predetermined plans rather than encouraging them to shape the process.
- The local focus of such approaches may underplay local inequalities and power relations and also neglect national and international economic and political forces.
- The use of participative methods tends to focus on getting information for the design and monitoring of projects but they are used less for promoting joint decision making in the implementation of projects.

Fundamentally, the challenge for participatory development is not so much bringing together different stakeholders in a predetermined process (that may reflect the power/knowledge of only one group), but to bring together and facilitate the negotiation of power and interests of all different stakeholders. Some applications of participatory approaches to agriculture and natural resource management have been discussed later.

Opportunity presented by decentralisation for participatory planning

Decentralisation processes are bringing government decision-making processes closer to the people affected by these decisions and provide a unique opportunity for adopting participatory planning processes. Where governance is being decentralised, regions, districts and municipalities assume devolved responsibility for public policy and are required to prepare and implement development plans.

While decentralisation could mean a decentralisation of the top-down approach to development planning there is a growing movement that planning here should employ participatory processes.

A number of features of decentralisation make it amenable to applying participatory processes.

Responsiveness to local needs

Decentralisation provides a mechanism that allows local actors to influence government services so that they are responsive to local conditions.

Empowering the poor

Decentralisation provides a greater opportunity for poor people to have access to decision-making structures.

Enable changes

Participation in local institutions could facilitate profound social change which development entails by facilitating the development of leadership and local support for change.

A number of obstacles must also be considered

- Capacity to undertake participatory planning could be weak and the resources to implement plans may be lacking.
- The extent that local development plans are constrained by the needs of harmonisation with higher-level plans may limit the extent to which they can reflect local conditions and priorities.
- There is also a risk that decentralised institutions could fall captive to local elites.

These risk factors need to be addressed to ensure that opportunities for participatory development are seized.

10.5 SUSTAINABLE LIVELIHOODS APPROACH

The *Sustainable Livelihoods Approach* to development planning and intervention has developed since the 1990s. As a methodology it is closely linked to participatory development, because it seeks to build on local knowledge and realities as opposed to perceived realities. Chambers and Conway (1992) provide an early definition of sustainable livelihoods, which has been adapted by agencies such as Oxfam, UK Department for International Development (DFID) and CARE in defining and developing their own approaches:

> *"A livelihood comprises the capabilities, assets (stores, resources, claims and access) and activities required for a means of living: a livelihood is sustainable which can cope with and recover from stress and shocks, maintain or enhance its capabilities and assets, and provide sustainable livelihood, opportunities for the next generation".*

While organisations have developed their own livelihood approaches, common factors in the approaches have been identified, by Conway et al. (2002), as follows:

- An understanding of the household and the resources it owns or can access is the basis for analysing development problems and processes. It expands analysis beyond looking at people's incomes to look at their possibilities based on assets, capabilities and activities and the risks they face.
- The approach is people-centred.
- It recognises the diversity of livelihood strategies and contexts within and between households.
- It looks at dynamics within households and the balance of short-, medium- and long-term perspectives in order to manage poverty and vulnerability.
- Its approach to development problems transcends individual sectors (e.g., agriculture, health, education).
- It pays attention to the institutional context including economic, social and political relationships that determine the livelihood strategies available to households and the linkages between micro and macro.

Figure 10.2 diagrammatically illustrates the methodological framework used by DFID to underpin its approach to programme and project design. The framework is intended to help users think through the different aspects of livelihoods, and particularly those factors that cause problems or create opportunities. It also gives an impression of how different factors relate to each other, and it is intended to stimulate debate and reflection, which should result in more effective programmes for poverty reduction. Adopting the approach means taking a wide view, considering the various factors that affect livelihoods and not being bound by any existing ideas about what is important to people, what they do or what they are trying to achieve. It is intended that using the framework to analyse livelihoods does, however, indicate which types of development activity can do the most to eliminate poverty and identify the different areas of interventions related to people's assets and institutions and processes.

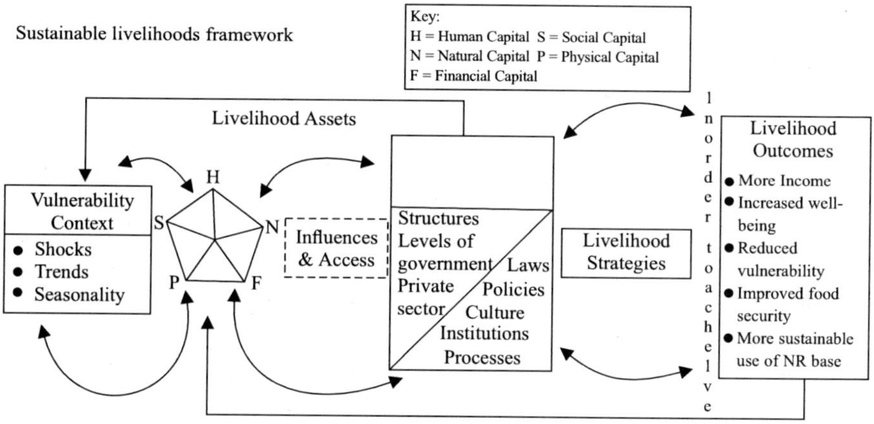

Source: DFID (1999)

Fig. 10.2 Sustainable Livelihoods Framework

The essence of a livelihood approach is working with people, taking their initial situation as a starting point and supporting them to build upon their own strengths and realise their potential, while simultaneously taking into account the effects of policies, external shocks, trends and institutional frameworks that affects their lives. This implies taking a *holistic* approach to rural development.

Intuitively the livelihoods approach is appealing and offers the following strengths, as outlined by Carney (1999):

- It is people centred.
- It provides a truer picture of rural life and rural poverty and the strategies people have.
- It highlights the importance of multiple actors.
- It looks at local, national and international linkages and their effects on local communities and individuals, and seeks to inform policy with this in mind.

- It looks at the multi-faceted nature of sustainability including vulnerability.

An underlying principle of the sustainable livelihoods approach is that it is to be operationalised in a participatory manner. People's livelihood objectives are to be identified through participatory activities; likewise participatory methods can be used to identify people's access to capital and how these are affected by the institutional, social and organisational environment.

10.6 COMPARISON BETWEEN SUSTAINABLE LIVELIHOOD AND INTEGRATED RURAL DEVELOPMENT APPROACHES

The *Sustainable Livelihood Approach* has much in common with the *Integrated Rural Development* (IRD) *Approach* of the 1970s. Both take account of the complexity of rural life and advocate for a broad based approach. However, proponents of the *Sustainable Livelihood Approach* contend that while building on the strengths of the IRD approach, the approach strives to avoid its weaknesses. In particular it is not intended to establish integrated programmes in rural areas, but rather to target a few key manageable areas such as agriculture production, income diversification and infrastructure. Essentially, the operationalisation of the approach is what matters. Key comparisons between IRD approach and *Sustainable Livelihood Approach* are presented in Table 10.3.

Table 10.3: Comparisons between sustainable livelihood and integrated rural development approaches

Area	*Integrated Rural Development (1970s)*	*Sustainable Livelihoods (late 1990s)*
Starting point	Structures, areas	People and their existing strengths and constraints
Conceptions of poverty	Holistic, multidimensional Recommendations suggest uniformity (an operational simplification)	Multidimensional, complex local. Embraces the concepts of risk and variability.
Problem analysis	Undertaken by planning unit in short period of time, viewed as conclusive	Inclusive process, iterative and incomplete.
Sectoral scope	Multi-sectoral, single plan. Sector involvement established at outset	Multi-sectoral, many plans. Small number of entry points. Sectoral involvement evolves with project

Level of operation	Local, area-based	Both policy and field level, clear links between the two
Partner Organization	National and local governments	Local and national governments. NGOs and civil society organisations, private sector
Project Management Structure	Dedicated project management unit, external to government	Project within partner organisation
Co-ordination (between sectors)	Integrated execution (donor-driven)	Driven by shared objectives, benefits of co-ordination identified by those involved
Sustainability	Not explicitly considered	Multiple dimensions. Core concern

Source: DFID (1999).

Notwithstanding its intuitive strength there are a number of difficulties and concerns with the *Sustainable Livelihood Approach,* not least of which is the feasibility of implementing the approach given its complex nature and the capacity and flexibilities required to work in a multi-sectoral and multi-actor environment. It has also been criticised as being neutral to justice issues such as the distribution of power.

It has been suggested that the SWAp approach, outlined previously, to development planning would seem intuitively at odds with the *Sustainable Livelihood Approach* since SWAps appears limited to the extent which participatory approaches can be applied. However, DFID contend that both can be mutually beneficial with the information collected in livelihood analyses enriching the sector programme and the SWAp framework providing the institutional arrangements for effective public management and co-ordination. In practise, reconciling the sustainable livelihood approach to sectoral programmes is challenging.

More recently, commentators, such as Conway et al. (2002), have extolled the virtues of combining a livelihood approach with a rights-based approach. Essentially, the livelihood approach focuses on practical means of development, building. On an analysis of existing circumstances to identify opportunities, while in contrast a rights-based approach focuses on the entitlements people should have and works back to identify what needs to be done to enforce these. In turn, a number of limitations have been identified with the rights-based approach:

- resources and capacity may not be available to guarantee rights;
- securing the rights of the current generation could jeopardise those of future generations; and
- a rights-based approach tends to emphasise the individual at the expense of the collective.

Looking at both theoretical frameworks the opportunities for complementing a livelihood approach with a rights-based approach have been identified as follows, by Conway et al. (2002)

- A rights approach to livelihoods provides a basis for focusing support on the poor as previously the approach did not explicitly identify distributional issues.
- While a rights approach poses a potential threat to public financial management and natural resources sustainability, combined with livelihood security it could redress.
- A rights approach could promote social and political stability.
- Securing livelihoods could be an important precondition to exercising rights.

An important underpinning of the theoretical framework of livelihoods approach is that it explicitly addresses the multidimensional nature of poverty and strives to include it in development planning.

In this chapter different approaches to planning were looked at. The examples looked at provided an overview of approaches in current use. Development planning remains useful because it provides a framework to guide development action.

The nature of this framework has changed dramatically, from being a detailed prescriptive centralised State plan, to being an indicative framework for building partnership between multiple partners. This change has made development planning a more complex activity.

Greater emphasis is now being placed on participatory processes, building consensus and ownership. This is not an easy task, but offers greater potential for success.

Decentralisation has brought planning and decision making closer to the people. This presents its own challenges in terms of local capacity and coherence with national policies, but offers the potential of ensuring that activities and interventions are appropriate to local conditions and priorities thereby affording greater opportunity to succeed.

CHAPTER 11

Policies and Strategies for Rural Development

CHAPTER OUTLINE

- Factors Affecting Environment and Poverty
- Rural Development Policies and Strategies
  - Need for Government Intervention
  - Need for Rural Development Policies
  - Strategies for Rural Development

11.1 FACTORS AFFECTING ENVIRONMENT AND POVERTY

Scherr (1999) outlines the following key factors as influencing poverty-environment interactions:

1. The characteristics of the natural resource base and farming systems of the poor.
2. Farmers' awareness and assessment of the importance of environmental degradation.
3. The availability of sustainable production technologies and their suitability for the poor.
4. Farmers' capacity to mobilise investment resources.
5. Economic incentives for conservation management.
6. Security of tenure and rights of access to resources for the poor.
7. The institutional capacity within communities to support adaptive responses by the poor.
8. The degree of political inclusion of the rural poor in decisions affecting resource policies.

According is Scherr understanding these factors, it is possible to design policies and programmes that have positive environmental and poverty outcomes. Amongst the strategies proposed are:

1. Co-invest in on-farm natural resource assets of the poor, e.g., soil conservation.
2. Employ the poor in projects to improve the resource base.

3. Develop and promote agriculture technologies with environmental benefits.
4. Promote low risk perennial production in poor and marginal areas, e.g., community woodlots, fruit trees.
5. Compensate the poor for conserving and managing resources, e.g., looking after water sources.
6. Facilitate access of the poor to agriculture-related natural resources, e.g., more secure access to water, more secure land rights.

11.2 RURAL DEVELOPMENT POLICIES AND STRATEGIES

11.2.1 Need for Government Intervention

According to classic microeconomic textbooks free market under its assumptions will result in the most efficient production and distribution of goods; in which: it is not possible to make some one better off without making some body worse off and it is not possible to increase the production of one good without reducing the production of other goods. The important question is that why do we need government involvement in economic development or general development of rural areas? The reasons for government intervention could be related to the following highly interrelated factors

1. How to create an egalitarian society? The final distribution of benefits, through free working of market forces, may not be egalitarian, if the initial distribution of capabilities (education, wealth, asset, social network and so on) is not egalitarian. And this may not be acceptable to society given the fact that the social weight of the poor's benefit may overweigh the social weight of the same level of loss to the rich. So even if market are working perfectly there is role for government to distribute the consumption of goods and services and capability from the rich to the poor. But if markets are imperfect the skewed distribution of wealth and living standard could result from market power of the better off than from its contribution to iota productivity and social good. In such a case redistribution is advocated even by those who accept the market allocation of wealth and living standard as legit.

2. How to deal with imperfect information and risk? Rural areas are identified by their high dependence on agricultural income. But agricultural output is dependent on random status of the weather, insects and other natural calamities. Thus, whatever the level of effort is exerted by the farmer the output is highly determined by factors out of the farmer's control. But far worst given lower price elasticity of demand (higher quantity elasticity of price), small change in output will result in large fluctuations on price. So farmers will face a very random income and quality of life due to random but also correlated moments of prices and outputs. But what makes it complicated is that insurance and credit market which can reduce risk of both production and consumption sides are highly missing in rural area. This is related to the common problem of moral hazard and adverse selection which is somehow mitigated in urban areas. But in rural areas given lower level of population density the administrative cost of providing insurance and banking services will be high and such markets are observed to be missing in rural areas. But two additional markets of information and future markets are also working suboptimally or missing in rural areas. The private information market is suboptimal given public good nature of information and its capacity to create market power. But, far worst, the missing future markets will result in suboptimal prediction of future prices. So the farmer is operating without proper knowledge on his output and price and if he faces a downturn he can't insure him/herself or borrow to escape the bad day. So in such a condition not only the farmer will suffer if he/she is left to the vengeance of market forces but also resource allocation will be suboptimal. It means that there is a wide gap in market allocation that needs to be filled by the state intervention.

3. Why is it necessary to create rural- urban balance? The existence of widespread market failures will result on unequal distribution of goods and services by the private sector between the rural and urban areas. In rural areas where the density is low and public goods are undersupplied; the transaction cost of doing business will be high, which 'will result in market failure and missing markets. But the less densely populated rural areas will have weak political voice on allocation, of public goods and the per capita cost of supplying public goods will be higher. So there will be a natural tendency for both private and public sectors to undersupply the rural areas compared to urban areas, which is commonly called urban bias. So the government intervention is required in empowering the rural people and correction of the state and market failures in order to create proper rural-urban balance.

4. How to provide public goods and services. Some goods and services are public by the nature. If one or few are able to provide the good or service they can't exclude others from consuming it and the consumption of the good by one individual does not reduce the capacity of the other individuals to use it. In this list are defense, street light, police service and so on. Ration agents will be better off, if they did not spend on these goods and are able to enjoy from the spending of others. But if all individuals did the same and try to be a free rider the good will not be supplied. So the invisible hand of the market will fail to coordinate the free and selfish motive of individuals to be in line with social optimal decision and allocation. So visible hand of the sate is needed to coordinate the allocation and provision of public goods and services by collecting mandatory taxes from citizens and users.

5. What is the need for leap frogging and compressing the time needed for development? The important point about market is that it will lend to solve its own failures in the very long run. So markets if are left for themselves can solve their own problem and in a long run and they can lead to economic development. But market forces in order to correct their own failures and achieve development may need more than 200 years. But with appropriate and selective adjustment of the market forces incentives by the government can possibly shorten the gestation, period of development in to maximum of 50 years (e.g., Japan) or minimum of 20 to 30 years (e.g., South East Asia). But in developing countries like India where majority of the population is living in rural areas, and leap forging effort which does not focus on the rural areas is a faulty business. So the need for leap forging will call for optimal government intervention in rural areas.

11.2.2 Need for Rural Development Policies

Before the need for rural development policy is explained, it is imperative to understand what policy is and how it differs from program and project. Policy is a definite course of action chosen from alternatives course of actions; and in the light of a given condition to guide and usually determine present and future decisions. So rural development policies are actions taken or planned to be taken by government, institutions, individuals and group of individuals with rural development objectives.

From the general guidelines developed by policies, different programmes will be formulated which are narrow in scope but in-depth details like what, how, where and by whom to be done. And a given programme will have a number of projects which are specific in terms of objectives, location, duration, funds and execution agency. And the executive agency deals with planning, financing and execution.

So the question that arises is why do we need policies or guidelines for government intervention. The reasons could be manifold:

(a) As the reasons for intervention are different the goals of government intervention are also different and sometimes conflicting. In such case identification of optimal intervention will need a reference guide, which is provided by the rural development policy. Means it will avoid interventions by clearly putting the importance of different objectives and the way to achieve them.

(b) Development needs a coordinated effort of private sector, community, and government. So government is not working in vacuum but in a complex social, political and economic matrix. In such an environment coordination will need clear flow of information between stake holders. In short, the non-governmental development agents will find it hard to contribute to development, if the intention and direction to government work is not clear. So clear rural development policy will not only help government to make consistent intervention but also it will improve the complementary role of the private sector, community and civic society, in achieving rural development.

(c) Government is not a single entity. It is a system built on different bodies. This includes bureaucrats, politicians and different institutions. It is built of different ministers, departments and agencies and the rural development effort will need a coordinated effort of all government bodies. And general guidelines will be provided by rural development policy will help to coordinate the development effort of different government parts.

11.2.3 Strategies of Rural Development

(a) **Growth oriented strategy.** This assumes that rural people are rational decision makers who will try to maximize their income. What is needed is adequate opportunities and a proper environment. The role of the state is to build infrastructure and maintain a favourable climate to stimulate the growth of rural enterprises. And given high potential areas can give quick result for government intervention on infrastructure, price incentive and technological diffusion, so it will concentrate on high potential areas, assuming growth will trickle down to other areas too. This trickle down will work through observation of surplus labour, provision of cheap food and transfer of technology and capital for search of cheap labour. A weak trickle-down effect will result in increased personal and regional income inequality, (an example of such effect the Indian green revolution experience).

(b) **Welfare oriented and patronistic strategy.** The welfare oriented strategy insists that government policy must be a Rawlsian in which it will minimize the maximum suffering that anyone can face than maximization of output or income. So government or economic objective must be that every individual has enough access to basic goods and services. Moreover, given the observed close to zero nutrition elasticity of income, the provision of income will not solve the problem because, people are observed to use additional income on things which does not improve their welfare as defined by specialists. Therefore, people are not that rational and they are not competent to identify and resolve their problems so government specialist can identify their problem and solve it with financial and administrative resource available to government. When such strategy is followed it creates dependence problem and its cost becomes unsustainable on government budget. The patronist strategy is more general than welfare oriented and it does not simply focus on short run welfare improvement but on guiding farmers. In such a strategy government will not only create incentive and informatics but also will determine what kind of technology farmers must use, what kind of resource they must employ and what kind output they must produce. Such policies will lead to massive inefficiency on the whole.

(c) **Responsive strategy.** The critical assumption of this strategy is that rural people will identify and resolve their problem if provided with minimum support and otherwise left to their own devices and initiatives. The role of government is to facilitate the self help effort of villagers by providing technologies and resources that are not locally available.

(d) **Holistic strategy.** This rejects development effort of only economic growth and income. Here development means social, economic, political and cultural development. It focuses on simultaneous improvement of rural quality of life and production capability by investing in elements of rural development like education, health, infrastructure, new technology, empowerment, recreation and so on, at the same time. It is very costly it solve all rural development problems at the same time and it will not be financially sustainable.

(e) **Integrated strategy.** The critical assumption of this strategy is that government can restructure social power relationships and the bureaucrats can share power with community groups. This approach focuses on both growth and distribution by making the community partner of the government. It deals with poverty, unemployment growth and inequality through integrated approach of physical, economic, technological social, motivational, organizational and political bases of the problem. The main idea is that improvement in one element of rural development will not only directly improve rural quality of life but will make the improvement in other elements too. By providing safe drinking water in rural areas quality of life improves and reduces the time wasted by rural women in fetching water. And this will improve girls' access to education.

CHAPTER 12

Rural Development in India

CHAPTER OUTLINE

- Important Institutions and Organisations of Rural Development in India
- Mahatma Gandhi National Rural Employment Guarantee Act (MGNREGA)
- National Rural Livelihood Mission (NRLM)- Aajeevika
- Pradhan Mantri Gram Sadak Yojana (PMGSY)
- Sansad Aadarsh Gram Yojana (SAGY)
- Deen Dayal Upadhyaya Grammen Kaushalya Yojana (DDU- GKY)
- Indira Awas Yojana (IAY)
- National Social Assistance Programme (NSAP)
- Total Sanitation Campaign (TSC)
- National Rural Drinking Water Programme (NRDWP)
- Provision of Urban Facilities in Rural Areas (PURA)
- CAPART—Council for Advancement of People's Action and Rural Technology
- DRDA Administration
- Integrated Watershed Management Programme (IWMP)
- Pradhan Mantri Krishi Sinchayee Yojana (PMKSY)
- Land Reforms
- Centrally Sponsored Scheme for Computerisation of Land Records (CLR)
- Centrally Sponsored Scheme for Strengthening of Revenue Administration Updating of Land Records (SRA & ULR)
- National Land Records Modernisation Programme (NLRMP)
- Panchayati Raj Institutions (PRIs)

Indian economy means – the rural economy and urban economy. How can we think of overall development of Indian economy without the development of rural economy, particularly in a country where around 65 per cent population resides in rural areas?

Long time ago Mahatma Gandhi very rightly said "India lives in villages". Still his statement is valid. So it is for sure that without the development of the rural areas nobody can imagine for the overall development of the Indian economy. There is a wide gap in the quality of life in rural and urban areas. So to minimise this striking gap the policy makers should formulate concrete and effective policies and they should be genuinely implemented and monitored. Here, it is utmost imperative to recall the statement of Late Prime Minister Rajiv Gandhi, who very innocently and honestly admitted that "only 20 per cent funds are reaching to the rural poor." Today also the scenario is more or less the same.

Poverty is indeed a global issue. Its eradication is considered integral to humanity's quest for sustainable development. Reduction of poverty in India is, therefore, vital for the attainment of international goals. Poverty alleviation has been one of the guiding principles of the planning process in India. This can be substantiated by the fact that anti-poverty programmes have been internalised in the (particularly the ninth) five year plan.

One of the unceasing objectives of the Government of India is integrated rural development. The Central Government's National Common Minimum Programme takes cognizance of the fact that for various reasons rural areas have not been able to keep up with the development carried out in urban areas. It emphasised the importance of villages to the overall development of the country and aims to work to bring about the development of rural areas.

The Ministry of Rural Development, adhering to the above-mentioned commitment of the Government, places supreme stress on the development of rural areas and wiping away the ills of poverty and hunger that plague our rural sphere. A number of initiatives have been taken in the recent years for creating social and economic infrastructure in rural areas to bridge the rural-urban divide as well as to provide food security and other basic needs of the rural populace.

The continuous expansion in the allocation of resources for implementation of poverty alleviation programmes highlights the emphasis placed by the government on rural development. The tentative Gross Budgetary Support (GBS) for the Ministry of Rural Development for the Twelfth Five Year Plan (2012-17) is ₹4,43,261 crore (against the ₹2,91,682 crore of Eleventh Plan period) which includes the major programmes. The plan outlay for 2015-16 of the Department of Rural Development is ₹71,642.00 crore.

An important component of the programme of development of the rural sector which brings about improvement in the economic condition of the people is dealing with the problem of unemployment. Two major rural development programmes focus on employment creation. MGNREGA offers the wage employment and National Rural Livelihoods Mission (NRLM) aims to generate sustainable livelihood for the poor (BPL) by mobilizing them in to self-help groups (SHGs) and creation of their federations. Self-employment is provided under Swarnjayanti Gram

Swarozgar Yojana (SGSY). Besides generating employment these wage employment schemes also ensure creation of durable assets in rural areas. Initiatives are also taken by the Ministry to build and upgrade the basic rural infrastructure through various schemes. Under Pradhan Mantri Gram Sadak Yojana (PMGSY) construction and repairing of rural roads is taken up to ensure rural connectivity. It is expected under the scheme that an expanded and renovated rural road network will lead to an increase in rural employment opportunities, better access to regulated and fair market, better access to health, education and other public services so as to accelerate the pace of economic growth in rural areas.

Social security and pension is provided under the National Social Assistance Program (NSAP) which is an integral element of India's battle against poverty and distress to provide succour to senior citizens, differently abled people and others who have suffered due to mishaps in their life through unconditional cash transfers. Similarly, basic amenities for housing, drinking water and toilets, etc., are provided under Indira Awaas Yojana (IAY), Accelerated Rural Water Supply Programme (ARWSP) and Total Sanitation Campaign (TSC) to enhance the welfare and well-being of the vulnerable sections of rural population. In order to check the diminishing productivity of wasteland and loss of natural resources area development is given a boost by the watershed programmes.

12.1 IMPORTANT INSTITUTIONS AND ORGANISATIONS OF RURAL DEVELOPMENT IN INDIA

Rural Development In India- Schemes

- **Mahatma Gandhi National Rural Employment Guarantee Act (MGNREGA):** The National Rural Employment Guarantee Act, 2005 (NREGA) later renamed as the "Mahatma Gandhi National Rural Employment Guarantee Act" (or, MGNREGA) guarantees 100 days of employment in a financial year to any rural household whose adult members are willing to do unskilled manual work. The Act came into force initially in 200 districts, and was extended gradually to other areas notified by the Central Government.
- **National Rural Livelihood Mission (NRLM) – Aajeevika:** Aajeevika - National Rural Livelihoods Mission (NRLM) was launched by the Ministry of Rural Development (MoRD), Government of India in June 2011. Aided in part through investment support by the World Bank, the Mission aims at creating efficient and effective institutional

platforms of the rural poor enabling them to increase household income through sustainable livelihood enhancements and improved access to financial services.

- **Swaranjayanti Gram Swarozgar Yojana (SGSY):** This was implemented as a total package with all the characteristics of self-employment such as proper training, development of infrastructure, planning of activities, financial aid, credit from banks, organizing self-help groups, and subsidies.
- **Pradhan Mantri Gram Sadak Yojana (PMGRSY):** Rural connectivity is a key component of rural development and poverty alleviation in India. The main mechanism for enhancing rural connectivity in a more systematic way has been the Pradhan Mantri Gram SadakYojana (PMGSY), a Centrally Sponsored Scheme (CSS), launched on 25 December 2000.
- **National Social Assistance Programme (NSAP):** National Social Assistance Program (NSAP) is an integral element of India's battle against poverty and distress to provide succour to senior citizens, differently abled people and others who have suffered due to mishaps in their life through unconditional cash transfers.
- **Indira Awas Yojana (IAY):** Rural Housing: Housing is considered to be a basic need for everyone. Considering this, at present the Indira Awaas Yojana (IAY) provides financial assistance of ₹ 70,000/- in plain areas and ₹ 75,000/- in hilly/difficult/IAP districts (w.e.f. from 1st April 2013) to BPL families in rural area.

Rural Development in India: Organisations

- **Council for Advancement of People's Action and Rural Technology (CAPART):** The main purpose of this organisation is to promote and organise the joint venture, which is emerging between the Government of India and the voluntary organizations pertaining to the development of the rural sector.
- **Department of Rural Development in India (DRDA) Administration:** This department provides services such as training and research facilities, human resource development, functional assistance to the DRDA, overseas the execution of projects and schemes
- **National Bank for Agriculture and Rural Development (NABARD):** NABARD is set up as an Apex Development Bank with a mandate for facilitating credit flow for promotion and development of

agriculture, small-scale industries, cottage and village industries, handicrafts and other rural crafts. It also has the mandate to support all other allied economic activities in rural areas, promote integrated and sustainable rural development and secure prosperity of rural areas. It was established on 12 July 1982 by a special Act of Parliament and its main focus was on the upliftment of rural India by increasing the credit flow for elevation of agriculture & rural non-farm sector and completed its 34 years on 1 Jan 2016.

- **Panchayati Raj Institutions (PRI's):** In India, the Panchayati Raj institutions function as a system of governance in which gram panchayats are the basic unit of local administration. The system has three levels: gram panchayat (village level), mandal parishad or block samiti or panchayat samiti (block level) and zila parishad (district level). It was formalized in 1992 by the 73rd amendment to the Indian Constitution.

12.2 MAHATMA GANDHI NATIONAL RURAL EMPLOYMENT GUARANTEE ACT (MGNREGA)

Mahatma Gandhi National Rural Employment Guarantee Act (MGNREGA) is a rights-based wage employment programme aiming at enhancing livelihood security by providing at least one hundred days of guaranteed wage employment in a financial year to every rural household whose adult members volunteer to do unskilled manual work. In the first phase, MGNREGA was implemented in 200 most backward districts with effect from February 2, 2006 and was extended subsequently to additional 113 and 17 districts with effect from April 1st 2007 and May 15th 2007, respectively. The remaining districts were included under the Act with effect from April 1, 2008. Thus, the Act now covers all the rural districts (644) of the country. The financial outlay (B.E.) under Mahatma Gandhi NREGA for 2015-16 is ₹ 34,699 crore.

The core objectives of the Scheme are:

- Providing not less than one hundred days of unskilled manual work as a guaranteed employment in a financial year to every household in rural areas as per demand, resulting in creation of productive assets of prescribed quality and durability.
- Strengthening the livelihood resource base of the poor;
- Proactively ensuring social inclusion and
- Strengthening Panchayati Raj Institutions.

The major goals of MGNREGA are to:

- Enhance livelihood security of the rural poor by generating wage employment opportunities in works that develop the infrastructure base of the area concerned.
- Rejuvenate the natural resource base of the area concerned.
- Create a productive rural asset base
- Stimulate the local economy by providing a safety net to rural poor.
- Ensure empowerment to women.
- Strengthen grass-roots democratic institutions.

The key achievements of the programme are:

- Since its inception in 2006, around ₹ 1,63,754.41 crore have been disbursed directly as wage payments to rural worker households.
- 1,657.45 crore person-days of wage employment has been generated.
- On an average, five crore rural households have been provided with wage employment each year since 2008.
- Scheduled Castes and Scheduled Tribes participation has been 48 per cent till 31st March, 2014.
- Women have accounted for 48 per cent of the total person-days generated. This is well above the mandatory 33 per cent as required under the Act.
- Since the beginning of the programme, 260 lakh works have been taken up under the Act.
- Average wage per person-day in the FY 2013-14 was ₹ 132.59 which is double the average wage rate paid in FY 2006-07. The notified wage today varies from a minimum of ₹ 153 in Meghalaya to ₹ 236 in Haryana.
- An Electronic Fund Monitoring System (eFMS) and Electronic Muster Management System (eMMS) has been introduced to ensure quick and transparent operations. Also, Aadhaar enabled direct electronic crediting of account payments to workers provides interoperability among banks and business correspondents (BC).

Outcomes during the Financial Year 2013-14

The outcomes of programme implementation in the financial year 2013-14 are as follows:

- **Employment Generated:** In 2013-14, 4.76 crore households were provided employment and 217.66 crore person-days of employment were generated.
- **Increasing Outreach to the poor and marginalized:** Self targeting in nature, the programme had high work participation from marginalized groups like SC/ST (40%), women (53%).

- **Strengthening Natural Resource Base:** In 2013-14, 138.49 lakh works were undertaken, of which 37% were for water conservation, 12% were for the provision of irrigation facilities on land owned by SC/ST/BPL and IAY beneficiaries, 11% were for rural connectivity and 5% were for land development.
- **Financial Inclusion of the Poor:** With a view to universalising the system of wage payments through institutional accounts, it has been recommended to all States to disburse wages through Post Office or Bank Accounts. Around 9.38 crore bank and post office accounts of workers have been reported on MGNREGA soft for disbursement of wages.

The MGNREGA Outcomes for the fiscal year 2013-14 is given below in Table 12.1.

Table 12.1: The MGNREGA outcomes FY 2013-14

S. No.	*States*	*Employment Generated Person-days in Lakhs*				*Average Person-days per Household*
		Total	*% of SC participation*	*% of ST participation*	*% of Women participation*	
1.	Assam	314.04	6.00	20.82	26.01	24
2.	Bihar	940.97	26.86	1.95	30.63	42
3.	Chhattisgarh	1294.85	8.92	39.81	48.53	52
4.	Haryana	128.87	50.70	00.00	36.86	36
5.	Jammu and Kashmir	365.56	5.80	15.28	19.88	51
6.	Madhya Pradesh	1387.58	18.82	28.54	42.41	42
7.	Rajasthan	2203.33	19.65	24.22	68.95	51
8.	Uttar Pradesh	1411.85	33.73	1.04	19.70	35
	Total	**21766.12**	**26.63**	**17.10**	**52.90**	**46**

Source: Rural Development Report, MRD 2013

Findings from the field, independent studies and MIS data on the impact of MGNREGA

The main findings from the field, independent studies and MIS data, on the impact of MGNREGA are:

i. **MGNREGA provides work when there are limited alternate employment opportunities available:** Reports indicate that when MGNREGA work is taken up by beneficiaries, there are very few

Alternate Employment Opportunities (AEO). In other words, MGNREGA has added to the employment opportunities available and not substituted other forms of employment including, agriculture employment. An NSSO panel survey found that in some of the high demand MGNREGA states, there were few AEOs available outside MGNREGA; only around 6%, 14% and 2% of the MGNREGA workers in Andhra Pradesh, Rajasthan and Madhya Pradesh, had other forms of employment available during the time they performed MGNREGA works. Importantly, MGNREGA also provided more number of work days at a higher average per day wage rate than any other type of work available at the same time.

ii. **Increase in agriculture wage and gender parity in wages:** The fact that MGNREGA has reversed the stagnation of agricultural wages of the early 2000s is well established by data and research. An analysis by Shri Jean Drèze observes that the pre-MGNREGA (2000–01 to 2005-06) growth rate of real agricultural wages was around 0.1 per cent per year for men and negative for women. After the implementation of MGNREGA (2005-06 to 2010-11), the growth rate for agricultural wages for men increased to 2.7 % per year and for women to 3.7% per year.

MGNREGA has also reduced traditional gender discrimination in wages. As per NSSO 66th round, the average wage for labour in MGNREGA was ₹ 90.9 per day for men, and for women it was ₹ 87 per day. The wage difference was larger for labour in other public works; ₹ 98.3 per day for men and ₹ 86.1 per day for women.

iii. **Increase in choice of work and participation rate of marginalized:** Preference for unskilled manual labour by surplus labour or by small, marginal or daily wage farmers in debt or bondage under MGNREGA, is reflective of an active choice in favour of non-exploitative and decent work. As per a recent Performance Audit conducted by the C&AG, around 90 % of the beneficiaries were either casual labourers or Small and Marginal Farmers (SMF). MGNREGA is also an important source of income for families who undertake distress migration due to limited work opportunities. Evidence also supports the fact that MGNREGA is succeeding in effectively targeting Scheduled Castes (SCs) and Scheduled Tribes (STs).

iv. **High work participation of women in MGNREGA:** With an average annual participation rate of 45-50%, evidence suggests that women are participating in the Scheme more actively than in other works.

Research also indicates that MGNREGA is an important work opportunity for women who would have otherwise remained unemployed or underemployed.

v. **Increase in agriculture production & productivity:** MGNREGA with its focus on agriculture related works can play a significant role in supporting agriculture and raising farm productivity. Several micro-level studies support this claim; a study conducted in Sidhi in Madhya Pradesh found that around 55% of the 240 respondents together reported an increase of 372 acres under crops. And around 56 % of the respondents reported diversification of crops over previous years. Crops like Jowar, Bajra, Kodo, Makka and Arhar were replaced by wheat, gram and vegetables due to increased availability of irrigation water.

vi. **Water related works:** Since the programme's inception around 50% of the total works taken up have been water related works. In addition to this around 13% of the works have been on land development. Micro-level field studies suggest that these works have led to a rise in availability of water for irrigation, improvement in soil quality, etc. This has further led to an increase in area under cultivation. For instance, studies in Bihar and Madhya Pradesh have shown an increase in net sown area and gross cropped area.

Challenges experienced in implementation of MGNREGA

Major challenges experienced in implementation of MGNREGA are as under:

- Low awareness about the programme and public participation
- Capacity building of functionaries
- Quality, durability and usefulness of assets
- Delays in wage payment
- Shortage of staff
- Improper planning and fund constraints
- Lack of outcome-based monitoring
- Inadequate coverage of persons with disabilities (PWDs) and women (in some states)
- Non-compliance with transparency & accountability provisions (social audit)
- Lack of ICT infrastructure

Recent Initiatives to Strengthen MGNREGA

Over the last few years, based on reports from the field and research inputs on implementation issues and challenges, the Ministry has taken initiatives to strengthen the implementation at grass roots level. Some new initiatives taken under MGNREGA are:

1. **Delay in payment of wages:** To reduce delay in payment of wages, the Ministry has initiated:
   - Electronic fund management system (e-FMS) that captures real time transactions and eliminates delays in wage payments and leakages.
   - e-FMS with post offices (Sanchaya Post) were attempted to ensure real time fund flow to the workers' post office accounts.
   - 16 states have made substantial progress in implementing the e-FMS.
2. **e-Muster Roll:** To overcome the problem of fake muster rolls and ghost workers, Ministry has introduced Electronic Muster Roll (e-MR). e-MRs are pre-printed muster rolls digitally populated with the names of the workers who demand works under MGNREGA. e-MRs are generated through NREGA Soft. Besides reducing processing time for payment of wages, e-MRs help in eliminating fake muster rolls, reducing ghost workers and improving data entry into NREGA Soft.
3. **Social Inclusion:** To achieve social inclusion of the marginalized and vulnerable groups, Ministry has taken the following steps:
   - To increase women participation in the scheme, major initiatives are being suggested including, opening individual bank/post office accounts for all women workers, identifying and providing job cards of distinct colour to widowed, deserted and destitute women, who qualify as a household under the Act.
   - In order to access the entitlements under MGNREGA, the wage seekers need to be made aware of various provisions of the Scheme. Thus, during FY 2013-14, the States have been asked to organize MGNREGA workers into labour groups. This would provide the workers a platform for articulating a collective voice and facilitating registration of wage demand in rural areas.
   - Since disabled and other vulnerable persons have specific needs, the States have been advised to create an enabling environment for their inclusion in MGNREGA activities. The States are to conduct a Work and Time Motion Study and prepare a separate Schedule of Rates (SoR) for physically challenged and other vulnerable sections of the society.

12.3 NATIONAL RURAL LIVELIHOOD MISSION (NRLM)–AAJEEVIKA

During 1980s, Integrated Rural Development Programme (IRDP) used to be one of the major programmes of this Ministry that directly targeted poor families for creation of assets, skill development and self-employment. The Planning Commission set up a committee under the chairmanship of Prof. S R Hashim in 1997, the report of which formed the basis for shifting from an individual beneficiary approach to a group-based approach for poverty alleviation. The **Swarnjayanti Gram Swarozgar Yojana (SGSY)**, became major sustainable income generating scheme through self-employment and micro-enterprise development programme to be implemented by the states, with effect from April, 1999. The cornerstone of the SGSY strategy was that the poor need to be organized into Self Help Groups (SHGs) and their capacities built up systematically so that they can access self-employment opportunities and establish effective linkages between the various components of the programme such as availability of credit, technology transfer/upgradation, marketing and infrastructure.

Performance of SGSY was assessed through concurrent evaluations, various studies and reports. Prof. Radhakrishna Committee on Credit Related Issues Related to SGSY, set up by the Ministry of Rural Development in April, 2008 reported the shortcomings in the implementation of SGSY like uneven mobilisation of rural poor and formation of SHGs across the States, insufficient capacity building of beneficiaries, low credit mobilization and lack of professionals to implement the programme. Based on the findings of the report, SGSY was restructured as **National Rural Livelihoods Mission (NRLM)**, subsequently renamed as "**Aajeevika**", to implement it in a mission mode across the country. The programme was formally launched on 3rd June, 2011. A further restructuring of NRLM based on the lessons from early implementation took place in May, 2013. The central outlay for the National Rural Livelihood Mission/Aajeevika for 2015-2016 was ₹ 2505.00 crore out of which ₹ 210.50 crore was earmarked for North Eastern Region and Sikkim.

Key Features of NRLM

The distinguishing features of NRLM are as follows:

i. **Universal Social Mobilization**-At least one woman member from each identified rural poor household is brought under the Self Help Group (SHG) network in a time bound manner. Special emphasis is on the poorest of poor and most vulnerable communities such as manual scavengers, victims of human trafficking, Particularly Vulnerable Tribal Groups (PVTGs), Persons with Disabilities (PwDs) and bonded labour. NRLM has devised special strategies to reach out to these communities and help them graduate out of poverty.

ii. **Participatory Identification of Poor (PIP):** The target group under NRLM is determined by a well-defined, transparent and equitable process of participatory identification of poor, at the level of the community. All households identified as poor through the PIP process are part of NRLM Target Group and are eligible for all the benefits under the programme. The NRLM Target Group derived through the PIP is de-linked from the BPL list. The PIP exercise is carried out by the primary federation, i.e., at least 6-12 months after village entry. The list of poor identified through the PIP is vetted by the Gram Sabha and approved by the Gram Panchayat.

iii. **Universal Financial Inclusion:** NRLM works on both demand and supply sides of financial inclusion. On the demand side, it promotes financial literacy among the poor and provides catalytic capital to the SHGs and their federations. On the supply side, it coordinates with the financial sector and encourages use of business correspondents (and community facilitators like 'Bank Mitras') Information, Communication & Technology (ICT) based financial technologies, business correspondents and community facilitators like 'Bank Mitras'. It also works towards universal coverage of rural poor against loss of life, health and assets. Further, it works on remittances, especially in areas where migration is endemic.

iv. **Implementation by the Poor:** The Mission is designed to mainstream the role of poor in its implementation. Key processes of NRLM are driven by the institutions of rural poor women, especially by women who have come out of poverty and whose lives have been transformed by this very process. Thus, it is a programme for the poor, of the poor and by the poor.

Recent Initiatives undertaken in the Budget 2015-16

- **"Mahila Kisan Sashaktikaran Pariyojana" (MKSP)** has been initiated as a sub-component of the NRLM to meet the specific needs of women farmers and achieve socio-economic and technical empowerment of the rural women farmers, predominantly small and marginal farmers.
- Another scheme under NRLM is for setting up of **Rural Self Employment Training Institutes (RSETIs)**, one in each district of the country, for basic and skill development training of the rural BPL youth to enable them to undertake micro enterprises and wage employment.

- Under NRLM, 25% of funds are available for **placement linked skill development and innovative special projects**. The objective of each special projects for skill development would be to ensure a time-bound training and capacity building programme for bringing a specific number of Below Poverty Line (BPL) families above the poverty line through placement ensuring regular wage employment.
- The Ministry of Rural Development is also implementing a new scheme titled "Skill Empowerment and **Employment in J&K (SEE J&K) 'Himayat'**. It envisages covering one lakh youth from rural & urban areas of J&K in the next five years. It will cover all youth with diverse education background, i.e. school dropouts, under graduates, etc.

Progress during 2013-14 (NRLM)

As of March 2014, all States except Goa have transited to NRLM (have set up a SRLM as society/company, appointed CEO and core team, and prepared action plan). Among the Union Territories, Puducherry has transited to NRLM. Goa and the remaining union territories (except Chandigarh and Delhi) are expected to transit in FY 2014-15.

Footprint of NRLM

During 2013-14, NRLM implementation commenced in 261 new blocks, making the cumulative NRLM footprint to1303 bocks. It has entered 32,573 villages spread across these blocks. NRLM has supported additional 2.92 lakh SHGs (either newly formed or strengthened) during the year. Further, NRLM has provided funds amounting to ₹ 204.56 crore to the SHGs/ Federations during 2013-14.

Table 12.2: Footprint of NRLM in FY 2013-14

Category	*Progress in FY 13-14*	*Cumulative progress*
Blocks entered	261	1303
Villages entered	52573	97391
SHGs formed/strengthened (in Lakh) *	2.92	19.3
Capitalization amount disbursed (in ` Crore)**	204.56	264.75

*Includes blocks under Externally Aided Projects (EAP)

**Excludes EAP blocks

Source: Ministry of Rural Development

State wise details of the credit disbursed to SHGs for the years 2011-12 and 2012-13 are given below in Table 12.3:

Table 12.3: Credit (SHG bank credit) disbursed to SHGs (in lakhs)

S. No.	*States*	*2011-12*	*2012-13*	*Credit Linkage Target (FY 13-14)*
1.	Madhya Pradesh	95.44	137.96	395
2.	Uttar Pradesh	445.41	450.98	948
3.	Chhattisgarh	92.58	70.13	224
4.	Bihar	398.61	222.01	670
5.	Jharkhand	127.41	75.36	214
6.	Odisha	540.98	473.28	909
7.	Jammu & Kashmir	8.04	8.44	14
Total		**16551.44**	**205.68**	**2991.25**

Source: Ministry of Rural Development

Sthree Nidhi – A Women Cooperative Bank

Sthree Nidhi Credit Cooperative Federation Ltd. is promoted by federations of Self Help Groups (SHGs) at Mandal level, in association with the Government of Andhra Pradesh with an authorized capital of ₹500 crore and a paid capital of ₹261 crore. SHGs access hassle-free credit from Sthree Nidhi Credit through federations as and when required using their mobile and therefore do not borrow from other sources at usurious rates of interest. Sthree Nidhi is in a position to extend credit to the SHGs even in far flung areas of the state in 48 hours to meet credit needs for exigencies like health, education and other income generation needs like agriculture, dairy and other activities. It provides an alternative low cost delivery solution against the private micro finance lending. Sthree Nidhi provides timely and affordable credit to the poor SHG members as a part of the overall strategy for poverty alleviation.

During the year 2013-14, Sthree Nidhi lent approximately ₹1000 crore to its member organisations – the federations.

Source: Annual Report- 2013-14, MoRD

Skill Development

Aajeevika Skills is the skill and placement initiative of Ministry of Rural Development, Government of India (MoRD). It is part of the National Rural Livelihood Mission (NRLM)-Aajeevika. It evolved out of the need to diversify incomes of the rural poor and to cater to the occupational aspirations of their youth. It aims to skill rural youth who are poor and provide them with jobs having regular monthly wages at or above the minimum wages. The programme's focus is on skilling and placement in the formal sector for rural youth who are poor. During the year 2013-14 a target of 5 lakh was set against which 2,08,843 persons were trained and 1,39,076 were placed till March, 2014.

ROSHNI: A new skill development scheme for the rural youth has been launched by this Department for tribal areas and critical LWE affected districts. This scheme is named 'Roshini' that takes into account the peculiar situation in selected critical Left Wing Extremist affected (LWE) districts. It is a special initiative under Aajeevika Skills launched on 7th June, 2013 for training and placement of youth from 27 most critical LWE affected districts. Six districts each from Jharkhand and Odisha, five from Chhattisgarh, two from Bihar and one each from Andhra Pradesh, Uttar Pradesh, West Bengal, Madhya Pradesh and Maharashtra have been chosen for the scheme. Under the scheme, at least 40% of the candidates covered need to be women. Special efforts are being made to proactively cover Particularly Vulnerable Tribal Groups (PVTGs) on a priority basis. NIRD &PR has been designated as the monitoring and coordinating agency for Roshni. The scheme is aimed at addressing the infrastructure, education and health deficiencies in these areas, and leveraging the availability of natural resources and traditional skills and knowledge.

Source: Ministry of Rural Development, GOI.

12.4 RURAL ROADS: PRADHAN MANTRI GRAM SADAK YOJANA (PMGSY)

The Government of India, as part of poverty reduction strategy, launched the Pradhan Mantri Gram Sadak Yojana (PMGSY) on 25th December 2000 as a centrally sponsored scheme to assist states, though roads other than National Highways are in the State List under the Constitution. The primary objective of the programme is to provide good all weather connectivity to all eligible unconnected habitations in the core network with a population of 500 (Census- 2001) and above. In respect of the Hill States (North-East, Sikkim, Himachal Pradesh, Jammu & Kashmir and Uttarkhand), Desert areas (as identified in the Desert Development Programme), and Tribal (Schedule V) Areas and Selected Tribal and Backward Districts (as identified by Ministry of Home Affairs and Planning Commission), the objective is to connect habitations with a population of 250 (Census 2001) and above. The programme envisages single all weather connectivity. The country has now a network of about 3,99,979 km of such roads.

With a view to ensuring full farm-to-market connectivity, the programme also provides for the upgradation of the existing 'Through Routes' and Major Rural Links to prescribed standards, though it is not central to the programme.

The total outlay for 2015-2016 is ₹ 14291.00 crore, out of which ₹ 1155.00 crore have been earmarked for North Eastern Region and Sikkim. A total of 1,78,184 habitations are targeted for providing road connectivity under PMGSY. The programme also has an upgradation component with a target to upgrade 3.75 lakh km of existing rural roads (including 40% renewal of rural roads to be funded by the states) in order to ensure full farm to market connectivity.

The impact of rural roads becomes visible not so much during or immediately after construction as after a few years, when the traffic picks up and market access is fully exploited by the rural economy. Maintenance of roads plays an important role in exploiting the full potential of socio-economic development leading to poverty alleviation.

During the year 2013-14 (up to March, 2014), project proposals for over ₹ 31,333 crore sent by states were cleared by the Ministry. State-wise details of outcome targets and achievements during the year 2013-14 up to March, 2014 have been given in the Table 12.4.

Table 12.4: Pradhan Mantri Gram Sadak Yojana: Outcome targets and achievements during 2013-14

S. No.	*State*	*Length (km)*		*No. of Habitations*		*Expenditure up to Mar'14 Rs. In Cr.*
		Target for 2013-14	*Length completed up to Mar'14*	*Target for 2013-14*	*Habitations connected upto Mar'14*	
1.	Assam	650	958	160	257	699.01
2.	Bihar	2800	2637	730	901	1685.37
3.	Chhattisgarh	1900	1292	235	896	713.58
4.	Jammu & Kashmir	1295	892	100	143	534.01
5.	Odisha	3460	3063	400	700	1605.72
6.	Madhya Pradesh	3350	3006	400	411	1393.07
7.	Rajasthan	1580	2290	184	579	718.35
8.	Uttar Pradesh	2320	1110	130	0	824.25
Total		27000	25316	3500	6560	13095.29

Source: Ministry of Rural Development, GOI

PMGSY II: PMGSY II was launched in May, 2013 and envisages consolidation of the existing rural roads network to improve its overall efficiency as a provider of transportation services for people, goods and services. During the 12th Five Year plan, upgradation of 50,000 km road length at an estimated cost of ₹ 33,030 crore is proposed to be covered. With a view to strengthen the quality of material and workmanship used in the construction of PMGSY roads, the Ministry of Rural Development released ₹ 33.75 crore during the financial year 2014-15 for the procurement of lab/survey equipment to 27 states.

Under PMGSY-II, 10,725 projects have been cleared out of eligible 50,000 projects. As on March 31, 2014, 97,838 habitations have been connected. New connectivity of 2,48,919 km has been achieved. The targets of the programme and present progress as on 31st March 2014 are given below in Table 12.5.

Table 12.5: Targets and achievements as on 31st March 2014

Activity	*Total Eligibility*	*Projects Cleared (Sanctioned)*	*Achievements*
PMGSY-I			
Habitations (No.)	1,78,184	1, 44,717 (81%)	97,838 (55% of eligible)
New Connectivity (km.)	-	**3,58,411**	2,48,919 (70% of sanctioned)
Upgradation (km)	2,24,906	1, 75,326 (78%)	1,51,060 (67% of eligible UG)
PMGSY-II			
Upgradation Length (km)	50,000	10,725 (21%)	NIL
Financial Progress			
Projects Cleared	*Funds released to the States*	*Expenditure by States*	*Balance work in Hand*
1,85,119	1,09,638.51	1,12,979.55	72,139

Source: Ministry of Rural Development, GOI

12.5 SANSAD ADARSH GRAM YOJANA (SAGY)

Sansad Adarsh Gram Yojana (SAGY) is a village development project launched by Government of India on 10th October 2014, under which each

Member of Parliament will take the responsibility of developing physical and institutional infrastructure in three villages by 2019. The goal is to develop three Adarsh Grams or model villages by March 2019, of which one would be achieved by 2016. Thereafter, five such Adarsh Grams (one per year) will be selected and developed by 2024.

This Rural Development Scheme has a holistic approach towards development. It broadly focuses on the development in the villages which includes social development, cultural development and spread motivation among the people on social mobilization of the village community. It envisages integrated development of the selected villages across multiple areas such as agriculture, health, education, sanitation, environment, livelihoods, etc. Far beyond mere infrastructure development, SAGY aims at instilling and nurturing values of national pride, patriotism, community spirit, self-confidence people's participation, dignity of women, etc., in the people.

The main objectives of SAGY are:

- To trigger processes which lead to the holistic development of the identified Gram Panchayats
- To generate models of local level development and effective local governance which can motivate and inspire the neighbouring Gram Panchayats to learn and adapt.
- To substantially improve the standard of living and the quality of life of all sections of the society through improved basic amenities, higher productivity, wider social mobilisations, etc.

Prior to this, a scheme called **Pradhan Mantri Adarsh Gram Yojana (PMAGY)** was launched in March, 2010 on a pilot basis, for the integrated development of 1000 villages each with more than 50% scheduled caste (SC) population. Under this scheme, each village would be able to avail gap funding of ₹ 10 lakh over and above the allocations under Rural Development and Poverty Alleviation Schemes. The scheme was implemented in five states, viz., Assam (100-villages), Bihar (225-villages), Himachal Pradesh (225-villages), Rajasthan (225-villages) and Tamil Nadu (225-villages). The expected time-frame for implementation of the pilot phase was 3 years. Expansion of the scheme was to be based on successful implementation of the pilot phase. PMAGY also focuses on basic needs—housing, sanitation, water supply, electricity, communications, banking, infrastructure connectivity, healthcare, nutrition, etc., and aims for convergence of existing programmes in these sectors.

12.6 DEEN DAYAL UPADHYAYA GRAMEEN KAUSHALYA YOJANA (DDU- GKY)

Deen Dayal Upadhyaya Grameen Kaushalya Yojana or DDU-GKY is a Government of India rural youth employment scheme. It was launched by on 25 September 2014 by the Ministry of Rural Development. It is a Placement Linked Skill Development Scheme for rural youth who are poor. This initiative is a part of the NRLM. It has its origin in the wage employment linked special project for skilling component of Swaranjayanti Gram Swarozgar Yojana (SGSY) which was subsequently renamed Aajeevika skills when SGSY was converted as NRLM. It is an important component of the national skill development policy. As a poverty alleviation initiative, DDU-GKY proposes to make skill acquisition aspirational amongst the rural poor and thereby helping create a highly skilled and productive workforce.

Against an annual target of 2.10 lakh candidates during 2014-15, a total of 46,918 candidates have been trained and a total of 23,001 candidates have been placed in regular jobs.

A total of ₹ 538.80 crore was released for implementation of projects under DDU-GKY in the period from 1st April 2014 till 30th November, 2014.

12.7 RURAL HOUSING: INDIRA AWAS YOJANA (IAY)

The outlay for 2015-2016 for Rural Housing was ₹ 10025.00 crore, out of which ₹ 1003.00 crore was earmarked for North Eastern Region and Sikkim.

As part of a larger strategy of the Ministry's poverty eradication effort, *Indira Awaas Yojana (IAY)*, a flagship scheme of the Ministry of Rural Development, has since inception been providing assistance to the BPL families who are either houseless or having inadequate housing facilities, for constructing a safe and durable shelter.

Ministry's commitment of 'shelter for all' gained momentum when India became a signatory to the Istanbul Declaration on Human Settlement in June 1996 recognizing thereby the need for access to safe and healthy shelter and basic services as essential for a person's physical, psychological, social and economic well-being. The object of the habitat approach is to achieve adequate shelter for all, especially the deprived urban and rural poor through an enabling approach leading to development and improvement in access to basic facilities like infrastructure, safe drinking water, sanitation, electricity, etc.

The Central Government has been implementing IAY as part of the enabling approach to 'shelter for all', taking cognizance of the fact that rural housing is one of the major anti-poverty measures for the marginalized. The house is recognized not merely as a shelter and a dwelling place but also as an asset which supports livelihood, symbolizes social position and is also a cultural expression. A good home would be in harmony with the natural environment protecting the household from extreme weather conditions and it would have the required connectivity for mobility and facilities for economic activities.

The objective of Indira Aawas Yojana (IAY) is primarily to provide assistance for construction of dwelling units and upgradation of existing unserviceable kachha houses for Scheduled Castes/Scheduled Tribes and non-SC/ST rural families living below the poverty line. From 1995-96, the IAY benefits have been extended to the families of the members of armed and paramilitary forces killed in action. A minimum of 60% of the funds under the scheme are earmarked for assistance to SC/ST families living below the poverty line. 3% of funds are reserved for disabled living below the poverty line in rural areas. The IAY funds and physical targets are also earmarked for the BPL Minorities (15%).

The financial assistance provided under the scheme for each house is ₹ 70,000 in plain areas and ₹ 75,000 in hilly/difficult areas/Left Wing Extremist (LWE) districts. For upgradation of kaccha/dilapidated house ₹ 15000 provided. Sanitary latrine is now a mandatory requirement of an IAY house in convergence with "**Swatch Bharat Abhiyan**".

Achievements

IAY has been implemented with the objective of providing adequate, affordable and durable homes to BPL families, addressing on priority the urgent needs of the poorest and the marginalized, particularly STs, SCs, Minority families in rural areas, including such families that have been rendered houseless due to man- made or natural calamities. Rural housing is one of the components of Bharat Nirman, which was launched in 2005 as a time bound action plan for rural infrastructure.

- In phase I of Bharat Nirman 60 lakh houses were to be constructed under IAY (in the period 2005-2009). Against this, 71.76 lakh houses were constructed with an expenditure of ₹ 21720.39 crore.
- In phase II of Bharat Nirman (2009-14) the target was fixed at 120 lakh houses under IAY. Against this target, 121.31 lakh houses have been constructed with an expenditure of ₹ 62042.25 crore.
- In the year 2013-14, 13.73 lakh houses have been constructed.

State-wise physical progress for the year 2013-14 is given below in Table 12.6.

Table 12.6: Indira Awas Yojana—State-wise physical progress 2013-14

S. No.	*States*	*Houses Completed*	*% of Target Achieved*
1.	Assam	62390	44.98
2.	Bihar	275869	45.56
3.	Chhattisgarh	21281	44.33
4.	Jammu & Kashmir	429	2.69
5.	Jharkhand	45347	67.53
6.	Madhya Pradesh	46896	41.52
7.	Uttar Pradesh	147742	49.71
	Total	1562611	62.99

Source: Rural Development Report, 2013

Best Practices

1. **Additional assistance from State resources** IAY beneficiaries receive additional assistance in many State Govts. ranging from ₹5,000 to ₹3.25 lakh. Details are as follows:

State/UTs	*Additional Assistance Given*
Andhra Pradesh	₹ 30,000 for SC
	₹ 35,000 for ST
Goa	₹ 25,000
Haryana	₹ 11,000
Karnataka	₹ 50,000
Kerala	₹ 1,30,000 for SC and general
	₹ 1,80,000 for ST
Maharashtra	₹ 25,000
Rajasthan	₹ 5,000
Sikkim	₹ 3,25,000
Tamil Nadu	₹ 50,000
Puducherry	₹ 30,000

2. **Housing Agencies/Corporation** In Andhra Pradesh and Karnataka, the scheme is implemented by a public corporation. These corporations have

taken up centralised procurement and supply of material and also provide technical support during construction. The release of instalments directly to the bank account of beneficiaries is done electronically and is linked to the progress of the houses as recorded by means of a geo-tagged photograph. A robust system of monitoring is also in place.

3. Quality inputs

- In Tamil Nadu temporary shelters are provided to the needy beneficiaries by the Gram Panchayats during the construction of IAY units.
- Tamil Nadu Government also encourages construction of Green Houses by using recycled, reused eco-friendly materials for IAY beneficiaries. Social audit is conducted in Gram Sabha by submitting their work performance, financial allocation, expenditure level, etc., in a transparent manner.
- Under the Chief Minister's Rural Housing Mission (CMRHM), the State Government of Sikkim aims to achieve the status of a Kutcha House free State by 2015 along with a qualitative improvement in the housing status of the poor in the State. The unit cost of a house comes to ₹3.25 lakh.

The CMRHM builds on tradition of community support by allowing co-financing in cash and kind from all quarters in the village.

Source: Annual Report- 2013-14, MoRD

12.8 NATIONAL SOCIAL ASSISTANCE PROGRAMME (NSAP)

Article 41 of the Constitution of India directs the State to provide public assistance to its citizens in cases of unemployment, old age, sickness, and disablement and also in other cases of undeserved want within the limit of its economic capacity and development. It is in accordance with these noble principles that the Government of India on 15th August 1995 included the National Social Assistance Programme (NSAP) in the Central Budget for 1995-96. This programme was meant for providing social assistance benefit to the aged, the BPL households in the case of death of the primary breadwinner and for maternity. The provisions were aimed at ensuring minimum national standards in addition to the benefits that the states were then providing or would provide in future. The NSAP now comprises Indira Gandhi National Old Age Pension Scheme (IGNOAPS), Indira Gandhi National Widow Pension Scheme (IGNWPS), Indira Gandhi National Disability Pension Scheme (IGNDPS), National Family Benefit Scheme (NFBS) and Annapurna. The financial outlay (B.E.) under NSAP for 2015-16 was ₹ 2505.00 crore.

The total coverage of beneficiaries under the scheme of NSAP as on 14.10.2014 was 275 lakh, which was 216 lakh in the year 2009-10.

- In July 2013, Direct Benefit Transfer (DBT) was launched in 121 pilot districts of the country covering 26 states / UTs. The bank accounts of beneficiaries are being brought under DBT so that the pension is directly transferred to the account of the beneficiaries by the disbursing office. As per NSAPMIS, direct transfer of pensions into accounts of pensioners, as on 31 March, 2014 was ₹ 213.89 crore, and the number of pensioners was ₹ 35.35 lakh.
- Further, as on 31st March, 2014, digitization of 92% of the beneficiaries' database has been completed, out of which, 45% of the beneficiaries have accounts in bank and 34% of the beneficiaries have accounts in post office. A total of 14.34 lakh beneficiaries have Aadhaar number out of which 46.36% beneficiaries have linked their Aadhaar number with bank accounts and 36.42% beneficiaries have linked their Aadhaar number with post office account.

Physical Achievements: Total number of beneficiaries reported by all the States/UT's, for the year 2014-15 is as follows:

Table 12.7: Total number of beneficiaries under NSAP, 2014-15

IGNOAPS	*IGNWPS*	*IGNDPS*	*NFBS*	*ANNAPURNA*
1,84,27,379	57,13,859	9,51,819	1,51,651	4,19,811

Source: http://rural.nic.in/netrural/rural/sites/online_eBook/MORD.html#p=60

Financial Progress: The total outlay for 2015-2016 for National Social Assistance Programme (NSAP) was ₹ 9082.00 crore, out of which ₹ 909.00 crore was for North Eastern Region and Sikkim. The scheme-wise release and expenditure reported by all the States/UT's for the year 2014-15 is as follows:

Table 12.8: Scheme-wise release and expenditure under NSAP, 2014-15

IGNOAPS		*IGNWPS*		*IGNDPS*		*NFBS*		*ANNAPURNA*	
Released	*Exp. Reported*	*Released*	*Exp. Reported*	*Released*	*Exp. Reported*	*Released*	*Exp. Reported*	*Released*	*Exp. Reported*
3425.10	3077.85	1509.65	1021.68	273.22	151.22	451.67	251.52	37.87	7.52

Source: http://rural.nic.in/netrural/rural/sites/online_eBook/MORD.html#p=60

12.9 TOTAL SANITATION CAMPAIGN (TSC)

The Total Sanitation Campaign (TSC) was launched in 1999 as a demand-driven, community-led programme with major IEC inputs to make sanitation a felt need of the people. The TSC has been able to accelerate sanitation coverage from 22 per cent as per the 2001 Census to 31 per cent in 2011, with over 28,000 PRIs becoming 'Open Defecation Free' (ODF).

The progress of the campaign remains far from satisfactory. Open defecation by around 600 million people is our biggest national shame. Latest Census data reveals that the percentage of households having access to television and telephones in rural India in 2011 exceeds the percentage of households having access to toilet facilities and tap water. Access to household amenities in ten worst performing states in terms of toilet facilities in rural India in the year 2011 (percentage of rural households) is given below (Table 12.9).

Table 12.9: Access to household amenities in worst performing states in terms of toilet facilities in rural India, 2011 (percentage of rural households)

Rank (Worst as 1)	*State*	*Toilet Facilities*	*Tap Water*	*Telephone*
1	Jharkhand	7.6	3.7	38.7
2	Madhya Pradesh	13.1	9.9	36.4
3	Odisha	14.1	7.5	33.6
4	Chhattisgarh	14.5	8.8	21.2
5	Bihar	17.6	2.6	53.5
6	Rajasthan	19.6	26.9	66.2
7	Uttar Pradesh	21.8	20.2	63.6
8	Tamil Nadu	23.2	79.3	66.3
9	Karnataka	28.4	56.4	62.6
10	Andhra Pradesh	32.2	63.4	54.8

Source: Census of India, 2011

A study, supported by UNICEF in 2008 revealed that in 56 per cent of NGP Gram Panchayats 70 per cent families were still defecating in the open and only 6 of the 162 NGPs had been able to sustain the NGP status. In a study for the Ministry of Drinking Water and Sanitation, the Centre for Media Studies (2010) found that the key factors explaining the gap between access to and usage of sanitation facilities were poor quality of construction and unfinished toilets, a major reason for which was the very low incentive provided under the TSC. The percentage of households with no latrine facilities in rural India in 2011 is given below (Table 12.10):

Table 12.10: Percentage of households without latrine facilities in rural India, 2011

S. No.	*State*	*2011*	*2001*
1.	Jharkhand	92.4	93.4
2.	Madhya Pradesh	86.9	91.1
3.	Odisha	85.9	94.8
4.	Chhattisgarh	85.5	94.8
5.	Bihar	84.2	86.1
6.	Rajasthan	80.0	85.4
7.	UP	78.2	85.4
8.	Tamil Nadu	76.8	85.6
9.	Andhra Pradesh	69.8	81.9
10.	**India**	**69.2**	**78.1**

Source: Census of India, 2011.

One of the limitations of the TSC is the narrow range of technology options offered in a country with such immensely diverse geographic, hydrologic, climatic and socio-economic conditions (high water table, flood prone, rocky ground, desert/water scarce areas and extreme low temperatures). This has led to many problems, including non-acceptance by local communities, water pollution especially in shallow water table regions, and waste of public funds. There is need to broaden the range of models permissible under TSC. Finally, the absence of a dedicated implementation agency at either the State/district or GP level, to implement TSC has emerged as a major bottleneck affecting quality of outcomes.

12.10 NATIONAL RURAL DRINKING WATER PROGRAMME (NRDWP)

The National Rural Drinking Water Programme (NRDWP) is a flagship programme of the Ministry of Drinking Water and Sanitation, and a component of the 'Bharat Nirman'. The objective of the programme is to ensure provision of safe and adequate drinking water supply through hand pumps, piped water supply schemes, etc., to all rural areas and households. Under the programme, financial assistance is provided to states/UTs for provision of drinking water supply to rural areas of the country under the components of: (i) coverage of partially covered rural habitations with water supply, (ii) coverage of quality affected rural habitations with water supply, (iii) taking up source and system sustainability measures, (iv) supporting operation and maintenance of existing water supply schemes, (v) water quality monitoring and surveillance and (vi) support activities like IEC, training, MIS, computerisation, R&D, etc. Assistance is provided in the ratio of 50:50 between Centre and States for the components of coverage, water quality and O&M except for North Eastern States and Jammu & Kashmir, to whom assistance is provided in the ratio of 90:10. Sustainability, water quality monitoring and surveillance, and support components are funded on a 100% basis by the Central Government. Out of 16.97 lakh rural habitations in the country as on 01.04.2014, 12.50 lakh habitations were fully covered with safe and adequate drinking water supply. For 2015-16, a provision of ₹ 2611.00 crore has been made for NRDWP and the rural water supply sector, including ₹ 261.00 crore for North Eastern Region and Sikkim. Further, 22% and 10% of the total allocation are earmarked for meeting expenditure on Scheduled Caste Sub-Plan and Tribal Sub-Plan respectively. During 2015-16 the thrust will be on coverage of rural population with piped water supply schemes, completion of on-going schemes, prioritising coverage of quality affected habitations, focusing on convergence of water supply with rural sanitation, planning for the optimum use of the sustainability component especially in water stressed blocks and effectively using incentive funds to promote decentralization of management of water supply schemes.

12.11 PROVISION OF URBAN FACILITIES IN RURAL AREAS (PURA)

Lack of livelihood opportunities, modern amenities and services for decent living in rural areas leads to migration of people to urban areas. There are wide gaps in the availability of infrastructure between rural and urban areas. To address these issues, the former President of India Dr. A.P.J. Abdul Kalam highlighted a vision of transformation of rural India through launching a mega mission for Provision of Urban Amenities in Rural Areas (PURA).

Seven pilot projects were implemented during the 10th Five Year Plan in Basmath (Maharashtra), Bharthana (Uttar Pradesh), Gohpur (Assam), Kujanga (Odisha), Motipur (Bihar), Rayadurg (Andhra Pradesh) and Shahpura (Rajasthan). Based on the findings of the evaluation study and feedback/ comments received during consultations with officials of State Governments, the scheme of PURA was restructured for implementation on pilot basis during 11th Five Year Plan. The scheme is being implemented on pilot basis.

Mission and Objectives of the PURA Scheme

Mission: Holistic and accelerated development of compact areas around a potential growth centre in a Gram Panchayat (or a group of Gram Panchayats) through Public Private Partnership (PPP) framework for providing livelihood opportunities and urban amenities to improve the quality of life in rural areas.
Objectives: The primary objectives of the scheme are the provision of livelihood opportunities and urban amenities in rural areas to bridge the rural-urban divide.

The illustrative list of amenities and economic activities proposed to be provided under PURA are given in the Table 12.11.

Table 12.11: Amenities and economic activities proposed to be provided under PURA

Amenities to be provided under MoRD Schemes (Compulsory Activities)	*Amenities to be provided under Non-MoRD Schemes*	*Add-on Projects (Revenue earning, people centric projects)*
• Water and Sewerage • Construction and maintenance of Village Streets • Drainage • Solid Waste Management • Skill Development • Development of Economic Activities	• Village Street Lighting • Electricity • Telecom, etc.	• Village Linked Tourism • Integrated Rural Hub, Rural Market. • Agri -Common Services Centre, • Warehousing, etc. • Any other rural-economy based project

Source: Ministry of Rural Development, GOI

12.12 COUNCIL FOR ADVANCEMENT OF PEOPLE'S ACTION AND RURAL TECHNOLOGY (CAPART)

Council for Advancement of People's Action and Rural Technology (CAPART) is an autonomous body working under the aegis of the Ministry of Rural Development, Govt. of India. It was set up in September 1986, as a supporting and funding agency for voluntary organisations. It aims at involving the people through non-government voluntary organizations in the implementation of development programmes as also in need based innovative projects. CAPART works towards creating a people's movement for development in the rural areas by means of a higher degree of social mobilization, lowering of social barriers and empowerment of the rural poor.

The primary objective is to promote voluntary action through community participation and to propagate appropriate rural technologies for the benefit of rural masses. It has a network of regional centres at Jaipur, Lucknow, Ahmedabad, Bhubaneswar, Patna, Chandigarh, Hyderabad, Guwahati and Dharwad. The total plan outlay for budget 2015-2016 was ₹ 10.00 crore.

THE OBJECTIVES OF CAPART INCLUDE:

- Encouragement, promotion and assistance to voluntary efforts in rural development with focus on injecting new technologies.
- Acting as conduit for transfer of appropriate technologies to the public and concerned organisation.
- Disseminate knowledge on rural technologies.
- Creation of employment opportunities.
- Conservation of environment conducting training programme including training for trainers.
- Carried out research studies, publishing research and study paper.
- Creating awareness on Intellectual Property Rights (IPR).

12.13 DISTRICT RURAL DEVELOPMENT AGENCY (DRDA) ADMINISTRATION

A centrally-sponsored scheme, District Rural Development Agency (DRDA) administration was launched on 1 April 1999 with the objective of strengthening the DRDA's and making them more professional in their functioning.

The primary objective of the Scheme of DRDA administration is to professionalise the DRDA so that they are able to effectively enhance the quality of implementation of anti-poverty programmes of the Ministry of Rural Development. The DRDAs are also expected to coordinate effectively with the line departments, the Panchayati Raj Institution, the banks and other financial institutions, the NGOs as well as the technical institutions with a view to gathering support and resources required for poverty reduction effort in the district.

The finding pattern of DRDA administration is in the ratio of 75:25 between the Centre and the States. During 2013-14, the BE was ₹ 250.00 crore. An amount of ₹ 400.01 crore was released to 593 DRDAs as on 31.3.2014. This amount includes ₹ 150.01 crore which has been approved by the Ministry of Finance while approving the 2nd Supplementary Grants.

12.14 INTEGRATED WATERSHED MANAGEMENT PROGRAMME (IWMP)

It is a modified programme of erstwhile Drought Prone Areas Programme (DPAP), Desert Development Programme (DDP) and Integrated Wastelands Development Programme (IWDP) of the Department of Land Resources. This consolidation is for optimum use of resources, sustainable outcomes and integrated planning. The scheme was launched during 2009-10. The programme is being implemented as per Common Guidelines for Watershed Development Projects 2008. The main objectives of the IWMP are to restore the ecological balance by harnessing, conserving and developing degraded natural resources such as soil, vegetative cover and water. The outcomes are prevention of soil erosion, regeneration of natural vegetation, rainwater harvesting and recharging of the groundwater table. This enables multi-cropping and the introduction of diverse agro-based activities, which help to provide sustainable livelihoods to the people residing in the watershed area.

During 2014-15, an allocation (RE) of ₹ 2319.00 crore has been made for the Integrated Watershed Management Programme (IWMP). Under IWMP, an amount of ₹ 2117.85 crore was released to various States up to 31.12.2014.

As per the Budget announcement for 2015-16, IWMP was made a component of Pradhan Mantri Krishi Sinchayee Yojana with an allocation of ₹ 1500.00 crore.

In the twelfth five year plan, the distinguishing characteristic of the new IWMP approach is its emphasis on livelihoods, especially for families without any assets. There are many government and non-government organizations in India who have done pioneering work in this regard and the Department of Land Resource (DoLR) is facilitating partnerships of each State government with selected institutions to carry this process forward with momentum.

12.15 PRADHAN MANTRI KRISHI SINCHAYEE YOJANA (PMKSY)

Pradhan Mantri Krishi Sinchayee Yojana (PMKSY) has been formulated amalgamating ongoing schemes, viz., Accelerated Irrigation Benefit Programme (AIBP) of Ministry of Water Resources, River Development & Ganga Rejuvenation; Integrated Watershed Management Programme (IWMP) of Department of Land Resources; and On Farm Water Management (OFWM) component of National Mission on Sustainable Agriculture

(NMSA) of Department of Agriculture and Cooperation. PMKSY is to be implemented in an area development approach, adopting decentralized state level planning and projectised execution, allowing the states to draw their irrigation development plans based on district/blocks plans with a horizon of 5 to 7 years. States can take up projects based on the District/ State Irrigation Plan. All the States and Union Territories including North Eastern States are covered under the programme.

Provision has been made under PMKSY during 2015-16 for carrying out extension activities in the field with special focus on water harvesting, water management and crop alignment for farmers and grass root level field functionaries.

It has been launched with an outlay of ₹ 50,000 crore for a period of 5 years (2015-16 to 2019-20) to achieve convergence of investments in irrigation at the field level.

12.16 LAND REFORMS

For land reforms, financial assistance is being provided to the States/UTs under the National Land Records Modernization Programme (NLRMP), inter-alia, for computerization of the Records of Rights (RoRs), digitization of maps, survey/resurvey using modern technology, computerization of registration, training and capacity building of the concerned officials and functionaries, connectivity amongst the land records and registration offices and modern record rooms/land records management centres at tehsil/ taluk/circle/ block level. States may pool in higher resources for NLRMP in view of enhanced devolution of Union taxes as per the recommendation of 14th Finance Commission. The Department of Land Resources has formulated the National Rehabilitation and Resettlement Policy (NRRP), 2007 with the objective of minimizing displacement and to promote, as far as possible, non-displacing or least-displacing alternatives, to ensure adequate rehabilitation package and expedite the rehabilitation process.

Computerisation of Land Records (CLR) and Strengthening of Revenue Administration and Updating of Land Records (SRA & ULR) are two centrally sponsored schemes that are administered by Land Reforms Division in the Department of Land Resources.

12.17 CENTRALLY SPONSORED SCHEME FOR COMPUTERISATION OF LAND RECORDS (CLR)

With the aim of removing inherent flaws in the existing land records system and bringing efficiency, transparency and easy accessibility to the system of land records, the centrally sponsored scheme on Computerization of Land Records (CLR) was launched in 1988-89.

Pilot projects were initiated in 8 districts, one each in 8 states, and the scheme was subsequently extended to the rest of the country.

Up to 2007-08, 583 districts in the country were covered under the programme. Also funds were provided to the States/UTs for setting up data centres at tehsils/taluk, sub-division and districts. Since the inception of the scheme, the Ministry released had ₹ 586.61 crore as on 31.03.2008. The utilization of funds reported by the States/UTs is ₹ 536.41 crore which is approximately 91.44% of the total funds released.

The scheme of Computerization of Land Records (CLR) has been merged with the National Land Records Modernization Programme (NLRMP) during 2008-2009.

12.18 CENTRALLY SPONSORED SCHEME FOR STRENGTHENING OF REVENUE ADMINISTRATION AND UPDATING OF LAND RECORDS (SRA&ULR)

The centrally sponsored scheme for Strengthening of Revenue Administration and Updating of Land Records (SRA & ULR) was started in 1987-88 with the objective of helping the States in updating and maintenance of land records, strengthening and modernizing revenue machinery, carrying out survey and settlement operations and strengthening training infrastructure. Funding under the scheme was on 50:50 sharing basis between the Centre and the states. The Union Territories were provided full Central assistance.

Funds were provided under the Scheme to all the States/UTs. As on 31.3.2008, funds to the tune of ₹ 475.36 crore were released to the States/ UTs as Central Share. The utilization of funds reported by the States/UTs is ₹ 439.24 crore which is about 92.40% of the total funds released.

The scheme of SRA&ULR has also been merged with the National Land Records Modernization Programme (NLRMP) during 2008-2009.

12.19 NATIONAL LAND RECORDS MODERNISATION PROGRAMME (NLRMP)

The Department was administering two centrally sponsored schemes, viz., Computerization of Land Records (CLR) and Strengthening of Revenue Administration and Updating of Land Records (SRA&ULR) up to 2007-08. During 2008-09, a modified centrally-sponsored scheme in the shape of the National Land Records Modernization Programme (NLRMP) was launched combining the key components of the aforesaid two schemes, adding new components such as integration of textual and spatial records, computerization of registration and inter-connectivity between revenue and registration systems, firming up modern technology options for survey and core GIS.

The activities being supported under the programme, *inter alia,* include computerization of the records of rights (RoRs), digitization of maps, survey/resurvey using modern technology including aerial photogrammetry, computerization of registration, training and capacity building of the concerned officials and functionaries, connectivity amongst the land records and registration offices and land records management centres at tehsil/taluk/circle/block level.

The activities to be undertaken under the NLRMP are to converge in the district and district is the unit of implementation. All the districts in the country are expected to be covered under the programme by the end of the 12th Plan. The ultimate goal of the NLRMP is to usher in the system of conclusive titling, to replace the current system of presumptive titles in the country.

An outlay of ₹ 181.00 crore (RE) was approved for 2014-15 for the National Land Records Modernization Programme (NLRMP) which includes ₹ 20.23 crore for Tribal Sub Plan and ₹ 30.11 crore for Special Component Plan for Scheduled Castes. The plan outlay under NLRMP for 2015-16 was ₹ 97.77 crore.

12.20 PANCHAYATI RAJ INSTITUTIONS (PRIs)

In the history of Panchayati Raj in India, on 24th April 1993, the Constitutional (73rd Amendment Act), 1992 came into force to provide constitutional status to the Panchayati Raj Institutions. The Act aims to provide a 3-tier system of Panchayati Raj for all States having population of over 2 million. The 3-tier system of Panchayati Raj consists of:

a. Village Level Panchayat
b. Block Level Panchayat
c. District Level Panchayat

Panchayats are more than instruments for implementation of the Act; they have an intrinsic value in realising the expected outcome of enhanced livelihood security for the poor. The Department of Rural Development has provided centrality to Panchayati Raj Institutions (PRIs) in the planning, implementation and monitoring of schemes like MGNREGA, NRLM, IAY, NSAP, etc. Through such processes PRIs have been strengthened.

The Central Plan outlay of Ministry of Panchayati Raj for the year 2015-16 is ₹ 94.00 crore out of which ₹ 10.00 crore has been earmarked for North Eastern Areas including Sikkim. An important function of the Ministry of Panchayat Raj is to monitor the implementation of Part IX of the Constitution inserted by the Constitution (73rd Amendment) Act, 1992, provisions of the Panchayats (Extension to the Scheduled Areas), Act, 1996 and Article 243 ZD in Part IX-A of the Constitution relating to District Planning Committees.

PRI's and MGNREGA

An important goal of MGNREGA is to deepen democracy at the grassroots level, and bring about greater transparency, responsiveness and accountability in local governance. MGNREGA provides a powerful, legal entitlement and opportunity to realise the objectives of the 73rd Amendment of the Constitution. The Act formally declares the Panchayats at the three levels as "principal authorities for planning and implementation of the Schemes made under this Act" and this provision is backed up by substantial guaranteed resources. Panchayati Raj Institutions (PRIs) have been entrusted with following roles and responsibilities in the implementation of Mahatma Gandhi NREGA:

As per the Act, Panchayats are the principal authorities to implement various provisions of MGNREGS. These institutions have emerged as principal authorities in the implementation of the Act as is evident from the fact that the maximum works have been done by the Panchayats and maximum funds have also flowed to them. During 2013-14, a total of 93,60,426 works have been done, out of which 8553574 (91.38%) works have been carried out by the Gram Panchayats. As regards flow of funds, a total of ₹ 3934536 lakh of fund (in terms of cost of work done) flowed to different implementing agencies, out of which ₹ 3623763 lakh (92.10%) have flowed to Gram Panchayats.

Best Practices: Implementation of MGNRGA by Panchayat (Springs Revival for Rural Water Security in Sikkim)

The villagers of Chuba Phong Gram Panchayat in Namthing block of South Sikkim district have transformed a community which used to suffer from regular droughts. About 120 household's level water storage tanks of 10000 litres capacity each have been constructed. These tanks are filled from revived springs and used to meet their household water requirements. The panchayats investment in water storage infrastructure has paid immediate dividends. Chuba Phong Gram Panchayat is one of many gram panchyats in Sikkim that have benefited from the Dhara Vikas programme launched by the State's Rural Management and Development Department. Hundreds of water storage tanks of 10,000 litres, 34,000 litres and 40,000 litres capacity have been constructed with funds from MGNREGA and the NRDWP among other sources. A sum of INR 75 million has been invested so far under MGNREGS.

Source: Annual Report, 2013-14, MoRD

Bibliography

BOOKS AND PAPERS

Abasiekong, Edet M.: 'Integrated Rural Development in the Third World: Its Concepts, Problems and Prospects'. Smithtown NY: Exposition Press, 1982.

Adelman, Irma and Steven Vogel: The Relevance of ADLI in Sub-Saharan Africa. In *Industrialisation based on Agriculture Development: African Development Perspective Yearbook*, 1990/91.

Aggarwal, A.N: The Economics of Underdevelopment, Oxford University Press, Bombay, 1969.

Antholt, Charles. H.: 'Getting ready for the Twenty-First Century: Technical Change and Institutional Modernisation in Agriculture', *World Bank Technical Paper 217*. Washington D.C.:World Bank, 1994.

Altieri, Miguel A.: Developing sustainable agricultural systems for small farmers in Latin America, Natural Resources Forum, Volume 24, Issue 2, pages 97–105, May 2000.

Arora, R.C: 'Integrated and Rural Development' S. Chand and Co. Ltd., New Delhi, 1979.
-'Industry and Rural Development' S. Chand and Co. Ltd., New Delhi, 1985.

Bandyopadhyaya, J.: 'The Poverty of Nations: A Global Perspective of Mass Poverty in the Third World', Allied Publications Pvt. Ltd., Calcutta, 1988.

Balakrishna, S. 'Some development features of Rural India, Rural Development of India, Some Facts', National Institute of Rural Development, Hyderabad, 1979.

Basu. A.S.: 'Tribal development programme in Himachal Pradesh: A case study of Bharmaur', A doctoral thesis, Punjab University, Chandigarh, 1981.

Behari Bipin: 'Rural Industrialisation in India', Vikas Publishing, New Delhi, 1997.

Bhatia, B.M.: Poverty, Agriculture and Economics Growth, Vikas Publishing House, New Delhi, 1977.

Bhattachary, B.N.:	'Indian Rural Economics', Metropolitan Book Co., New Delhi, 1984.
Bhattachary, S.N.:	'Rural Development in India and developing countries', Metropolitan Book Co., New Delhi, 1983.
Bhattachary, S.N.:	'Community Development: An Analysis of the Programme in India', Academic Publishers, Calcutta, 1970.
Bhattachary Sibnath:	'Rural Industrialisation in India: Its nature and problems', B.R. Publishing Corporation, Delhi, 1980.
Bruce R. Crouch & Sankariah Chamala:	'Extension Education & Rural Development', John Willey & Sons Ltd., New York, 1981.
Carney, Diana:	'Sustainable Rural Livelihoods: What Contribution Can We Make?' Department for International Development, Cornell University, 1998.
Chambers, Longhurst & Pacey:	'Seasonal Dimensions to Rural Poverty', S. Chand & Co. Ltd., New Delhi, 1985.
Chisholm, Nancy S.:	'A Future for Public Housing', Real Estate Economics Volume 11, Issue 2, pages 203–220, June 1983.
Dakshinamurthi C., Michael, A.M. & Shri Mohan:	'Water Resources of India and their Utilisation in Agriculture', Water Technology Centre, IARI, 1973.
Dak, T.M.:	'Management in Rural Development' Oxford and IBH, New Delhi, 1983.
Dandekar, V.M.& Rath, N. Das Gupta, P.K.:	'The impact of Industrialisation on a tribe in south Bihar', Anthropological Survey of India, Calcutta, 1978.
Dasgupta, Partha.:	'An enquiry into Well-being and Destitution'. Oxford University Press, New York, 1993.
Dasgupta, Partha and Maler, Goran. K.,:	'Net national product, wealth, and social well-being'. Environment and Development Economics, pp. 69-93, February 2000.
Dasgupta, Partha, and Maler. K.G. :	The Environment and Emerging Developing Issues.' *Proceedings of the World Bank Annual Conference on Development Economics 1990. Supplement to the World Bank Economic Review and the World Bank Research Observer*, pp. 101-32, 1991.
Deogaonkar, S.G.:	'Administration for rural development of India', Concept, New Delhi, 1980.
Deininger, Klaus:	*Land policies for growth and poverty reduction.* A World Bank policy research report. Washington, DC : World Bank Group, 2003.

Delgado, M. Rosegrant, H. Steinfeld, S.Ehui, VC. Courbois: 'Livestock to 2020. The next food revolution', International Food Policy Research Institute, Food and Agriculture Organisation of the United Nations, International Livestock Research Institute, Washington, D.C., 1999.

Desai, A.R.: Rural sociology in India, Popular Prakashan, Bombay, 1983.

Desai, D.K.: 'Management in Rural Development', Oxford and IBH, New Delhi, 1983.

Desai, S.S.M.: 'Rural banking in India', Himalaya Publishing House, Bombay, 1983.

Desai Vasant: 'Rural Development'
Vol. 1-Issues and Problems
Vol. 2-Programmes and Strategies
Vol. 3-Organisation and Management
Vol. 4-Experiment in Rural Development
Vol. 5-Rural Development through Plans.
Vol. 6-Rural Development in the Seventh Plan
Himalaya Publishing House Bombay, 1988.
-A study of Rural Economics, Himalaya Publishing House, Bombay.
-Rural Banking in India, HPH, Bombay.
-Financing Rural Development, HPH, Bombay.
-Fundamentals of Rural Development
-Issues in Agriculture & Forestry
-Indian Agriculture: Its Nature & Problems
-Forestry Management in India
-Agriculture Economics.

Dholakia & Iyengar: 'Planning for Rural Development-Issues and Case Studies', Himalayas Publishing House, Bombay, 1989.

Dube and Murdia(e.d.): 'Land Alienation and Restoration in Tribal Communities in India', Himalaya Publishing House, Bombay, 1982.

D. Vasudeva Rao: 'Rural Development through Irrigation', Ashish Publishing House, New Delhi, 1988.

'Facts of Rural Development', Ashish Publishing House, New Delhi, 1972.

E.M. Sminger, Douglas: 'Rural India in transition', All India Panchayat Parishad, New Delhi, 1972.

Elic, A.N.: 'Operational Problems of Rural banking', Vora & Co., Bombay, 1967.

Elliot, Charles: 'Problems of Poverty in Third World: A Study of Social Economics Stratificat-Ion', Praeger, New York, 1975.

Fan, S., P. Hazell: 'Linkages between government spending, growth and poverty in rural India', IFPRI Research Report 110, Washington D.C.: International Food Policy Research Institute, 1999.

Fonseca, A.J.(e.d): 'Challenge of Poverty in India', Vikas Publishing House, New Delhi, 1971.

Franda, M.: 'Small is Plitics: Organisational Alternatives in India's Rural Development', Wiley Eastern Ltd., New Delhi, 1987.

Gadgil, D.R.: 'District Development Planning', Asia Publishing House, Bombay, 1967.

Gaikwad, V.R.: 'Panchayati Raj and Bureaucracy', National Institute of Community Development, Hyderabad, 1969.

Ghandhi, Rajiv & Singh, Rao Birendra: 'Agricultural Development and the small Farmer', S. Chand & Co. Ltd., New Delhi, 1984.

Garg, Usha & Jagdish Vibhakar: 'Poverty of Nations and Third World', UDH Publishers, New Delhi, 1985.

Gedem, R.M.: 'Poverty Economic Development and Industrialisation', Deep & Deep Publications, New Delhi, 1988.

Ghate, Prabhu: 'Direct Attack on Rural Poverty: Policy Programmes and Implications', Concept, New Delhi, 1984.

Giriappa, S.: 'Income Saving and Investment Pattern in Rural India', Ashish Publishing House, Bombay, 1988.

'Rural Energy Crisis', Himalaya Publishing House, Bombay, 1988.

Grewal, P.S.: 'Rural Banking in India', Kalyani Publishers Ludhiana, 1985.

-Rural Economic, Kalyani Publishers Ludhiana, 1983.

Gupta & Gupta: 'Rural Development in India-Poverty and Development', Himalaya Publishing House, Bombay, 1988.

G. Morley Mohan Lal: 'Poverty Alleviation Indian Experience', Himalaya Publising House, Bombay, 1988.

Hague, M.L.: 'The Poverty Curtain', National, New Delhi, 1988.

Hanumappa, H.G. (ed): 'Sericulture for Rural Development, Himalaya Publishing House, Bombay, 1986.

Hardin, Garitt.: 'Tragedy of the Commons', Science (AAAS) 162 (3859): 1243–1248., December 1968.

Hariharn, C.: 'Panchayati Raj and Rural Development—A Study of Tamil Nadu', Concept, New Delhi, 1983.

Harison, Paul: 'Inside Third World: The Anatomy of Poverty', Second Edition, Penguin, 1981.

Hayami, Y.: 'Development Economics: From the poverty to the Wealth of Nations', Oxford: Clarendon Press, 1997.

Hinchcliffe, F., I.Gujit, J.N. Pretty, and Shah: 'New Horizons: The Economic, Social and Environmental Impact of Participatory Watershed Development', International Institute for Environment and Development, London, 1995.

Jain, L.C., Krishnamurthy, & Tripathi, P.M.: 'Grass without Roots-Rural Development under Government Auspices', Sage Publications Pvt. Ltd., Delhi, 1985.

Jain, S.C.: 'Community Development and Panchayati Raj in India', Allied Publishers, Bombay 1975.

Jayne, T. S., and S. Jones : Food Marketing and Pricing Policy in Eastern and Southern Africa: A Survey. World Devlopment 25: 1505-1527, 1997.

Johnstor, Bruce F. and William, C. Clark: 'Redesigning Rural Development: A Strategic Prespective', The John Hopkin University Press, Baltimore, 1982.

Joshi, Navin Chandra: 'Indian Rural Economy', Young Asia Publications, New Delhi, 1980.

Kashyap, C.I.: 'Management and Planning of Rural Development in India', Ashish Publishing House, New Delhi, 1989.

Kaur, Satnam: 'Women in Rural Development', Mittal Publications, New Delhi, 1988.

K. Manu.: 'Tribal Women in Changing Society; Mittal Publications, New Delhi, 1988.

Kherallah, Mylene: Reforming Agricultural Markets in Africa, Baltimore: Johns Hopkins University Press, 2002.

Kocher, E. James: 'Rural Development, Income Distribution and Fertility Decline,' The Population Council, 1970.

Lakshman & Narayan (Ed.): "Rural Development in India-A Multidimensional analysis", Himalaya Publishing House, Bombay, 1988.

Lal,A.K,: 'Politics of Poverty: A study of bounded Labour', Chetana Publications, New Delhi, 1977.

Lal, Mohan.: 'Rural Industrialisation & Regional Development,' Deep & Deep Publication, New Delhi, 1987.

Lele; Uma.,: 'Design of Rural Development – Lessons from Africa", John Hopkins University Press, London, 1975.

Long, N.,: An Introduction to the Sociology of Rural Development, Tavistock Publications Ltd., London, 1982.

Madan, G.R.,: 'India's Developing Villages,' National, New Delhi, 1986.

Mahajan, V.S.,: 'Studies in Indian Agriculture & rural Development', Deep & Deep Publications, Neew Delhi, 1988.

Maheshwari, S.R.,: 'Rural Development in India – A Public Policy Approach', Sage Publications (India) Pvt. Ltd., New Delhi, 1985.

Mardal, R.B.,: 'Planned Development of Rural Settlements', Concept, New Delhi, 1981.

Marriott, Mckim: 'Village India', The University of Chicago Press, USA, 1963.

Mathew, T. (E.d.): 'Rural Development in India', Publishers Academy, New Delhi, 1986.

Maxwell, S., and R. Herber-Percy: New trends in development thinking and implications for agriculture. In Food agriculture and rural development: *Current and emerging issues for economic analysis and policy research*, ed. K. Stamoulis. Rome: Food and Agriculture Organisation of the United Nations, 2001.

Mehta, B.C. Awadh Prashad: 'Agrarian relations and Exploitation', Ashish Publishing House, New Delhi, 1988.

Mehta, N.C. and Panandikar: 'Rural Banking', National Institute of Bank Management, Pune, 1974.

V.A. Pai, Mehta, S.R.: 'Rural Development Policies and Programmes', Sage Publications, New Delhi, 1984.

Mehta, V.D.: 'Growth Agriculture Employment in Rural India', Prateeksha Publications, Jaipur, 1988.

Mellor, John, W.: The Economics of Agricultural Development, 1964.

Minhas, B.S.: 'Planning and the Poors', S. Chand & Co. Ltd., New Delhi, 1988.

Mishra, G.P., Rai, R.P. and Bajpai, B.K.: 'Village Industries and Agriculture in Changing Agrarian Situation', Ashish Publishing House, New Delhi, 1989.

Mishra, R.P. and Sundaram, K.V.,: 'Rural Area Development –Perspective and Approaches', Sterling Pulishers (P) Ltd., New Delhi, 1979.

Mishra, R.P.: Rural Development –Capitalist and Socialist Paths, Vols. 1-5, Concept Publishing Co., New Delhi, 1985.

Mishra, S.N.: 'Rural Development and Panchayati Raj', Concept, Publications, New Delhi, 1981.

Mohapatra, P.C.: 'Economics Development of Tribal India', Ashish Publishing House, New Delhi, 1988.

Mohsin, Nadeem,: 'Rural Development through Governmental Programmes', Concept, New Delhi, 1985.

Moris, Jone: 'Managing Induced Rural Development', International Development Institute, Indiana University, Bloomington, 1981.

Mosher, A.T.,: 'Thinking About Rural Development', Agricultural Development Council, New York, 1976.

Mosier, A.R. and Delgado, J.A.: 'Methane and nitrous oxides fluxes in grasslands in western Puerto Rico', *Chemosphere*, 35: 2059-2082, 1997.

Moynihan, Daniel P.,: 'On Understanding Poverty: Perspective from the Social Sciences', Basic Books, New York, 1969.

Mydral, Gunnar: - 'Asian Drama: An Enquiry into the Poverty of Nations'(3 Vol.) Penguin., New York, 1968.

-The Challenge of World Poverty', Penguin, 1970.

NABARD: 'Vikas Volunteer Vahini – Genesis and Methodology', Bombay, 1984.

Naidu, L.K.,: 'Bank Finance for Rural Artisans', Ashish Publishing House, New Delhi, 1984.

Nanavati, B and Anjaria, J.J.,: 'The Indian Rural Problems, Indian Society of Agriculture Economics, Bombay, 1970.

Naoroji, Dadabhai,: 'Poverty and un-British Rule in India', Swan Sonnenschein, London, 1901.

N.I.R.D.: 'Rural Development in India: Some Facets', (Revised Ed.), National Institute of Rural Development, Hyderabad, 1986.

North, Douglass: 'Institutions, Institutional Change and Economic Performance', Cambridge University Press, October 1990.

Norton, Roger. D: 'Agricultural Development Policy: Concepts and Experiences', ISBN: 978-0-470-85778-6, December 2003.

Osmani, S.R.: Human Rights to Food, Health and Education, *Journal of Human Development* , Vol.1(2), pp. 271-96, 2000.

Ostrom, Elinor.: 'Governing the Commons: The Evolution of Institutions for Collective Action', Cambridge, UK: Cambridge University Press, November 1990.

Pais, H., & Singh, C.S.K.,: 'Poverty Alleviation Programmes: Feedback from Jhahna (M.P.)', National Labour Institute, New Delhi, 1986.

Pandey, B.N. (Ed.),: 'Role of Science and Technology In Rural and Economics Development in India', S. Chand & Co. Ltd., New Delhi, 1986.

Pareek, Udai: 'Education and Rural Development in Asia, Oxford and IBH Publications, New Delhi, 1982.

Patel, V.K., Shah, A.C., and D' Mello, L.: 'Rural Economics', Himalaya Publishing House, Bombay, 1987.

Poulton C, Dorward A, Kydd J, Poole N, Shah, P., G. Bharadwaj and R. Ambastha: 'Participatory impact monitoring of a soil and water conservation programme by farmers, extension volunteer and AKRSP' RPA Notes, vol. 13, 1995.

Smith L et al.: 'A New Institutional Economics Perspective on Current Policy Debates, Smallholder Cash Crop Production under Market Liberalisation: A New Institutional Economics Perspective', Wallingford, 1998.

Pretty, J. N., & Chambers, R.: 'Towards a learning paradigm: New professionalism and institutions for sustainable agriculture'. IDS Discussion Paper DP 334. Brighton: IDS. 1994.

Radhy, Kishore C.: 'Commercial Banks and Rural Development', Asian Publications Services, New Delhi, 1980.

Rao, R.V.: 'Rural Industrialisation in India: The Changing Profile', (2nd Ed), Concept, New Delhi, 1987.

Rao, V.K.R.V.: 'Food Nutrition & Poverty in India, Vikas Publishing House, New Delhi, 1982.

Rao, Vasudeva, D: 'Rural Development through Irrigation', Ashish Publishing House, New Delhi, 1987.

Rao, Vasudeva, D: 'Facets of Rural Development', Concept, New Delhi, 1986.

Robery, Chambers.: 'Rural Development, Longman, London, 1983.

Reardon. T.: 'African agriculture: Productivity and sustainability issues'. In *International agricultural development*, ed. C. K. Eicher and J. Staatz. Baltimore : John Hopkins University Press, 1998.

Sharma, S.K. (Ed.): 'Dynamics of Rural Development', Concept, New Delhi, 1977.

Sharma, S.K. and Malhotra, S.L.: 'Integrated Rural Development: Approach, Strategy and Perspectives' Abhinav Publications, New Delhi, 1977.

Shah, S.M.:	'Rural Development and Planning and Reforms', Abhinav Publications, New Delhi, 1977.
Singh, Ajit:	Rural Development & Banking in India', Deep & Deep Publications, New Delhi, 1985.
Singh, Mohinder,:	'Rural Development Administration & Anti Poverty Programme', Deep & Deep Publications, New Delhi, 1988.
Singh Katar:	'Rural Development –Principals, Policies and Management', Sage Publications, (India) Pvt. Ltd. New Delhi, 1988.
Sinha, A.K.:	'Mass Media and Rural Development –A study of village Communication in Bihar', Concept, New Delhi, 1985.
Singh, G.S.:	'Rural Modernisation, Contradiction and Change', Intellectual Publishing House, New Delhi, 1982.
Singh, A.K.:	'Agricultural Development and Rural Poverty', Ashish Publishing House, New Delhi, 1987.
Singh, Pramod:	'Ecology of Rural India', Ashish Publishing House, New Delhi, 1986.
Sirisikar, V.M.:	'The Rural Elite in Development Society', Orient Longmans Ltd. Bombay, 1976.
Singh, R.Y. & Singh A.K.:	'Planning in Integrated Rural Environment', Deep & Deep Publicatons, New Delhi, 1980.
Srinivas, M.N.	-India's Villages, Media Promoters and Publishers, Bombay, 1978.
	-India: Social Structure, Hindustan Publishing Corp. Delhi, 1982.
Sirivastav, M and Singh, A.K.:	'Rural Development in India', Deep & Deep Publications, New Delhi, 1988.
Stiglitz, Joseph E.; Meier, Gerald M.:	'Frontiers of Development Economics: the Future in Perspective'. Washington, D.C. Oxford New York: World Bank Oxford University Press, 2001.
Stiglitz, Joseph E.:	"Redefining the role of the state - What should it do? How should it do it? And how should these decisions be made?" England: Anthem Press, pp. 94–126, 2001.
Stiglitz, Joseph E.; Weiss, Andrew.:	"Credit rationing in markets with imperfect information". The American Economic Review (American Economic Association via JSTOR) 71 (3): 393–410.June 1981.

Subramanian, C.:	'Integrated Rural Development', Abhinav Publications, New Delhi, 1976.
Sudha, V. Rao.:	'Education and Rural Development', Sage Publications (India) Pvt. Ltd. New Delhi, 1985.
Swaminathan, M.S.:	'Science & Integrated Rural Development', Concept, New Delhi, 1982.
Tiwari, R.T. & Sinha, R.C.:	'Rural Development and Planning In India', Deep & Deep Publications, New Delhi, 1986.
Thakur, Devendra:	'Rural Development and Planning in India', Deep & Deep Publications, New Delhi, 1986.
Townsend, Peter:	'The Concept of Poverty', Heinamann, London, 1970.
Tripathi, P.C.:	'Rural Transport and Economic Development', S. Chand & Co. Ltd., New Delhi, 1972.
U.N.A. P.D.I.:	'Local Level Planning & Rural Development: Alternative Strategies', United Nations Asian & Pacific Development Institute (U.N.A.P.D.I.) Bankok, Concept, New Delhi.
Updhyaya, Rakesh:	'Integrated Rural Development Programmes: A Policy Approach', Himalaya Publishing House, Bombay, 1989.
Uphoff, Norman:	'Grassroots Organizations and NGO's in Rural Development: Opportunities with diminishing states and Expanding Markets' World Development 21 (4), 1993.
Venkaiah, V.:	'Impact of Agro-Based Industries on Rural Economy', Himalaya Publishing House, Bombay, 1987.
Venkatappaiah, B:	'Recent Trends in Rural Development Objectives and Programmes', Andhra University Press, Waltair, 1974.
Venkata Reddy, K.:	'Rural Development in India (Poverty & Development), Himalaya Publishing House, Bombay, 1988.
Vidyarthi, P.L.:	'Rural Development in South Asia' Concept, New Delhi, 1982.
Vivekananad, M.:	'Planning Unit Areas for Integrated Rural Development', Ashish Publishing House, New Delhi, 1986.
Wadhava, Charan, D.:	'Rural Banks for Rural Development: An Analysis of the working of Regional Banks in India, with two case Studies', MacMillan, New Delhi, 1980.
Wedderburn, Dorothy (ed):	'Poverty, Inequality and Class Structure', Cambridge University Press, London. 1974.
Whitby, M.C.:	'Rural Resource Development ', Mathuen and Co. Ltd. London, 1974.

Yerram Raju, B: 'Agricultural Finance: Commercial Banks and Rural Development –Issues and Trends', A Data News Features Publications, New Delhi, 1982.

Yujiro, Hayani, and Ruttan, Vernon W.: 'Agriculture Development: An International Perspective', The Johns Hopkins University Press, Baltimore, 1971.

Zaidi, Sayed, Sajid Husain,: 'Rural India and Malnutrition: Implications, Problems & Prospects', Concept New Delhi, 1982.

REPORTS

Adm. D.W. "policy Issues in Rural Finance and Development" Report of the Conference of Rural Finance Research, San Diego, California, 1977.

All India Rural Debt and Investment Survey (1971-72) "Indebtedness of Rural Households and Availability of Institutional Finance," R.B.I. Bombay, 1977.

All India Rural Credit Survey Committee Report Vol. 1, 2, 3, R.B.I., Bombay, 1954.

All India Rural Credit Survey Committee Report, R.B.I., 1969.

Annual Reports, Ministry of Rural Development, New Delhi.

Annual Reports, 2013-14, Ministry of Rural Development, New Delhi.

Bank of India, "Farm Business Finance –Background Paper" for Workshop on Financing Agriculture Organised at Orissa University of Agriculture and Technology. Bhubaneswar, 1986.

CGIAR Financial Reports, CGIAR Secretariat, Washington D.C., 1999.

Evaluation report on the Administrative Arrangements for Rural Development PEOs Study, 1983.

Financing Agriculture by Commercial Banks –Reports of a Seminar held on December 6-8, 1968, Bombay, 1968.

India, Government of, Ministry of Agriculture and Irrigation, reports of the National Commission on Agriculture, 1976.

Part II, Policy and Strategy.

Part V, Resource Development.

Part VI, Crop Production, Sericulture and Agriculture.

Part VII, Animal Husbandry.

Part VIII, Fisheries.

Part IX, Forestry.

Part X, Inputs.

Part XI, Research, Education and Extension.

Part XII, Supporting Services and Incentives.

Part XIII, Rural Employment and Special Area Programmes.

Part XV, Agrarian Reforms.

IFAD, "Rural Poverty Report, 2001: New Realities, New Challenges: New Opportunities for Tomorrow's Generation", 2011.

India, Government of, Directorate of Economics and Statistics, Ministry of Agriculture and Rural Development, Indian Agriculture in Brief, 1985.

India, Government of, Different Five Year Plan Reports.

India, Government of, Ministry of Education, Challenge of Education, New Delhi, 1985.

India, Government of, Royal Commission on Agriculture in India, Report, Calcutta, Central publications Bureau, 1928.

India, Government of, India 1987.

India, Government of, Report on India's Food Crisis and Steps to Meet It by the Agricultural Production Team sponsored by Ford Foundation, April, 1959.

India, Government of, Report on High-Yielding Varieties Programme (Studies in eight districts, Kharif, 1966-67.)

India, Government of, Report of the Expert Committee on Assessment and Evaluation of the Intensive Agricultural District Programme. (1960-68.)

India, Government of, Report of the Irrigation Commission, 1972.

India, Government of, The Advisory Board on Energy –Recommendations, Sept. 1983. and Feb. 1984.

Govt. of India, Planning Commission, 6th and 7th Five Year Plans, Yojna Bhawan New Delhi, 1989.

Govt. of India, Planning Commission, Faster, Sustainable and More Inclusive Growth, An Approach to the Twelfth Five Year Plan (2012-17) , Yojna Bhawan New Delhi, October, 2011.

Govt. of India, Planning Commission, Twelfth Five Year Plan (2012-17), Social Sectors, Yojna Bhawan New Delhi, 2013 .

Govt. of India, Planning Commission, "Evaluation Report on Integrated Rural Development Programme", Yojna Bhawan, New Delhi, May, 1985.

Govt. of India, Planning Commission, Report on Evaluation Study of Small Farmers, Marginal Farmers and Agricultural Labourers, Yojna Bhawan, New Delhi, 1979.

Govt. of India, Planning Group on District Planning", Vol. I & II, Yojna Bhawan, New Delhi, 1984.

Govt. of India, Ministry of Rural Development, "Important Circulars on IRDP (issued since 2.10.1980) Krishi Bhawan, New Delhi, July, 1982.

Govt. of India, Ministry of Rural Reconstruction, Manual on IRDP, Krishi Bhawan, New Delhi, 1980.

Institute of Financial Management & Research, "An Economic Assessment of Poverty Eradication & Rural Unemployment Programme and Their Prospects", Mimeo, Madras, April, 1984.

International Communication Agency, "Proceedings of Seminar on Dynamics of Rural Development," Missourie-U.S.A., May, 23-25, 1980.

International Labour Organisation, "Human resource Development, Objectives, Problems and Policies," Geneva, 1968.

Management Development Institute, "Backward Area Development: Strategies and Policies", Proceedings of a Seminar, New Delhi, 1977.

National Institute of Rural Development, "Rural Development Statistics", Hyderabad, 1984.

National Bank for Agriculture & Rural Development, "Study of the Implementation of IRDP", Mimeo, NABARD, Bombay, 1985.

NCEUS, Report on Conditions of Work and Promotion of Livelihoods in the Unorganised Sector, New Delhi, August, 2007.

ODI Annual Report, Research Reports and Studies, June 2002, ODI, UK.

Rath, N., "Re-orientation of the Rural Anti-Poverty Programme: A Note on Rural Development Vol. II, Dept. of Rural Development, Ministry of Agriculture, New Delhi, 1985.

Report of the Expert Group on "Alleviation of Poverty", Planning Commission, Yojna Bhawan, New Delhi, 1982.

Report of the Committee to Review the "Existing Administrative Arrangements for Rural Development and Poverty Alleviation Programmes, CAARD, 1985.

Report of the Working Group on the "Role of Bank in Implementation of New 20-Point Programme" (Ghosh Committee), Bombay, 1981.

Report of the Committee to Review Arrangement for Institution Credit for Agricultural and Rural Development, CRAFICARD, 1981.

Report of the Public Accounts Committee for the year 1987-88 on IRDP, Ministry of Agriculture, New Delhi, 1988.

R.B.I. Report on "Guidelines for Advances to Priority Sector", Bombay, 1984.

R.B.I.'s "Important Circulars for IRDP", Bombay, 1984.

R.B.I. Report on "Priority Sector Lending and the 20-point Economic Programme –Role of Banks", Bombay, 1981.

UNCTAD, "The least Developed Countries: 1984 Report", U.N.O., New York, 1984 Annex. 1985.

UNDP, "Human Development Report 2009: Overcoming Barriers: Human Mobility and Development", New York, 2009.

World Bank, "Demography and Poverty", World Bank Staff Working Paper No. 623 by Michael Lipton, Washington, D.C., 1983.

World Bank, "Poverty and Hunger: Issues and Options for Food Security in Developing Countries", Washington, D.C., 1986.

World Bank, Poverty Undernutrition and Hunger", World Bank, Staff Working Paper No. 597 by Michael Lipton, Washington D., 1988.

World Bank, "Rural Development: Sector Policy Paper", Washington D.C., 1975.

World Bank, "Agricultural Credit Sector Policy Paper", Washington D.C., 1975.

World Bank, "The Assault on World Poverty", Baltimore, John Hopkins University press, USA, 1975.

World Bank, "World Development Report 2011", Washington D.C., April, 2011.

Y. Venugopal Reddy, "Multilevel Planning with Special Reference to District Planning: Some issues", Seminar on District Planning, Lal Bhadur Shastri Academy of Administration, Mussoorie, 1973.

Index

L

M

N

O

P